Sabine Baring-Gould

In Troubadour-Land

A Ramble in Provence and Languedoc

Sabine Baring-Gould

In Troubadour-Land
A Ramble in Provence and Languedoc

ISBN/EAN: 9783337404321

Printed in Europe, USA, Canada, Australia, Japan

Cover: Foto ©Andreas Hilbeck / pixelio.de

More available books at **www.hansebooks.com**

TOWER OF ST. TROPHIME, ARLES.

IN TROUBADOUR-LAND.

A RAMBLE IN

PROVENCE AND LANGUEDOC.

BY

S. BARING-GOULD, M.A.,

AUTHOR OF "MEHALAH," "JOHN HERRING," "OLD COUNTRY LIFE," ETC.

ILLUSTRATED BY J. E. ROGERS.

"What is this life, if it be not mixed with some delight? And what delight is more pleasing than to see the fashions and manners of unknown places? You know I am no common gadder, nor have oft troubled you with travell."—*Tom of Reading*, 1600.

PREFACE.

WITH Murray, Bædeker, Guide Joanne, and half-a-dozen others—all describing, and describing with exactness, the antiquities and scenery—the writer of a little account of Provence and Languedoc is driven to give much of personal incident. When he attempts to describe what objects he has seen, he is pulled up by finding all the information he intended to give in Murray or in Bædeker or Joanne. If he was in exuberant spirits at the time, and enjoyed himself vastly, he is unable, or unwilling, to withhold from his readers some of the overflow of his good spirits. That is my apology to the reader. If he reads my little book when his liver is out of order, or in winter fogs and colds—he will call me an ass, and I must bear it. If he is in a cheerful mood himself, then we shall agree very well together.

S. BARING-GOULD.

LEW TRENCHARD, DEVON,
October 28, 1890.

CONTENTS.

CHAPTER I.

INTRODUCTORY.

The Tiber in Flood—Typhoid fever in Rome—Florence—A Jew acquaintance—Drinking in Provence—Buying *bric-à-brac* with the Jew—the *carro* on Easter Eve—Its real Origin—My Jew friend's letters—Italian *dolce far niente* . 1

CHAPTER II.

THE RIVIERA.

No ill without a counterbalancing advantage—An industry peculiar to Italy—Italian honesty—Buffalo Bill at Naples—The Prince and the straw-coloured gloves—The Riviera—A tapestry—Nice—Its flowers—Notre Dame—The château—My gardener—A pension of ugly women—Horses and their hats—Antibes—Meeting of Honoré IV. and Napoleon—The Grimaldis—Lérins, an Isle of Saints—A family jar—Healed 15

CHAPTER III.

FRÉJUS.

The freedman of Pliny—Forum Julii—The Port of Agay—The Port of Fréjus—Roman castle—Aqueduct—The lantern of Augustus—The cathedral—Cloisters—Boy and dolphin—Story told by Pliny—The *Chaine des Maures*—Désaugiers—Dines with the porkbutchers of Paris—Siéyès—*Sans phrase*—Agricola—His discoveries . . . 31

CHAPTER IV.

MARSEILLES.

The three islands Phœnice, Phila, Iturium—Marseilles first a Phœnician colony—The tariff of fees exacted by the priests of Baal—The arrival of the Ionians—The legend of Protis and Gyptis—Second colony of Ionians—The voyages of Pytheas and Euthymenes—Capture of Marseilles by Trebonius—Position of the Greek city—The Acropolis—Greek inscriptions—The lady who never "jawed" her husband—The tomb of the sailor-boy—Hôtel des Négociants—Ménu—Entry of the President of the Republic—Entry of Francis I.—The church of S. Vincent—The cathedral—Notre Dame de la Garde—The abbey of S. Victor—Catacombs—The fable of S. Lazarus . . . 42

CHAPTER V.

THE CRAU.

The Basin of Berre—A neglected harbour—The diluvium - Formation of the Crau—The two Craus—Canal of Craponne—Climate of the Crau—The *bise* and *mistral*—Force of the wind—Cypresses—A vision of kobolds 58

CHAPTER VI.

LES ALYSCAMPS.

Difficulty of finding one's way about in Arles—The two inns—The *mistral*—The charm of Arles is in the past—A dead city—Situation of Arles on a nodule of limestone—The Elysian Fields—A burial-place for the submerged neighbourhood—The Alyscamp now in process of destruction—Expropriation of ancient tombs—Avenue of tombs—Old church of S. Honoré—S. Trophimus—S. Virgilius—Augustine, apostle of the English, consecrated by him—The flying Dutchman—Tomb of Ælia—Of Julia Tyranna—Her musical instruments—Monument of Calpurnia—Her probable story—Mathematical *versus* classic studies—Tombs

CONTENTS.

of *utriculares*—Christian sarcophagi—Probably older than the date usually attributed to them—A French author on the wreckage of the Elysian Fields 67

CHAPTER VII.

PAGAN ARLES.

The Arles race a mixture of Greek and Gaulish—The colonisation by the Romans—The type of beauty in Arles—The amphitheatre—A bull-baiting—Provençal bull-baits different from Spanish bull-fights—The theatre—The ancient Greek stage—The destruction of the Arles theatre—Excavation of the orchestra—Discovery of the Venus of Arles—A sick girl—Palace of Constantine 84

CHAPTER VIII.

CHRISTIAN ARLES.

Sunday in France—Improved observance—The cathedral of Arles—West front—Interior—Tool-marks—A sermon on peace—The cloisters—Old Sacristan and his garden—Number of desecrated churches in Arles—Notre Dame de la Majeur—S. Cæsaire—The isles near Arles—Cordes—Montmajeur—A gipsy camp—The ruins—Tower—The chapel of S. Croix 98

CHAPTER IX.

LES BAUX.

The chain of the Alpines—The promontory of Les Baux—The railway from Arles to Salon—First sight of Les Baux—The churches of S. Victor, S. Claude, and S. Andrew—The lords of Les Baux claimed descent from one of the Magi—The fair maid with golden locks—The chapel of the White Penitents—The *deïmo*—History of the House of Les Baux—The barony passes to the Grimaldi—The ladies of Les Baux and the troubadours—Fouquet—William de Cabestaing—The morality of the loves of the troubadours—The

Porcelets—Story of a siege—Les Baux a place of refuge for the citizens of Arles—*Glanum Liviæ*—Its Roman remains—In the train—Jäger garments 114

CHAPTER X.

THE CAMPAIGN OF MARIUS.

The Trémaïé—Representation of C. Marius, Martha, and Julia—The Gaïé—The Teutons and Ambrons and Cimbri threaten Italy—C. Marius sent against them—His camp at S. Gabriel—The canal he cut—The barbarians cross the Rhone—First brush with them—They defile before him at Orgon—The rout of the Ambrons at Les Milles—He follows the Teutons—The plain of Pourrières—Position of Marius—The battle—Slaughter of the Teutons—Position of their camp—Monument of Marius—Venus Victrix—Annual commemoration 130

CHAPTER XI.

TRETS AND GARDANNE.

The fortifications of Trets—The streets—The church—Roman sarcophagus—Château of Trets—Visit to a self-educated archæologist—His collection made on the battle-field—Dispute over a pot of burnt bones—One magpie—Gardanne—The church—A vielle—Trouble with it—Story of an executioner's sword 156

CHAPTER XII.

AIX.

Dooll, but the mutton good—Les Bains de Sextius—Ironwork caps to towers—S. Jean de Malthe—Museum—Cathedral—Tapestries and tombs—The cloisters—View from S. Eutrope—King René of Anjou—His misfortunes—His cheeriness—His statue at Aix—Introduces the Muscat grape 168

CHAPTER XIII.

THE CAMARGUE.

PAGE

Formation of the delta of the Rhone—The diluvial wash—The alluvium spread over this—The three stages the river pursues—The zone of erosion—The zone of compensation—The zone of deposit—River mouths—Estuaries and deltas—The formation of bars—Of lagoons—The lagoons of the Gulf of Lyons—The ancient position of Arles between the river and the lagoons—Neglect of the lagoons in the Middle Ages—They become morasses—Attempt at remedy—Embankments and drains—A mistake made—The Camargue now a desert—Les Saintes Maries—No evidence to support the legend—Based on a misapprehension 177

CHAPTER XIV.

TARASCON.

Position of Tarascon and Beaucaire opposite each other—Church of S. Martha—Crypt—Ancient paintings—Catechising—Ancient altar—The festival of the Tarasque—The Phœnician goddess Martha—Story of S. Fronto—Discussion at *déjeûner* over the entry of M. Carnot into Marseilles—The change in the French character—Pessimism—Beaucaire—Font—Castle—Siege by Raymond VII.—Story of Aucassin and Nicolette 189

CHAPTER XV.

NIMES.

The right spelling of Nimes—Derivation of name—The fountain—Throwing coins into springs—Collecting coins—Symbol of Agrippa—Character of Agrippa—What he did for Nimes—The Maison Carrée—Different idea of worship in the Heathen world from what prevails in Christendom—S. Baudille—Vespers—Activity of the Church in France—Behaviour of the clergy in Italy to the King and Queen—The Revolution a blessing to the Church in

France—Church services in Italy and in France—The Tourmagne—Uncertainty as to its use—Cathedral of Nimes—Other churches—A canary lottery—Altars to the Sun—The sun-wheel—The cross of Constantine—Anecdote of Fléchier 203

CHAPTER XVI.

AIGUES MORTES AND MAGUELONNE.

A dead town—The Rhônes-morts—Bars—S. Louis and the Crusades—How S. Louis acquired Aigues Mortes—His canal—The four littoral chains and lagoons—The fortifications—Unique for their date—Original use of battlements—Deserted state of the town—Maguelonne—How reached—History of Maguelonne—Cathedral—The Bishops forge Saracen coins—Second destruction of the place—Inscription on door—Bernard de Treviis—His romance of Pierre de Provence—Provençal poetry not always immoral—Present state of Maguelonne . . . 219

CHAPTER XVII.

BÉZIERS AND NARBONNE.

Position of Béziers—S. Nazaire—The Albigenses—Their tenets—Albigensian "consolation"—Crusade against them—The storming of Béziers—Massacre—Cathedral of Béziers—Girls' faces in the train—Similar faces at Narbonne, in cathedral and museum—Narbonne a Roman colony—All the Roman buildings destroyed—Caps of liberty—Christian sarcophagi—Children's toys of baked clay—Cathedral unfinished—Archiepiscopal palace—Unsatisfactory work of M. Viollet-le-Duc—In trouble with the police—Taken for a German spy—My sketch-book gets me off 237

CHAPTER XVIII.

CARCASSONNE.

Siege of Carcassonne by the Crusaders—Capture—Perfidy of legate—Death of the Viscount—Continuation of the war—Churches of New Carcassonne—*La Cité*—A perfect

Mediæval fortified town—Disappointing—Visigoth fortifications—Later additions—The cathedral—Tomb of Simon de Montfort 251

CHAPTER XIX.

AVIGNON.

How Avignon passed to the Popes—The court of Clement VI.—John XXII.—Benedict XII.—Their tombs—Petrarch and Laura—The Palace of the Popes—The Salle Brûlée—Cathedral—Porch—S. Agricole—Church of S. Pierre—The museum—View from the Rocher des doms—The Rhone—The bridge—Story of S. Benezet—Dancing on bridges—Villeneuve—Tomb of Innocent VI.—The castle at Villeneuve—Defences—Tête-du-pont of the bridge . . 261

CHAPTER XX.

VALENCE.

A dull town—Cathedral—Jacques Cujas—His daughter—Pius VI.—His death—Maison des Têtes—Le Pendentif—The castle of Crussol—The dukes of Uzes—A dramatic company of the thirteenth century 283

CHAPTER XXI.

VIENNE.

Historic associations—Salvation Army bonnets—The fair—A quack—A vampire—The amphitrite—A *carousel*—Temple of Augustus and Livia—The Aiguille—Cathedral—Angels and musical instruments—S. André-le-Bas—Situation of Vienne—Foundation of the Church there—Letter of the Church on the martyrdoms at Lyons 294

CHAPTER XXII.

BOURGES.

The siege of Avaricum by Cæsar—The complete subjugation of Gaul—The statue of the Dying Gaul at Rome—Beauty of Bourges—The cathedral—Not completed according to design—Defect in height—Strict geometrical proportion in design not always satisfactory—Necessity of proportion for acoustics—Domestic architecture in Bourges—The house of Jacques Cœur—Story of his life—A rainy day—Why Bourges included in this book—A silver thimble—*Que de singeries faites-vous là, Madeleine ?*—Adieu . . 307

APPENDIX . 325

LIST OF ILLUSTRATIONS.

FULL PAGE ILLUSTRATIONS.

Tower of S. Trophimus, Arles	*Frontispiece*	
Abbey of S. Victor, Marseilles	*To face page*	55
Part of the North Cloister of Arles Cathedral .	,,	104
Les Baux	,,	118
The Pont du Gard	,,	208
Béziers from the River	,,	238
An Entrance to Carcassonne	,,	254
The Cathedral and the Palace of the Popes, Avignon	,,	268

GENERAL ILLUSTRATIONS.

	PAGE
The Carro	7
A Florentine Torch Holder	9
A Horse in a Hat	23
Lérins	25
Aqueduct of Fréjus.	35
Lantern of Augustus	36
Map of Massalia	47
Musical Instruments from the Tomb of Julia . .	75
Calpurnia's Monument	76
An Arelaise. (*From a Photograph.*) . . .	86
Part of the Amphitheatre of Arles . . .	88
Back of a House at Arles.	91
A Boat with two rudders at Arles . . .	96
On a House at Arles	99
Samson and the Lion, from the West door of the Cathedral of Arles	100
On a House at Arles	101
South Entrance to the Cloister, Arles Cathedral . .	103
Church of Notre Dame de la Majeur, Arles. . .	105

LIST OF ILLUSTRATIONS.

	PAGE
Tower of the desecrated Church of S. Croix, Arles	106
Part of the Courtyard of the Convent of S. Cæsarius, Arles	107
Church of the Penitents Gris, Arles	108
In the Cloisters, Montmajeur	111
In the Cloister at Arles	113
Les Baux	116
Range of the Alpines from Glanum Liviæ	129
Ruins S. Gabriel	130
La Trémaïé	131
Les Gaïé	134
Caius Marius. (*From a bust in the Vatican.*)	137
Orgon and the Durance	138
Mont Victoire and the Plain of Pourrières	144
Sketch Plan of the Battle-fields	146
Monument of Marius	148
Venus Victrix	149
Gardanne	158
The Vielle	160
Les Saintes Maries	186
Early Altar, Tarascon	189
Spire of S. Martha's Church, Tarascon	190
Iron Door to Safe in S. Martha's Church	191
King René's Castle, Tarascon	192
A bit in Tarascon	194
The Chapel of Beaucaire Castle	199
Beaucaire Castle from Tarascon.—Sunset	202
In the Public Garden, Nimes	205
The Maison Carrée, Nimes	209
Cathedral of Nimes.—Part of West Front	215
Aigues Mortes.—One of the Gates	220
Aigues Mortes.—Tower of the Bourgignons	221
Sketch Map of Aigues Mortes and its Littoral Chains	223
Original use of Battlements. (*From Viollet-le-Duc.*)	225
Second stage of Battlements	226
East End of the Church of Maguelonne	230
Béziers.—Church of S. Nazaire	241
Fountain in the Cloister of S. Nazaire, Béziers	242
Types of faces, Narbonne: Modern—Sixteenth-Century Tomb in Cathedral—Classic Bust in Museum	244
Freedmen's Caps, Narbonne	245
Children's Toys in the Museum, Narbonne	246
Towers on the Wall, Carcassonne	252

LIST OF ILLUSTRATIONS.

	PAGE
A Bit of Carcassonne	256
Inside the Wall, Carcassonne	258
Papal Throne in the Cathedral of Avignon	264
John XXII.	265
Benedict XII.	265
An Angle of the Papal Palace, Avignon	266
Lantern at the Cathedral, Avignon	269
Angel at West Door, Church of S. Agricole	270
A Bit of the Old Wall, Avignon	271
Part of Church of S. Didier, Avignon	273
Bridge and Chapel of S. Benezet	274
At Villeneuve	276
Castle of S. André, at Villeneuve	278
At Villeneuve	280
A Well at Villeneuve	281
Cathedral of Valence	284
Doorway in the House Dupré Latour, Valence	286
Doorway and Niche in the Maison des Têtes, Valence	289
House in Vienne	297
At Vienne	299
Hurdy-Gurdy Played by an Angel	303
Church of S. André-le-Bas.—The Tower	304
Porte de l'Ambulance, Vienne	305
A Street Corner, Bourges	310
Part of Jacques Cœur's House	316
Turret in the Hôtel Lallemand	319
Staircase in the Hôtel Lallemand	320
Sculpture over the Kitchen Entrance at Jacques Cœur's House	323
Jacques Cœur's Knocker	324

ERRATUM.

FRONTISPIECE.—*For* St. Trophine, *read* St. Trophimus.

IN TROUBADOUR-LAND.

CHAPTER I.

INTRODUCTORY.

The Tiber in Flood—Typhoid fever in Rome—Florence—A Jew acquaintance—Drinking in Provence—Buying *bric-à-brac* with the Jew—The *carro* on Easter Eve—Its real Origin —My Jew friend's letters—Italian *dolce far niente*.

CONCEIVE yourself confronted by a pop-gun, some ten feet in diameter, charged with mephitic vapours and plugged with microbes of typhoid fever. Conceive your sensations when you were aware that the piston was being driven home. That was my situation in March, 1890, when I got a letter from Messrs. Allen asking me to go into Provence and Languedoc, and write them a book thereon. I dodged the microbe, and went.

To make myself understood I must explain.

I was in Rome. For ten days with a sirocco wind the rains had descended, as surely they had never come down since the windows of heaven were opened at the Flood. The Tiber rose thirty-two feet. Now Rome is tunnelled under the streets with drains or sewers that carry all the refuse of a great city into the Tiber. But, naturally, when the Tiber swells high above the crowns of the sewers, they are choked. All the foulness of the great town is held back under the houses and streets, and breeds gases loathsome to the nose and noxious to life. Not only so, but a column of water, some twenty to twenty-five feet in height, is acting like the piston of a pop-gun, and is driving all the accumulated gases charged with the germs of typhoid fever into every house which has communication with the sewers. There is no help for it, the poisonous vapours *must* be forced out of the drains and *must* be forced into the houses. That is why, with a rise of the Tiber, typhoid fever is certain to break out in Rome.

As I went over Ponte S. Angelo I was wont to look over the parapet at the opening of the sewer that carried off the dregs of that portion of the city where I was residing. One day I looked for it, and looked in vain. The Tiber had swelled and was overflowing its banks, and for a week or fortnight there could be no question, not a sewer in the vast city would be free to do anything else but mischief. I did not go on to the

Vatican galleries that day. I could not have enjoyed the statues in the Braccio Nuovo, nor the frescoes in the Loggia. I went home, found Messrs. Allen's letter, packed my Gladstone bag, and bolted. I shall never learn who got the microbe destined for me, which I dodged.

I went to Florence; at the inn where I put up— one genuinely Italian, Bonciani's,—I made an acquaintance, a German Jew, a picture-dealer with a shop in a certain capital, no matter which, editor of a *bric-à-brac* paper, and a right merry fellow. I introduce him to the reader because he afforded me some information concerning Provence. He had a branch establishment—never mind where, but in Provence— and he had come to Florence to pick up pictures and *bric-à-brac.*

Our acquaintance began as follows. We sat opposite each other at table in the evening. A large rush-encased flask is set before each guest in a swing carriage, that enables him to pour out his glassful from the big-bellied flask without effort. Each flask is labelled variously Chianti, Asti, Pomino, but all the wines have a like substance and flavour, and each is an equally good light dinner-wine. A flask when full costs three francs twenty centimes; and when the guest falls back in his seat, with a smile of satisfaction on his face, and his heart full of good will towards all men, for that he has done his dinner, then the bottle is taken out, weighed, and the guest charged the amount of wine he has consumed. He gets a fresh flask at every meal.

" Du lieber Himmel!" exclaimed my *vis-à-vis.* " I

do b'lieve I hev drunk dree francs. Take up de flasche and weigh her. Tink so?"

"I can believe it without weighing the bottle," I replied.

"And only four sous—twenty centimes left!" exclaimed the old gentleman, meditatively. "But four sous is four sous. It is de price of mine paper"—brightening in his reflections—"I can but shell one copy more, and I am all right." Brightening to greater brilliancy as he turns to me: "Will you buy de last number of my paper? She is in my pocket. She is ver' interesting. Oh! ver' so. Moche information for two pence."

"I shall be charmed," I said, and extended twenty centimes across the table.

"Ach Tausend! Dass ist herrlich!" and he drew off the last drops of Pomino. "Now I will tell you vun ding. Hev you been in Provence?"

"Provence! Why—I am on my way there, now."

"Den listen to me. Ebery peoples hev different ways of doing de same ding. You go into a cabaret dere, and you ask for wine. De patron brings you a bottle, and at de same time looks at de clock and wid a bit of chalk he mark you down your time. You say you will drink at two pence, or dree pence, or four pence. You drink at dat price you have covenanted for one hour, you drink at same price anodder hour, and you sleep—but you pay all de same, wedder you drink or wedder you sleep, two pence, or dree pence, or four pence de hour. It is an old custom. You understand? It is de custom of de country—of La belle Provence."

"I quite understand that it is to the interest of the taverner to make his customers drunk."

"Drunk!" repeated my Mosaic acquaintance. "I will tell you one ding more, ver' characteristic of de nationalities. A Frenchman—*il boit;* a German—*er sauft;* and an Englishman—he gets fresh. Der you hev de natures of de dree peoples as in a picture. De Frenchman, he looks to de moment, and not beyond. *Il boit.* De German, he looks to de end. *Er sauft.* De Englishman, he sits down fresh and intends to get fuddled; but he is a hypocrite. He does not say de truth to hisself nor to nobody, he says, *I will get fresh,* when he means de odder ding. Big humbug. You understand?"

One morning my Jew friend said to me: "Do you want to see de, what you call behind-de-scenes of Florence? Ver' well, you come wid me. I am going after pictures."

He had a carriage at the door. I jumped in with him, and we spent the day in driving about the town, visiting palaces and the houses of professional men and tradesmen—of all who were "down on their luck," and wanted to part with art-treasures. Here we entered a palace, of roughed stone blocks after the ancient Florentine style, where a splendid porter with cocked hat, a silver-headed *bâton,* and gorgeous livery kept guard. Up the white marble stairs, into stately halls overladen with gilding, the walls crowded with paintings in cumbrous but resplendent frames. Prince So-and-So had got into financial difficulties, and wanted to part with some of his heirlooms.

There we entered a mean door in a back street,

ascended a dirty stair, and came into a suite of apartments, where a dishevelled woman in a dirty split dressing-gown received us and showed us into her husband's sanctum, crowded with rare old paintings on gold grounds. Her good man had been a collector of the early school of art; now he was ill, he could not attend to his business, he might not recover, and whilst he was ill his wife was getting rid of some of his treasures.

There we entered the mansion of a widow, who had lost her husband recently, a rich merchant. The heirs were quarrelling over the spoil, and she was in a hurry to make what she could for herself before a valuer came to reckon the worth of the paintings and silver and cabinets.

In that day I saw many sides of life.

"But how in the world," I asked of my guide, "did you know that all these people were wanting to sell?"

"I have my agents ebberywhere," was his reply.

I thought of the *Diable boiteux* carrying the student of Alcala over the city, Madrid, removing the roofs of the houses, and exposing to his view the stories of the lives and miseries of those within.

I was at Florence on Easter Eve. A ceremony of a very peculiar character takes place there on that day at noon. In the morning a monstrous black structure on wheels, some twenty-five feet high, is brought into the square before the cathedral by oxen, garlanded with flowers. This erection, the *carro*, is also decorated with flowers, but is likewise covered with fireworks. A rope is then extended from the *carro* to

INTRODUCTORY.

a pole which is set up in the choir of the Duomo, before the high altar. For this purpose the great west doors are thrown open, and the rope extends the whole length of the nave. Upon it, close to the pole, is perched a white dove of plaster.

Crowds assemble both in the square and in the nave of the cathedral. Peasants from the countryside come in in bands, and before the hour of noon every vantage place is occupied, and the square and the streets commanding it are filled with a sea of heads.

THE CARRO.

At half-past eleven, the archbishop, the canons, the choir, go down the nave in procession, and make the circuit of the Duomo, then re-enter the cathedral, take their places in the choir, and the mass for Easter Eve is begun. At the Gospel —at the stroke of twelve, a match is applied to a fusee, and instantly the white dove flies along the rope, pouring forth a tail of fire, down the nave, out at the west gates, over the heads of the crowd, reaches the *carro*, ignites a fusee there, turns, and, still propelled by its fiery tail, whizzes along the cord again, till it has reached its perch on the pole in the choir, when the fire goes out and it remains stationary. But in the meantime the match ignited by the dove has communicated with the squibs and crackers attached to the *carro*, and the whole mass of painted wood and flowers is enveloped in fire and smoke, from which issue sheets of flame and loud detonations. Meanwhile, mass is being sung composedly within the choir, as though nothing was happening without. The fireworks continue to explode for about a quarter of an hour, and then the great garlanded oxen, white, with huge horns, are reyoked to the *carro*, and it is drawn away.

The flight of the dove for its course of about 540 feet is watched by the peasants with breathless attention, for they take its easy or jerky flight as ominous of the weather for the rest of the year and of the prospects of harvest. If the bird sails along without a hitch, then the summer will be fine, but if there be sluggishness of movement, and one halt, then another, the year is sure to be one of storms and late frosts and hail.

Now what is the origin of this extraordinary custom—a custom that is childish, and yet is so curious that one would hardly wish to see it abolished?

Several stories are told to explain it, none very satisfactory. According to one, a Florentine knight was in the crusading host of Godfrey de Bouillon, and was the first to climb the walls of Jerusalem, and plant thereon the banner of the Cross. He at once sent tidings of the recovery of the Holy Sepulchre back to his native town by a carrier pigeon, and thus the Florentines received the glad tidings long before it reached any other city in Europe. In token of their gladness at the news, they instituted the ceremony of the white pigeon and the *carro* on Easter Eve.

Another story is to the effect that this Florentine entered the city of Jerusalem before the first crusade, broke off a large fragment of the Holy Sepulchre, and carried it to Florence. He was pursued by the Saracens, but escaped by shoeing his horse with reversed irons. Another version is that he resolved to bring back to Florence the sacred flame that burnt in the Church of the Holy Sepulchre. Accordingly he lighted thereat a torch, and rode back to Italy with the torch flaming. But to protect it from the wind, he rode with his face to the tail of his steed, screening the torch with his body. As he thus rode, folk who saw him shouted "Pazzi! Pazzi!"—Fool! Fool! and this name was assumed by his family ever after. The Pazzis of Florence every year paid all the expenses of the *carro* till quite recently, when the Municipality assumed the charge and now defray it from the city chest. Clearly the origin of the custom is forgotten; nevertheless it is not difficult to explain the meaning of the ceremony.

A FLORENTINE TORCH HOLDER.

In the Eastern Church, and still, in many churches in the West, the lights are extinguished on Good Friday, and formerly this was the case with all fires, those of the domestic hearth as well as the lamps in church. On Easter Day, fresh fire was struck with flint and steel by the bishop, and all candles, lamps and hearths were rekindled from this new light. At the present day one of the most solemn scenes in the Eastern Church is this kindling of the Easter fire, and its communication from one to another in a vast congregation assembled to receive it and carry it off to their homes. In the Church of the Holy Sepulchre at Jerusalem, the new fire kindled and blessed by the patriarch, is cast down from the height of the dome.

In Florence, anciently, it was much the same. The archbishop struck the Easter fire, and it was then distributed among the people; but there were inconveniences, unseemly scuffles, accidents even, and the dove was devised as a means of conveying the Easter fire outside the Duomo, and kindling a great bonfire, whereat the people might light their torches without desecrating the sacred building by scrambling and fighting therein for the hallowed flame. At this bonfire all could obtain the fire without inconvenience. By degrees the bonfire lost its significance, so did the dove, and fables were invented to explain the custom. The bonfire, moreover, degenerated into an exhibition of fireworks at mid-day.

One morning my Jew friend insisted on my reading a letter he had just received from his daughter, aged fourteen. He was proud of the daughter, and highly pleased with the letter.

It began thus: "Cher papa—nous sommes sauvés. That picture of a Genoese lady you bought for 200 francs, and doubted if you would be able to get rid of, I sold before we left home for Provence to an American, as a genuine Queen Elizabeth for 1,000 francs." Then followed three closely-written pages of record of business transactions, all showing a balance to the good, all showing a profit nowhere under thirty per cent. Finally, the letter concluded: "Mamma's back is better. Louis and I went on Sunday to see a farm. A cow, a stable, an old peasantess saying her rosary, a daughter knitting—all real, not waxwork. Votre fille très devouée, LEAH."

"That is a girl to be proud of," said my acquaintance. "And only fourteen! But hein! here is another letter I have received, and it is awkward." He told me that when he had been in London on business he had lodged in the house of a couple who were not on the best of terms. The husband had been a widower with one child, a daughter, and the stepmother could not abide the child. Whilst M. Cohen, my friend, was there, the quarrels had been many, and he had done his best to smooth matters between the parties. Then he had invited them over to visit the Continent and stay at his house. They had come, and he had again to exercise the office of mediator. "And now," lamented my good-hearted friend, "nebber one week but I get a letter from de leddy. Here is dis, sent on to me. Read it." The letter ran as follows :—

"Do write to me. I fear my last letter cannot have reached you, or you would have answered it. I am miserable. My husband is so cross about that little girl, because I cannot love the nasty little beast. Oh, Mr. Cohen, do come to London, or let me come abroad and live in your house away from my husband and that child. You were so sensible and so kind. I can't bear to be longer here in the house with my husband and the spoiled child."

My friend looked disconsolately at me.

"What am I to do?" he asked. "She writes ebery week, and I don't answer. And my wife sends on dese letters."

"Do?" said I. "Send this one at once to Madame Cohen, and ask her to answer it for you. That London lady will never trouble you again."

The following circumstance I relate, not that it has the smallest importance except as a characteristic sketch of Italian *dolce far niente*, and as a lesson to travellers. The proper study of mankind is man, and a little incident such as occurred to me, and which I will now relate, raises the curtain and shows us a feature of humanity in Italy. When I hurried from Rome, I sent off all my luggage by goods train to England, except such articles as I could compress into a Gladstone bag; a change of raiment of course was there. But mark the cruelty of fate. My foot slipped on a white marble stair, and I rent a certain garment at the knee. I at once dived into my Gladstone bag and produced another pair, but found with a shock that they also had suffered—become threadbare, and needed attention from a tailor. What was to be done? I had to leave Florence at noon. The discovery was made the night before. I rose early, breakfasted early, and hung about the shop door of a tailor at 8 A.M. till the door was opened, when I entered, stated my case, and the obliging *sartore* promised that the trifling remedy should be applied and I should have my garment again in one hour. "In one hour!" he said, holding up his hand in solemn asseveration.

Nine o'clock came; then ten, and my raiment had not returned. I flew to the tailor's shop and asked for my garment. "It was all right," said he, "only the thread being knotted. It should be sent to my inn." So I returned and waited. I had my lunch, paid my bill, packed my bag, looked at my watch. The omnibus was at the door. No garment. I ran to the tailor's. He listened to my tale of distress with an amiable smile on his face, then volunteered to come with me to my inn, and talk the matter over with the host. Accordingly he locked up his shop and sauntered with me to Bonciani's. Bonciani and he considered the circumstances at length, thrashed the subject thoroughly. Then, as the horses were being put into the omnibus—"Come," said the tailor, "I have a brother, a grocer, we will go to him."

"But why?" asked I. "Do you see, the boxes are being put on the omnibus. I want my—garment."

"You must come with me to my brother's," said the tailor. So to the grocer's went we. Vainly did I trust that the journeyman who was engaged on my article of apparel lodged there, and that, done or undone, I could recover it thence. But no—not so. The whole story was related with embellishments to the brother, the grocer, who listened, discussed, commented on, the matter.

"There goes the 'bus!" I shouted, looking down the street. "Even now, if you will let me have the article, I can run to the station and get off; I have my ticket."

"Subito! subito!" said the tailor.

Then the grocer said that the thing in request might be sent by post. "But," I replied, "I am going into France, to Nice, and clothes are subjected to burdensome charges if carried across the frontier."

"Ten minutes!" I gasped. "Almost too late."

A moment later—

"Appunto!"

"The clock is striking. I am done for."

"Appunto!" and he lighted a cigarette.

So I had to travel by night, instead of by day.

CHAPTER II.

THE RIVIERA.

No ill without a counterbalancing advantage—An industry peculiar to Italy—Italian honesty—Buffalo Bill at Naples—The Prince and the straw-coloured gloves—The Riviera—A tapestry—Nice—Its flowers—Notre Dame—The château—My gardener—A pension of ugly women—Horses and their hats—Antibes — Meeting of Honoré IV. and Napoleon — The Grimaldis—Lérins, an Isle of Saints—A family jar—Healed.

That was not all. The dawdling of the tailor not only made me lose the mid-day train, but delayed my arrival in Nice for twenty-four hours. I took the night train to Pisa, where I purposed catching the express from Rome. But the express came slouching along in a hands-in-the-pocket sort of way, and was over half-an-hour late, and would not bestir itself to pick up the misspent, lost moments between Pisa and Genoa, the consequence of which was that the train for Nice had gone on without waiting, and accordingly those who desired to prosecute their journey in that direction were obliged to loiter about in the small hours of the morning between a restaurant, half asleep, and a waiting-room where the electric light had gone out, till the hour of seven.

Before leaving Italy, I may mention an industry which I found cultivated there, original, and I believe unique. When I procured postage stamps at the post-offices, I was surprised, if I took them home with me, to find that their adhesive power had failed. I also received indignant letters from correspondents in England remonstrating with me for posting my communications to them unstamped. This surprised me, and at Rome, where I had been accustomed to purchase *franco-bolli* at the head office, I took them home and regummed them. But the remarkable phenomenon was, that such stamps as were purchased at tobacconists' shops had gum on them—only those acquired at the post-offices were without. I learned that the same peculiarity existed at Florence, and indeed elsewhere in Italy, and finally the explanation was vouchsafed to me. The functionary at the post-office passes a wet sponge over the back of the sheets of *franco-bolli* supplied to him, thus removing the adhesive matter. When he sells stamps at the window, he hopes that those who purchase will proceed at once to apply them to their letters, without perceiving their deficiencies. As soon as the stamp becomes dry it falls off, and quite a collection of stamps of sundry values can thus be gathered at every clearing of the box, and the postal clerk reaps thence a daily harvest that goes a long way towards the eking out the small pittance paid him by Government. It is interesting to see the directions taken by human enterprise.

Whilst I was in Rome, Buffalo Bill was in Naples exhibiting his troupe of horses and gang of Indians. The Italian papers informed the public of a remarkable exploit achieved by the Neapolitans. They had done Buffalo Bill out of two thousand francs. It had been effected in this wise. His reserved seats were charged five francs. Four hundred forged five-franc notes were passed at the door of his show by well-dressed Neapolitans, indeed, the *élite* of Neapolitan society; and the trick played on him was not discovered till too late. Now consider what this implies. It implies that some hundreds of the best people, princes, counts, marquesses at Naples lent themselves to see Buffalo Bill's exhibition by a fraud. They wanted to see and be seen there, but not to pay five francs for a seat. There must have been combination, and that among the members of the aristocracy of Naples. The Italian papers did not mention this in a tone of disgust, but rather in one of surprise that Italians should have been able to overreach a Yankee. But I do not believe such a fraud would have been perpetrated at Rome, Florence, or Milan. It was considered quite in its place at Naples.

A lady of my acquaintance was staying in a pension at Naples. There resided at the time, in the same pension, a prince—Neapolitan, be it understood. One day, just before she left, she brought in a packet of kid gloves she had purchased, among them one pair, straw-coloured. She laid them on the table, went out for two minutes, leaving the prince in the room with the gloves. On her return, the prince and the straw-coloured gloves were gone. She made inquiries of the landlady, who, when told that the prince had been in the room, laughed and said: "But of course he has them. You should never leave anything in the room unguarded where there is a prince." Two days after the departure of this lady, the straw-coloured gloves were produced by his highness and presented by him to a young lady whom he admired, then in the same pension.

No evil comes without a counterbalancing good. The day I was detained in Florence by that tailor, and the loss of the night train at Genoa were not immense evils. A furious gale broke over the coast, and when at seven in the morning we steamed out of Genoa, the Mediterranean was sullen, the rain poured down, and the mountains were enveloped in vapour. But as we proceeded along the coast the weather improved, and before long every cloud was gone, the sky became blue as a gentian, and the oranges flamed in the sunshine as we swept between the orchards. Had I gone by the noon train from Florence I should have travelled this road by night, had I caught the 3.27 A.M. train I should have seen nothing for storm and cloud. And—what a glorious, what an unrivalled road that is! It was like passing through a gallery hung with Rénaissance tapestry, all in freshness of colour. The sea deep blue and green like a peacock's neck, the mountains pale yellow, as shown in tapestry, with blue shadows; the silvery-grey olives, the glossy orange trees with their fruit—exactly as in tapestry. Surely the old weavers of those wondrous webs studied this coast and copied it in their looms.

I have said that the sea was like a peacock's neck; but it had a brilliancy above even that. As I have mentioned tapestry I may say that it resembled a sort of tapestry that is very rare and costly, of which I have seen a sample in a private collection at Frankfort, and another in the Palazzo Bardini at Florence. It consists of the threads being drawn over plates of gold and silver. In the piece at Florence the effect of the sun shining through a tree is thus produced by gold leaf under the broidery of tree-leaves. Silver leaf is employed for water, with blue silk drawn in lines over it. So with the sea. There seemed to be silver burnished to its greatest polish below, over which the water was drawn as a blue lacquer.

And Nice. What shall I say of that bright and laughing city—with its shops of flowers, its avenues of trees through which run the streets, its gardens, its pines and cactus and aloe walks? Only one blemish can I pick out in Nice, and that is a hideous modern Gothic church, Notre Dame, filled with detestable garish glass, so utterly faulty in design, so full of blemish of every sort, that the best wish one could make for the good people of Nice is that the next earthquake that visits the Riviera may shake this wretched structure to pieces, so as to give them an opportunity of erecting another in its place which is not a monstrosity.

The Avenue de la Gare is planted with the eucalyptus, that has attained a considerable size. It is not a beautiful tree, its leaves are ever on the droop, as though the tree were unhealthy or unhappy, sulky at being transplanted to Europe, dissatisfied with the climate, displeased with the soil, discontented with its associates. It struck me as very much like a good number of excellent and very useful souls with whom I am acquainted, who never take a cheerful view of life, are always fault-finding, hole-picking, worry-discovering, eminently good in their place as febrifuges, but not calculated to brighten their neighbourhood.

What a delightful walk is that on the cliff of the château! The day I was at Nice was the 9th of April. The crags were rich with colour, the cytisus waving its golden hair, the pelargonium blazing scarlet, beds of white stock wafting fragrance, violets scrambling over every soft bank of deep earth exhaling fragrance; roses, not many in flower, but their young leaves in masses of claret-red; wherever a ledge allowed it, there pansies of velvety blue and black and brown had been planted. In a hot sun I climbed the château cliff to where the water, conveyed to the summit, dribbled and dropped, or squirted and splashed, nourishing countless fronds of fern and beds of moss, and many a bog plant. The cedars and umbrella pines in the spring sun exhaled their aromatic breath, and the flowering birch rained down its yellow dust over one from its swaying catkins.

I see I have spoken of the cytisus. I may be excused mentioning an anecdote that the sight of this plant provokes in my mind every spring. I had a gardener—a queer, cantankerous creature, who never saw a joke, even when he made one. "Please, sir," he said to me with a solemn face, "I've been rearing a lot o' young citizens for you."

"Have you?" said I, with a sigh. "I fancy I'm rearing a middling lot of them myself."

"Please, sir," said he to me on another occasion, "that there lumbago be terrible trying to know what to do with it."

"Oh!" said I with alacrity, "nothing equals hartshorn and oil applied to the small of the back with a flannel. You have a wife ——"

"Yes, sir." He looked at me vacantly. "And yet, it's a beautiful thing."

"Well—yes, when it attacks one's deadly enemy."

"I've cut it down, and trimmed it out, and tied it up," said the gardener. He meant the *Plumbago capense!*

That man never would allow that he was beaten. My eldest boy one day held some pansies over the fumes of ammonia, turned them green, and showed them as a *lusus naturæ* to the gardener. He smiled contemptuously. "Them's the colour of biled cabbage," said he; "I grew them verdigris green—beds of 'em, when I was with Squire Cross."

One day he said to me: "The nurserymen call them plants big onias just to sell them, I call them little onias; you shall just see them I grow, them be the true big onias, as large as the palm of your hand."

I tumbled, by hazard, at Nice into a pension, where I believe I saw at *table d'hôte* a score of the ugliest women I have ever had the trial of sitting over against in my long career. I found out, in conversation with a porter at the station afterwards, that this pension was notorious for the ugly women who put up there, and it is a joke among the porters when they see one very ill-favoured arrive by the train, that she is going to be an inmate of the Hotel ———. The name I will not give, lest any of my fair readers, in that spirit of delighful perversity that characterises the sex, should go there and spoil the credit of the pension. I could not endure the *table d'hôte* there for many days. An ugly woman is, or may be, restful for the eye when her face is in repose—not when she is chewing tough beef or munching an apple. Besides, Lent was passed.

When I was in Rome there appeared in a comic paper at the beginning of Lent the picture of a very stout lady, who thus addressed her spouse. "Hubby, dear! you haven't kissed me." "Can't, love," he replies, "*fat* is forbidden in Lent." Ugliness was uncongenial to me in radiantly beautiful Nice, and in sparkling Easter—so I packed my Gladstone bag and went further.

The snow still lying on the crests of the Maritime Alps and the intermediate ranges broken into fantastic forms, the lovely range of red porphyry Esterel to the south, with the intensely blue sea drawing a thread of silver about its base, together made a picture of incomparable loveliness.

The sun was so hot that the horses had already assumed their summer hats. "A good man is merciful to his beast," and the good-hearted peasants of the Riviera and Provence, thinking that their horses must suffer from the burning heat of the sun, provide them with straw hats, very much the same sort of hats as girls wear, adorned also with ribbons and rosettes, but to suit the peculiarity of formation of the horse's head, two holes are cut in the hat through which the ears are drawn. The effect is comical when you are being driven in a carriage with a pair of horses before you wearing straw hats, and their ears protruding, one on each side, like the horns in the helmets of mediæval German knights. One lovely glimpse of the sea I got that I shall never forget. The blue sea was in the background gleaming; against it stood a belt of sombre cypresses; before the cypresses the silvery, smoke-grey tufts of olive, in a grove; and before the olive, in mid-distance, a field of roses in young claret-red foliage—a landscape of belts of colour right marvellous.

A HORSE IN A HAT.

Then Antibes—a blue bay with castle on one horn, on the other the little town, its lighthouse, and a couple of bold towers.

It was at Cannes that Prince Honoré IV. of Monaco encountered Napoleon in 1815, as he was returning from Paris in his carriage to take possession of his principality, that had been restored to him by the Treaty of Paris in 1814.

The Grenadiers of the Imperial Guard stopped his carriage, made the prince descend, and conducted him before a little man with clean-cut features, whom he at once knew as the Emperor—returned from Elba.

"Où allez-vous, Monaco?" asked Napoleon bluntly.

"Sire," replied Honoré IV., "je vais à la découverte de mon royaume."

The Emperor smiled.

"Voilà une singulière rencontre, monsieur," said Napoleon. "Deux majestés sans place ; mais ce n'est peut-être pas la peine de vous déranger. Avant huit jours je serai à Paris, et je me verrai forcé de vous renverser du trône, mon cousin. Revenez plutôt avec moi, je vous nommerai sous-préfet de Monaco, si vous y tenez beaucoup."

"Merci de vos bontés, sire," replied the prince in some confusion ; "mais je tiendrais encore plus à faire une restauration, ne dut-elle durer que trois jours."

"Allons! faites la durer trois mois, mon cousin, je vous garderai votre place de chancellier, et vous viendriez me réjoindre aux Tuileries."

The two monarchs separated after having shaken hands amicably. The story would be spoiled by translation.

The Grimaldis anciently possessed much more extensive territories than at present. At Cagnes, near Vence, is their ancient château, now converted into a hospital and barrack, and they owned considerable property, manors and lordships near Cannes and Vence. We shall meet them again as Princes of Les Baux.

The present reigning family are not properly Grimaldis. The last representative was a daughter, married to the Count of Thorigny in 1715, who, on the extinction of the male line in 1731, assumed the name of Grimaldi, and succeeded to the principality.

Everywhere, for the mere delight of the eye, not from thought of any gain gotten out of it, is the Judas tree covered with pink flowers, standing among the cool grey olives. Here and there is a mulberry bursting into fresh, green, vivid leaf; in every garden the palms are rustling their leaves in the pleasant air, and are glistening in the sun. Out at

LÉRINS.

sea lies the low, dull island of Lérins; but, though low and dull, full of interest, as taking the place to Provence occupied by Iona to Scotland and Lindisfarne to Northumberland, a cradle of Christianity, a cradle rocked by the waves. I cannot do better than quote Montalembert's words on this topic. "The sailor, the soldier, or the traveller who proceeds from the roadstead of Toulon to sail towards Italy and the East, passes among two or three islands, rocky and arid, surmounted here and there by a slender cluster of pines. He looks at them with indifference, and avoids them. However, one of these islands has been for the soul, for the mind, for the moral progress of humanity, a centre purer and more fertile than any famous isle of the Hellenic Archipelago. It is Lerins, formerly occupied by a city, which was already ruined in the time of Pliny, and where, at the commencement of the fifth century, nothing more was to be seen than a desert coast. In 410, a man landed and remained there; he was called Honoratus. Descended from a consular race, educated and eloquent, but devoted from his youth to great piety, he desired to be made a monk. His father charged his eldest brother, a gay and impetuous young man, to turn him from his purpose; but, on the contrary, it was he who won over his brother. Disciples gathered round them. The face of the isle was changed, the desert became a garden. Honoratus, whose fine face is described to us as radiant with a sweet and attractive majesty, opened here an asylum and a school for all such as loved Christ."

From this school went forth disciples, inspired with the spirit of Honoratus, to rule the churches of Arles, Avignon, Lyons, Vienne, Fréjus, Valence, Nice, Metz, and many others. Honoratus himself, taken from his peaceful isle to be elevated to the metropolitan see of Arles, had for his successor, as Abbot of Lerins, and afterwards as Bishop of Arles, his pupil and kinsman S. Hilary, to whom we owe the admirable biography of his master. Hilary was celebrated for his graceful eloquence, his unwearied zeal, his tender sympathy with all forms of suffering, his ascendency over a crowd, and by the numerous conversions which he worked. But, indeed Lerins was a hive whence swarmed forth the teachers and apostles of Southern Gaul. Hence came the modest Vincent of Lerins, the first controversialist of his time, who at the head of his greatest work inscribed a touching testimony of his love for that poor little isle where he had spent so many years, and learned so much. Salvian, also, the "Master of Bishops," as he was called, though himself only a priest, was held to be the most eloquent man of his day, only second to S. Augustine. S. Eucherius of Lyons, S. Lupus of Troyes, who had married the sister of S. Hilary, were other prelates trained in this holy isle. When Troyes was threatened by Attila and his Huns, Lupus boldly went forth to meet him. "Who art thou?" asked the bishop. "I am Attila, the Scourge of God," was the reply. The intrepid gentleness of the bishop disarmed the ferocious invader. He left Troyes without injuring it, and drew back to the Rhine. And this isle through Lupus claims some regard from a native of Britain, for Lupus, trained in it, was chosen by the Council of Arles in 429 to combat the Pelagian heresy in Great Britain, along with S. Germanus of Auxerre.

Into the same carriage with me, at Nice, got a pair —a young couple ; he, with an amiable but weak face ; she heavy featured, her only charm her eyes. There had been a breeze between the pair, evidently, before they took their places, and she was sulky. He, poor fool, endeavoured by every means to allay her ruffled temper, always ineffectually. He pulled out his Guide

Joannot, and endeavoured to interest her in the places we passed, their history, their antiquities; in vain, she sat scowling, with pursed lips. He called her attention to the red porphyry cliffs of Esterel with purple shadows in their hollows, to the blue bays opening between their red horns—all to no purpose, she would not look out at the window. He produced a box of jujubes, and offered her one between his thumb and forefinger. She refused it, but thrust her fingers into the box and extracted one for herself. Then she leaned back in the carriage, drew her hat over her face, and exposed to view only a chin and a mole under it, that moved up and down as she sucked her jujube.

Next, the feeble, amorous husband, endeavoured to get hold of her hand. She snatched it away vixenishly. Hectic spots formed on his cheeks, and perspiration stood in great drops on his brow. This was clearly the first ruffle he had experienced on the hymeneal sea. He got out of the carriage at Cannes, and hung about the buffet till the extreme moment, hoping to betray her into tokens of uneasiness lest he should miss the train. As it was, at the final moment he swung himself into another carriage. She thrust her hat a little on one side, protruded an eye to see what became of him, then covered it once more. He got in at the next station, breathless, in pretended agitation. He had nearly lost his place—he was all but left behind. Had he been so left, what would she have done? She vouchsafed no reply. Tired, however, of looking into the crown of her hat, she now removed it and placed it on her lap. The face was still sullen, with the jowl hanging down, the coarse lips set in defiance, and an ugly flicker in the eyes. Now the hectic-cheeked husband became boisterous in merry conversation with other travellers near him, but always with an eye reverting at periods to his wife, whose lips retained a contemptuous curl. Then he sulked in his turn, folded his arms, thrust forth his feet under the seat opposite, and looked gloomily into the space between them. Thereat she began to hum an air from "La Traviata," when suddenly the situation was altered. By some marvellous instinct she discovered that I had been observing the little play; the comedy *à deux*, and had made my comments thereon—not in her favour.

Instantly the expression of her countenance changed. She turned to her husband. "Gustave!" said she, "Je souffre," and she laid her head on his shoulder. A flash in his face, full of surprise sliding into ecstasy. He could not understand this sudden change in her disposition, and I am quite sure she never gave him the key.

I left the carriage at Fréjus, and at parting caught her eye. She laughed, so did I. We understood each other. Now, as it happened, at Nice, when I was seeking a carriage, I entered one where were a lady and an elderly gentleman.

At the first glance I recognised a "Milord Anglais," the lady was his daughter. At the same moment that I said to myself, "This carriage will never do for me," the lady addressed me, "Monsieur! ce voitoore est réservée à noos doox."

If I had gone to Fréjus with them, I should have

missed that little episode of the young married couple and that would have grieved me, and the reconciliation would not have been brought about before Marseilles. Oh, how grateful I was to fate, that the lady had said, " Monsieur! ce voitoore est réservée à noos doox."

CHAPTER III.

FRÉJUS.

The freedman of Pliny—Forum Julii—The Port of Agay—The Port of Fréjus—Roman castle—Aqueduct—The lantern of Augustus—The cathedral—Cloisters—Boy and dolphin—Story told by Pliny—The *Chaine des Maures*—Désaugiers—Dines with the porkbutchers of Paris—Siéyès—*Sans phrase*—Agricola—His discoveries.

IT was strange. The first person I thought of, on arriving at Fréjus, was not Julius Cæsar the founder of this old port —no, nor Agricola, a native of Fréjus, who is so associated with British history, especially with Scottish — no! it was Pliny's sick freedman, about whom that polished orator wrote in his nineteenth letter, in Book V. of his collected epistles. Pliny was a native of Como, he had two villas on the lake. He was a kindly, honourable, somewhat bumptious man — but what great talkers think small matter of themselves? He had a slave, a Greek, named Zosimus, of whom he writes to his friend Paulinus, who had an estate at

Fréjus: "He is a person of great worth, diligent in his services, and well skilled in literature; but his chief talent is that of a comedian. He pronounces with great judgment, propriety, and gracefulness; he has a very good hand too upon the lyre, and performs with more skill than is necessary for one of his profession. To this I must add, he reads history, oratory, and poetry. He is endeared to me by ties of long affection, now heightened by the danger in which he is."

Pliny had given Zosimus his liberty, but Zosimus remained attached to his service as freedman. Some years before, this accomplished slave had overstrained his voice, and begun to spit blood. Thereupon Pliny sent him to Egypt, where in the dry air he seemed better, and after a while Zosimus returned to his master, apparently completely restored. Pliny goes on, in his letter: "Having exerted himself again beyond his strength, there was a return of his former malady and a spitting of blood. For this reason, I intend to send him to your farm at Forum Julii (Fréjus), having often heard you mention the exceeding fine air there, and recommend the milk of that place as very salutary in disorders of this nature. I beg you will give directions to your people to receive him into your house, and to supply him with what he shall have occasion for: which will not be much; for he is so temperate as not only to abstain from delicacies, but even to deny himself the necessaries his ill health requires. I shall supply him with all that is needful for his journey. Farewell."

Now, on reaching Fréjus on a balmy day in April, when the air was soft as butter-milk, and the sun was hot, not scorching, my thoughts went at once to poor Zosimus, with his hacking cough, his delicate complexion, come here to inhale the soft air and drink the warm milk. And I thought of him the more from certain experiences of my own relative to Como. I went to that city in January from England, thinking that it lay in a warm nook, and that there I might bask for a few weeks, when recovering from an attack of bronchitis, till I was able to go further south.

I went into an hotel where I had stayed in summer and been comfortable; but—oh!—never shall I forget the horrors of that hotel in January! I was the sole person staying in it. There was no bedroom that had in it a stove. In the *salle-à-manger* the fire was lighted for half-an-hour at nine in the morning, then let out and not rekindled through the day. The fountain in the square was frozen. An icy wind descended from the Alps. My bedroom was a tomb; brick-floored, stone vaulted. My bed measured two feet across, and the sheet and crimson *duvet* were so nicely adjusted as exactly to fit the bed, when unoccupied. When I lay in the bed, that *duvet* was balanced like a logan stone on the ridge of my body shivering under it, and it oscillated as I shivered. Then it slid gently to the floor, and left me with a chill and damp linen sheet over me, the thermometer being below zero, and I—afflicted with a cough.

Next morning I fled—fled to Milan—was stabbed there by the Tramontana, fell ill, escaped to Genoa, and there recovered.

Now, perhaps, the reader will understand how it was that naturally, and at once, my mind turned to poor Zosimus, as I entered Fréjus. His dust is laid there—I doubt not. He had wandered there—some eighteen hundred years ago, and, like me, had inhaled the sweet scent of the flowering beans, looked on the Esterel chain glowing as if red-hot in the sunshine, and had entertained, like me, kindly, affectionate thoughts of that somewhat pedantic, conceited, but eminently worthy Caius Plinius Cæcilius Secundus.

Although Julius Cæsar is said to have formed the port at Forum Julii, and to have given the place his name, it is probable that there was a settlement there earlier. He, however raised it into consideration by the construction of the harbour. The port is there still, within its moles, and guarded by two castles on heights above it, but—alas for the well being of Fréjus, the harbour is filled with sand and soil brought down by the river Argens and washed in by the waves, and is now a level meadow, every portion belonging to a farmer cut off from another portion by a ditch, in which spring the rushes and croak the frogs. Augustus enlarged the port, and after the decisive battle of Actium (B.C. 31) sent thither the galleys captured from Anthony. The sea is now two miles distant.

The mistake of making ports at the mouths of rivers was one constantly made by the Romans. The Greeks knew better—Marseilles has not been choked.

Hard by, at Agay, is a perfect natural harbour. The red porphyry mountains rise in fantastic shapes above it, and plunge in abrupt crags into the deep blue water. It is a little harbour that calls out

"Come and rest in me from every wind." Now a lighthouse has been erected at the extremity of one of the natural moles of rock, a coastguard establishment crowns the heights, two or three fishermen's cottages nestle in the lap of the bay—that is all.

On the south of the port of Fréjus is an old castle. There must have existed there originally a nodule of rock, but out of this a platform has been formed artificially of earth gathered from the port, and this platform was converted in Roman times into a fort. On one side may be seen a curious contrivance for resisting the outward pressure of the earth heaped up within. The basement wall has not buttresses thrust forth, but consists of a series of semicircular concave depressions in its face. In Mediæval times a strong castle with circular towers was erected on the ancient basement, that also is now in ruins, the ledges where the old Roman wall ended and the Mediæval wall sprang at half the thickness of the former were, when I saw them, dense with white irises.

AQUEDUCT OF FRÉJUS.

Fréjus was supplied in Roman times with an aqueduct, the arches of which, broken and ruinous, still stretch across the plain, and were destined to convey into the town the waters of the Siagnole, from a distance of about fifty miles. The arcade is about forty-five feet high.

Following a path that leads along the ancient mole one reaches a quadrangular tower of Roman masonry with a stone conical roof, which goes by the name of the Lantern of Augustus, and is supposed to have served as lighthouse at the entrance of the harbour, but the height is too insignificant for this purpose, it is not over thirty-five feet, and there is no indication of any contrivance whereby it could have been utilised for the purpose of a pharos. In the Torlonia Museum at Rome is a bas-relief

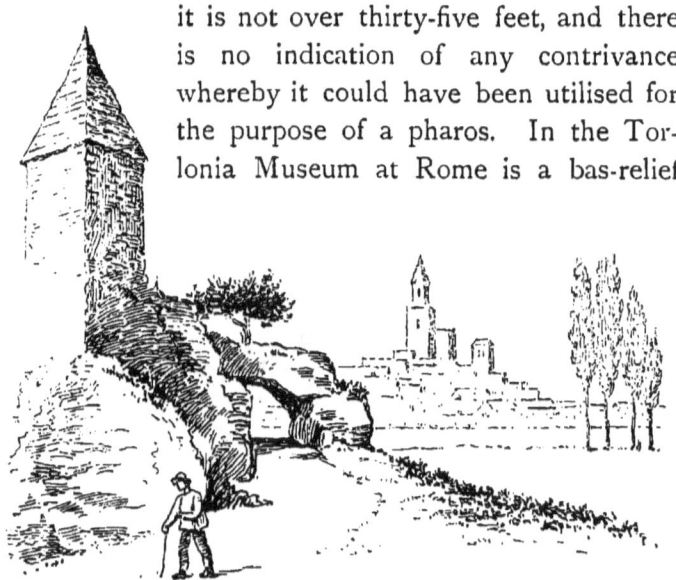

LANTERN OF AUGUSTUS.

representing the port of Ostia, with its pharos; that is a structure of several stages, each receding as it is superposed on the other, and the topmost sustains the ever-burning fire—quite a different sort of building from this tower at Fréjus.

Fréjus is a cathedral city, though numbering only 3,500 inhabitants, but it is an ancient see, dating from about 374, when it was an important maritime place. Its fortunes had gone down in the Middle Ages, and the citizens and prelates were never in a position to build much of a cathedral. The present church is of the eleventh century, both small and plain. It contains little of interest save a fine painting on gold ground of S. Margaret and other saints, brought from the ancient Monastery of Lerins. The organ gallery is supported on granite pillars, Classic, found among the ruins of the amphitheatre. The baptistery is surrounded by eight porphyry columns with Corinthian capitals taken from a pagan temple.

The carved doors of the cathedral deserve to be seen, they are of rich Rénaissance work. In the north aisle of the cathedral to the west is the tomb of two bishops of the seventeenth century, Bartholomew and Peter de Camelin, kneeling; and at the east end are two alabaster monuments of bishops three centuries earlier. The cloisters are of the usual Provençal type, the arcade resting on double columns, but walls have been erected blocking up the spaces, and the interior yard is turned into the bishop's fowl-house.

But—is not that sufficient? I am not writing a guide book; and I enter into these details here solely because the guide books pass over the cathedral very slightingly, and concern themselves chiefly with the Roman antiquities. Of these latter, besides what I have mentioned, there is the Porte Dorée, one arcade only of what was formerly a noble portico facing the harbour; also a fine amphitheatre, now traversed by a highway, not however as perfect as those of Nimes and Arles. Fragments also remain of the ancient theatre, but they are unimportant.

Hard by the Hotel de Ville is a beautiful red porphyry figure of a boy and a dolphin which one would have taken to have been Rénaissance work, but that the Rénaissance artists would hardly have taken the pains to sculpture such intractable material as porphyry for a petty town of the size of Fréjus. The group recalls that very odd story told by Pliny in one of his letters, which, as it may not be familiar to many of my readers, I will venture here to repeat. He says that the story "was related to him at table by a person of unsuspected veracity." At Hippo, in Africa, when the boys were playing in the lake that communicates with the sea, and the lads were contending together which could swim furthest, one boy found a dolphin play about him as he swam, and he ventured to climb on the back of the fish. The dolphin was not alarmed, but conveyed the little fellow on his back to the shore. The fame of this remarkable event spread through the town, and crowds came down to the water's edge to see the boy and ask him questions. Next day he went into the water again, and once more the dolphin appeared, played round him, and again took him on his back. This happened several times, and the circumstance was bruited throughout the neighbourhood, so that great numbers of people came in from the countryside to see the fish play in the water with the children, and carry them on its back. At last the authorities of the town, annoyed at the concourse of the curious, destroyed the playful dolphin, a bit of barbarity that excites Pliny's wrath.

To the south-west of Fréjus lies the Chaine des Maures, the outline of which is by no means so bold as that of the porphyry Esterel, but the mountains rise in sweeping lines from a broad and fertile plain covered and silvered with olives, growing out of rich red soil, like the old red sandstone of Devonshire. The red sandstone rocks through which the line passes are ploughed with rains. On the right appears the wonderfully picturesque little town of La Pauline, with an extensive ruined castle, and the walls and towers of the town in tolerable condition. Above it rises a stately peak capped with the white limestone that forms the mountains about Toulon and Marseilles, and having all the appearance of a flake of snow.

When we reach the basin between Aubaine and Camp-Major we are surrounded by these barren white ranges, so white that they look as if a miller had shaken his flour-bag over them.

But I have not quite done with Fréjus yet. I fear the reader will think I have given him a dull chapter of antiquarian and historical detail, so I will here add an anecdote, to spice it, concerning a worthy of Fréjus, Désaugiers, one of the liveliest of French poets. He was born at Fréjus in 1772. One day he was invited to preside at the annual banquet of the pork-butchers. At dessert everyone present was expected to pronounce an epigram or sing a song; and when the turn came to Désaugiers, he rose, cleared his throat, looked around with a twinkle in his eye, and thundered forth " Des Cochons, des Cochons."

The pork-butchers bridled up, grew red about the cheeks and temples, believing that an insult was intended, when Désaugiers proceeded with his song :—

"Décochons les traits de la satire."

Siéyès was another native of Fréjus, that renegade priest, to whom is attributed the ferocious saying, when called on to give his vote on the condemnation of Louis XVI., " La mort—sans phrases." Some few years after the Directory sent Siéyès as ambassador to Berlin. He invited a prince of the blood royal of Prussia to dine at the embassy with him ; but the prince took the invitation and scored across it his answer :—

" Non—sans phrases."

Napoleon as national recompense to Siéyès for the services he had rendered to France, and to himself personally, gave him the estate of Crosne. This gave rise to the epigram—

> " Bonaparte à Siéyès a fait présent de Crosne,
> Siéyès à Bonaparte a fait présent du trône."

But after all, it is chiefly as the birthplace of Agricola, that true model of a Roman soldier of the best description, that Fréjus interests us most. His father, Julius Græcinus, had fallen a victim to Caligula, because he refused to undertake the prosecution of a man the Emperor was determined to destroy, and there is some reason to suspect that Agricola himself was sacrificed to the suspicions and envy of Domitian. Like most good and honourable men, he had a good mother, whose virtues Tacitus records.

When Agricola was proconsul of Britain, his rule was mild, and he took pains to win the confidence of the provincials. He it was who drew a chain of forts from sea to sea between the Tyne and Solway, to protect the reclaimed subjects of the southern valleys from the untamed barbarians who roved the Cheviots and the Pentlands. He was not merely a conqueror, but an explorer and discoverer, in Scotland. In A.D. 83 he passed beyond the Frith and fought a great battle with the Caledonians near Stirling. The Roman entrenchments still remaining in Fife and Angus were thrown up by him. In 84 he fought another battle on the Grampians, and sent his fleet to circumnavigate Britain. The Roman vessels at all events for the first time entered the Pentland Frith; examined the Orkney islands, and perhaps gained a glimpse of the Shetlands.

It was interesting to tread the soil where the childhood was passed of a man who left such permanent marks in Britain, and to whom we are indebted for our first knowledge of Scotland.

CHAPTER IV.

MARSEILLES.

The three islands Phœnice, Phila, Iturium—Marseilles first a Phœnician colony—The tariff of fees exacted by the priests of Baal—The arrival of the Ionians—The legend of Protis and Gyptis—Second colony of Ionians—The voyages of Pytheas and Euthymenes—Capture of Marseilles by Trebonius—Position of the Greek city—The Acropolis—Greek inscriptions—The lady who never "jawed" her husband—The tomb of the sailor-boy—Hôtel des Négociants—Ménu—Entry of the President of the Republic—Entry of Francis I.—The church of S. Vincent—The Cathedral—Notre Dame de la Garde—The abbey of S. Victor—Catacombs—The fable of S. Lazarus.

The traveller approaching Marseilles from the sea observes three islets of bare limestone rock that are apparently a prolongation of that rocky promontory now crowned by the fortress of S. Nicolas, and that act as a natural breakwater against wave and storm from the S.E. They go by the names of Pomègue, Ratonneau, and Château d'If. But the classic geographers called the group the Little Stœchades, and named these islets Phœnice, Phila, and Iturium ; and these three appellations give us in a compact form the story of ancient Marseilles, founded by the

Phœnicians, refounded by the Greeks, and then made a dependency under the Roman empire.

That Marseilles was a Phœnician colony before the Phoceans settled there is shown by the monuments that have been exhumed from the foundations of the modern houses, and are now collected in the museum. There are some curious images of Melkarth and Melita, the Hercules and Venus of these Asiatic traders, known also to us through the Bible as Baal and Ashtaroth. But most curious of all is a long Phœnician table of charges made by the priests of Baal for the various sacrifices and oblations offered by the people. This tariff of charges was found in 1845. It consists of twenty-one lines, and begins :—

"The Temple of Baal.—This is the regulation relative to the dues legally established by Italis-Baal, the suffete, son of Bod-tanith, son of Bod-Milcarth, and by Italis-Baal.

"For an entire ox, the ordinary sacrifice, the priests are to receive ten shekels. At the sacrifice, in addition, three hundred mishekels of flesh.

"Item. For the ordinary sacrifice, of cereals and flour of wheat, also the hide, the entrails, and the feet of the victim. All the rest of the flesh goes to the master of the sacrifice."

So it continues to regulate the fees for a calf, a ram, a bird; also for cakes, and for offerings made by lepers and by common people. The table of fees is extremely curious and is, I believe, unique.

The Phœnician colony at Marseilles was probably in decline when, in B.C. 599, a Greek fleet left the port of Phocæa, one of the twelve Ionian cities of Asia

Minor, seeking new homes in the West. The colony was under the command of an adventurer named Protis. Attracted by the Bay of Marseilles, and the basin surrounded by hills that lay in its lap, the Greek colony disembarked.

And now for a legend.

The first measure taken by the new arrivals was to send a deputation to the King of the Segobrigæ, a Keltic race occupying what is now called Provence. The king was at Arles, which was his capital; his name was Nannos. By a happy coincidence the embassy arrived on the day upon which Nannos had assembled the warriors of his tribe, for his daughter, Gyptis, to choose a husband among them.

The arrival of the young Greek, Protis, in the midst of this banquet was a veritable *coup-de-théâtre*; he took his place at the board. His natural grace, his easy and polished manners, the nobleness and elegance of his person and features, contrasted strangely with the savagery and coarseness of the Gaulish warriors.

Free to choose whom she would, Gyptis rose from the table, filled a cup, and made the circuit of the board. Every eye was fixed on her; he was to be her choice to whom she offered the bowl. She did not hesitate for a moment, she went to the Greek stranger and extended it to him. Protis put the goblet to his lips, and the alliance was concluded.

The example of Gyptis was followed by some of her maidens. The Gauls agreed to receive the Greeks, and suffer them to colonise the basin of Marseilles

But the chiefs who had been set aside by the fair Gyptis bore a grudge against the new-comers. The growing prosperity and rapid development of the new settlement aroused their jealousy, which was probably augmented by the defection of some of their wives and daughters. Profiting by the Feast of Flora in May, they presented themselves at the gates of Marseilles in attendance on some waggons laden with green boughs, under which were their arms concealed. But love, that had founded the Ionian colony, was destined to save it. A young Gaulish woman revealed the plot to her Hellenic lover, and the Greeks laid their hands on the arms that were to have been employed against them, turned them against the intrusive Gauls, and massacred them to a man.

But having thus saved themselves from one danger they felt that they had incurred another. They had provoked the deadly animosity of the whole tribe of the Segobrigæ. They therefore appealed to their countrymen in Ionia to come to their aid. The appeal met with a ready response, a second fleet of colonists arrived. Marseilles was encompassed with walls on the land side, and thus made secure against the assaults of undisciplined barbarians.

Such is the graceful legend of the origin of Marseilles. It is only so far historical that it gives us in poetic and romantic form the main facts, that the first colony settled at Marseilles without opposition, that after a while it got embroiled with the Gaulish tribes of the neighbourhood, and that a second Ionian colony came to strengthen the first. But this second colony arrived B.C. 542, fifty-seven years after the first, and was due to the taking of Phocæa by the Medes and Persians.

As a Greek mercantile colony Marseilles flourished, and sent forth other colonies, that formed settlements along the Ligurian coast, as a Litoral crown from Ampurias and Rhodé in Catalonia to the confines of Etruria. Free, rich, protected by the Roman legions, these Greek settlements cultivated the arts and sciences with ardour, as well as carrying on the trade of the Mediterranean.

In the year B.C. 350 two of her most illustrious citizens, Pytheas and Euthymenes, explored the northern and southern Atlantic. Pytheas was charged to make a voyage of discovery towards the north. He coasted Spain, Portugal, Aquitania, Brittany, discovered Great Britain, coasted it, and reached Thule, which some have supposed to be Iceland, but others the Orkney Isles. In a second voyage he penetrated the Baltic by the Cattegat and Sound, and reached the mouths of the Dwina or the Vistula. On his return he composed two works, records of his discoveries, of which precious fragments have been preserved by Pliny and Strabo. Thanks to his labours, Marseilles was the first town whose latitude was determined with some precision.

About the same time, Euthymenes was commissioned to make explorations in the opposite direction. He sailed south-west, traced the western coast of Africa, and penetrated the mouths of the Senegal, whence he brought back gold dust.

Marseilles was taken, B.C. 49, by Trebonius, the lieutenant of Julius Cæsar. Two naval battles ruined her fleet; and, but for the clemency of Cæsar, the doom of the city would have been sealed. She had enthusiastically taken the part of Pompey, and had resisted Cæsar with unusual determination. But he appreciated the importance of the colony and the

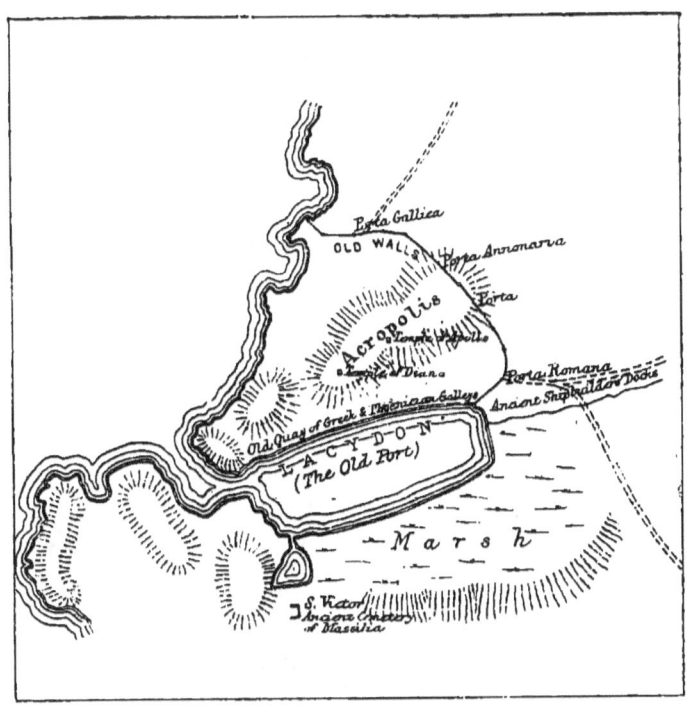

ANCIENT MASSILIA.

mercantile energy of her inhabitants, and he did not lay his hand in retribution too severely upon her.

The old Greek city of Massilia occupied the promontory which is still old Marseilles, clustered on the Butte St. Laurent and Butte des Moulins, where was the Acropolis, with the temples of Apollo and Diana, and the Butte des Cannes. The harbour was the natural fiord, which is now the Vieux port; and the modern splendid street Canebière runs along the site of the old shipbuilding-docks of the Greeks. Here was found a few years ago an ancient galley with keel and ribs of cedar, and coins in her of the date of Julius Cæsar. She is now in the museum. To the south of the old port was a marsh; the rectangular canal and the Bassin du Carénage mark the position of this marsh, now built over—a marsh that reached to the base of the limestone hills that rise to the peak now occupied by Notre Dame de la Garde.

The old Greek walls of Massilia ran in a sweep along where is now the Boulevard des Dames, Rue d'Aix, and reached the Vieux port at the Bourse.

Considering the importance of the Greek city, its wealth and splendour, it is surprising to find nowhere in Marseilles any ruins of its ancient founders. But Marseilles has traversed every historic period, in the midst of storm; and after a voyage of three thousand years through history, she has been plundered of every fragment of her ancient treasures. In Rome the Colosseum and the tomb of Augustus were robbed of their materials for the construction of houses; and in Marseilles every stone of her ancient temples and acropolis have been appropriated for baser purposes. She has passed through twenty fires, and as many sieges. Taken, sacked, decimated, she has been rebuilt over and over again, always hurriedly, consequently always with material taken where nearest at hand, without respect for her monuments and historic recollections. The disturbed soil of Marseilles is not even a heap of ruins, for every stone found in the soil has been utilised as material for construction. Nevertheless some traces of the Greek founders remain in the beautiful coins of the colony, and in inscriptions that have been picked out of the walls or foundations of mediæval houses. The coins, stamped with classic beauty, are well-known to numismatists.

We have space to notice only one or two inscriptions. One is the sign of Athenades, son of Dioscorides, professor of Latin grammar, probably set up two thousand years ago over his door; another is a notice of a young lad, Cleudemos, son of Dionysius, having gained a prize. A curious Greek inscription is found at Carpentras, a colony from Marseilles, that illustrates the manner in which foreign religions got mixed up with those that were proper to the Greeks.

"Blessed be Thebe, daughter of Thelhui, laden with oblations for the God Osiris—she never jawed her husband—she was blameless in the eyes of Osiris, and receives his benediction."

Truly such a wife deserved that her conduct towards her husband should be commemorated through ages upon ages, and we may thank good fortune that it has preserved to us the name of this incomparable lady.

As I am on the subject of Greek inscriptions, I may quote the following touching one, that has been found built into the wall of a house at Aix.

"On the banks, beaten by the waves, a youth appeals to thee, voyager! I, beloved by God, am no more subject to the domination of Death. I passed my life sailing on the sea, myself a sailor, like to the youthful gods, the Amyclæans, saviours of sailors, free from the yoke of matrimony. Here in my tomb, which I owe to the piety of my masters, I rest sheltered from all maladies, free from toil, from cares, from pains; whereas in life, all these woes fall on our gross envelopes of matter. The dead, on the other hand, are divided into two classes, of which one returns to the earth, whereas the other rises to join the dance with the celestial choirs; and it is to this latter class that I belong, having had the good fortune to range myself under the banners of the Divinity."

Clearly this was the tomb of a young sailor-boy, a native of Aix, who had served in a merchant vessel of Marseilles. There is something graceful and pathetic in the monument.

But enough of the past. Now for the present, and in considering the present let us attend to that which feeds and builds up that gross envelope of matter the young Greek sailor had laid aside.

At Marseilles I put up at the Hôtel des Négociants, in the Cours Belzunce. Let me observe that I do not see the fun of going to hotels of the first class. Not only is one's expense doubled, but one is thrown among English and American travellers, and sees nothing whatever of the people in whose country one is travelling. Now, here in this commercial inn, I had for dinner the following dishes, which I am quite sure I should not have had in the Grand Hôtel de Noailles, where a dinner is six francs, whereas at my inn I paid just half. I must also observe that the dinners were abundant and excellent, but among the dishes were some that were peculiar to the Provençal cuisine, for instance :—

Bread slices sopped in saffron, with fish, garnished with small crabs, to be chewed up, shell and all.

Artichokes, raw, with oil and vinegar.

Oranges with pepper and salt.

On the table were glass jugs with tar-water, and I observed that over half those present drank their wine diluted with this tar-water.

One day in summer I was at table-d'hôte in France when I saw a very fine melon on the table. Said I, in my heart of hearts, "I'll have some of you by-and-by!" But, to my consternation, the melon was taken round with stewed conger eel, and eaten with salt and pepper. I could not summon up courage to try the mixture, and the whole melon was consumed before the next course came on.

I was at Marseilles when M. Carnot, the President of the Republic visited it, April 16th. Great efforts were made to give him a splendid reception. Venetian masts were set up, strings of fairy lamps were suspended between them, and tricolours were hung as banners to the masts, or grouped together in trophies. But alas! No sooner were all preparations made, than a furious gale broke over the coast, the venetian masts swayed in the wind and were upset or thrown out of the perpendicular, the little lamps jingled against each other and were broken, such as were not shivered were filled with rain, the banners were lashed with the broken wires and torn to shreds, and when M. Carnot arrived, in a pouring rain, it was amidst a very wreckage of festival preparations, and he was received by a crowd of umbrellas. Under such circumstances enthusiasm was damped and ejaculations of welcome were muffled. The President occupied an open landau, and drove along the boulevards without umbrella or waterproof, bowing to right and left in a slashing rain. A deputation of flower women presented him with a sodden bouquet, by the hand of a dripping little girl in white that clung to her as a bathing gown. The President insisted on the maid being lifted to him into the carriage, where he hugged and kissed her, whilst the moisture ran out of her garments like a squeezed sponge, and this demonstration provoked some damp cheers.

I bought Henri Rochefort's paper next day, to see what his correspondent had to say about the visit. Some passages from it are too racy not to be quoted.

"Il faisait un temps à ne pas mettre un ministre dehors, lorsque le train présidentiel est arrivé en gare, et le défilé à la détrempe était pitieux à voir dans *le gargouillement et la transsudation de ce dégorgement cataractal.* Sadi Carnot avait donné l'ordre de laisser son landau découvert, afin de recevoir les ovations enthousiastes des parapluies.

"Bref, la Présidence est arrivée à la préfecture *trempée comme une soupe à l'oignon et fortement dessalée.*"

Verily there is no tongue like the French for saying nasty things in a nasty way.

I do not know whether it is fair for one to pass an opinion on a man from a sight of his face overrun with rain-water, and with his nose acting like a shoot from a roof; but certainly the impression produced on me by M. Sadi Carnot was that his features were wooden, and that he was but a very ordinary man—intellectually. I pass this opinion with hesitation. When dried possibly the sparks of genius may be discovered and may flare up; they were all but extinguished in the downpour when I saw him.

That cheerful king, Réné of Anjou and Provence, paid a visit to Marseilles in 1437, and made his royal entry on Sunday, December 15th. He was delighted with the reception accorded him, and in a gush of kindly feeling promised to make Marseilles his headquarters. But he forgot his promise, or circumstances were against his keeping it. He never revisited Marseilles. On January 22, 1516, Francis I. entered the town and was received by children carrying banners and garlands, and troups of young girls in white, then followed archers, arquebusiers, the consuls, and the clergy bearing the relics of S. Lazarus and S. Victor. A theatre was erected at every street corner, on which were presented to his sight incidents from the life of S. Louis. The procession ended with a battle of oranges and lemons, in which the king gave and received a good many blows on the head with the golden fruit.

At the head of the Allées des Capucins, a fine street planted with trees and with a handsome fountain in the place where the Allées de Meilhan unites with it, is a really fine modern Gothic church with twin west spires of open tracery. They are perhaps too thin, a usual fault with modern work, but otherwise the church is very good and stately. It is as fine within as without, but sorely disfigured by the coloured glass, which is garish. French painted glass is very bad. It is precisely the sort of stuff that was turned out by

English glass-painters about thirty years ago, the colours crude and distressing to the eye—windows that our more cultured taste cannot now endure. But the French artists have not advanced, the windows put in to-day are as detestable as those they put in at the beginning of the revival. Unfortunately, every cathedral is crowded through the length and breadth of France with this abominable stuff, that is only tolerable in a modern tasteless church, vulgar in its architecture and insipid in its sculpture, but is painfully out of place in a venerable minster.

The city of Marseilles has been lucky in securing a good architect for the Church of S. Vincent de Paul, but in another architectural venture Marseilles has been unfortunate. She was resolved to have a cathedral, and she gave the designing of it to a man void of taste, who has built a hideous erection on the quay in what he is pleased to call Byzantine style. I am quite sure any Byzantine architect would cheerfully have jumped into the Bosphorus rather than disfigure a city with such a structure as Notre Dame.

The Germans have a saying that the higher a monkey climbs the more he exposes his monkeyishness; and unfortunately this architect has been allowed to climb very high. He was given the peak of Notre Dame de la Garde, that towers over Marseilles, on which to erect a church. The site is exceptionally good, one on which a man of ordinary genius would have done something, could hardly have failed to have done something, that would have been picturesque. But such is the perversity of this unfortunate man's talent that he has erected a structure on the limestone crag, of

ABBEY OF S. VICTOR, MARSEILLES.

almost miraculous hideousness. It is also in so-called Byzantine architecture. There is a dish-cover which serves as a dome, and a tower which would be comical if it were not irritating. It resembles the handle of a rénaissance knife or fork stuck into a sheath and standing upright with a figure at top. We have made a blunder at South Kensington in setting side by side a depressed dome—the Albert Hall, and the acute pinnacle of the Albert Memorial; but a road runs between them, and it is possible to shut one eye and see one of these two structures apart from the other. But in Notre Dame de la Garde the two are combined in one building, and tease the eye from every point in Marseilles.

I ascended the steep crag to the church and found it full of a devout congregation. The service was the "Salut," and the Host was being elevated to the strains of "The Last Rose of Summer," on the hautbois stop of the organ.

The view from the platform of the church, of Marseilles, the coast, the blue Mediterranean and the islands is beautiful. Below Notre Dame de la Garde, and above the old port, stands the ancient Abbey of S. Victor; this abbey, of which the church alone remains, occupies a site where the successive generations of Massaliots buried their dead from the earliest pagan times, and here the first Christians formed catacombs of which some traces remain under the church, subterranean passages bearing some resemblance to those in the outskirts of Rome. The abbey itself was founded by Cassian, in the fourth century, over these galleries containing the bones of the first Christians, but his monastery was wrecked by the Saracens four hundred years later, and it was rebuilt in the eleventh and thirteenth centuries. What remains of this famous Abbey of S. Victor has rather the appearance of a fortress than a church; the walls and ramparts date from 1350, and were the work of William de Grimoard, who was prior of the monastery before he was elevated to be pope under the title of Urban V. The heavy, clumsy pile is a type of the architecture, at once military and ecclesiastical, that characterises most of the churches along the coast.

Externally the venerable church is devoid of beauty. No attempt at decoration has been made. It seems a shapeless pile of towers and machicolated and battlemented curtains, falling into almost complete ruin. But on passing through the single entrance, one finds oneself in a well-proportioned church of nave and side aisles, a south chapel, and an apse. Each buttress of the apse is battlemented outside and forms a turret, and two strong towers are adapted internally to serve as a transept and a porch.

Marseilles claims to have had as its first apostle Lazarus, whom Christ raised from the dead. The foundation of this myth is that in the fourth century it perhaps had a prelate of the name of Lazarus, though the earliest known bishop was Orestius, A.D. 314. The fact is that the existence of S. Lazarus at Marseilles was unsuspected till the eleventh century. When Cassian founded his abbey he dedicated it to S. Victor. If he had known anything about Lazarus, almost certainly he would have dedicated the church to him; he erected moreover, two other chapels, one to SS. Peter and Paul, the other to the Blessed Virgin and S. John the Baptist. When, in 1010, Benedict IX. enumerates the glories of the abbey restored after the destruction by the Saracens, he does not make the most transient allusion to S. Lazarus. However, Benedict IX., in 1040, does mention the passion of this Lazarus raised from the dead by Christ, as one of the causes why the abbey was venerable. His relics were said to have been transported thence to Athens, to preserve them from the Saracens. We shall learn more about this fable when we come to the Camargue.

CHAPTER V.

THE CRAU.

The Basin of Berre—A neglected harbour—The diluvium—Formation of the Crau—The two Craus—Canal of Craponne—Climate of the Crau—The Bise and Mistral—Force of the wind—Cypresses—A vision of kobolds.

ON leaving Marseilles by train for Arles, the line cuts through the limestone ridge of the Estaque, and the traveller passes from the basin of Marseilles into the much more extensive basin of Berre, surrounded by hills on all sides, a wide bowl like a volcanic crater, with the great inland salt lake of the Etang de Berre occupying its depths. This is a great natural harbour, seven times the size of the port of Toulon, and varying in depth from 28 to 32 feet; it is perfectly sheltered from every wind, and entire fleets might anchor there in security, not only out of reach, but out of sight of an enemy, for the chain of l'Estaque intervenes between it and the sea. It would seem as though Nature herself had designed Berre as a safe harbour for the merchant vessels that visit the south coast of France. It is almost inconceivable how this sheet of water, communicating with the sea by the channel of Martignes, can have been neglected; how it is that its still blue waters are not crowded with ships, and its smiling shores not studded with a chain of industrial and populous towns. " The neglect of this little inland sea as a port of refuge," says M. Elisée Reclus, " is an economic scandal. Whilst on dangerous coasts harbours are constructed at vast expense, here we have one that is perfect, and which has been neglected for fifteen centuries." But though the Romans or Greeks had a station here, they did not utilise the lagoon. At S. Chamas are remains of the masters of the ancient world, but no evidence that they had there a naval station.

The line cuts again through the lip of the basin, and we are in the Crau.

At a remote period, but, nevertheless, in one geologically modern, the vast floods of the diluvial age that flowed from the Alps brought down incredible quantities of rolled stones, the detritus of the Alps. This filled up a great bay now occupied by the mouths of the Rhone, and spread in a triangle from Avignon as the apex, to Cette in the west, and Fos in the east. This rubble, washed down from the Alps, forms the substratum of the immense plain that inclines at a very slight angle into the Mediterranean, and extends for a considerable distance below the sea. Not only did the Rhone bring down these boulders, but also the Durance, which enters the Rhone above Arles, and formed between the chain of Les Alpines and the Luberon another triangular plain of rolled stones, with the apex at Cavaillon and the base between Tarascon and Avignon. But the Durance did more. There is a break in the chain on the south, between the limestone Alpines and the sandstone Trévaresse; and the brimming Durance, unable to discharge all her water, choked with rubble, into the Rhone, burst through the open door or natural waste-pipe, by Salon, and carried a portion of her pebbles into the sea directly, without asking her sister the Rhone to help her. Now the two great plains formed by the delta of the Rhone, and that of the Durance into the Rhone, are called the great and little Craus. They were known to the ancients, and puzzled them not a little. Strabo says of the Great Crau : " Between Marseilles and the mouth of the Rhone, at about a hundred stadia from the sea, is a plain, circular in form, and a hundred stadia in diameter, to which a singular event obtained for it the name of the Field of Pebbles. It is, in fact, covered with pebbles, as big as the fist, among which grows some grass in sufficient abundance to pasture herds of oxen."

Then we are given the legend that accounts for it. Here Hercules fought against the Ligurians, when the son of Jove, having exhausted his arrows, was supplied with artillery by a discharge of stones from the sky, showered on his enemies by Jupiter.

This desert, a little Sahara in Europe, occupies 30,000 acres. " It is composed entirely of shingle," says Arthur Young, " being so uniform a mass of round stones, some to the size of a man's head, but of all sizes less, that the newly thrown up shingle of a sea-shore is hardly less free from soil; beneath these surface-stones is not so much a sand as a cemented rubble, with a small admixture of loam. Vegetation is rare and miserable, some of the absinthium and lavender so low and poor as scarcely to be recognised, and two or three miserable grasses, with *Centaurea calycitropes* and *solstitialis*, were the principal plants I could find." A mineralogical examination of the rolled stones presents peculiar interest. In the Little Crau, the mouth of the Durance, are found prodigious numbers of green and crystalline rocks, granite and variolite brought down from the Alps of Briançon, but nine-tenths of the pebbles of the Great Crau are white quartz brought from the great chain of the Alps, together with mica-slate and calcareous stones, and only a few of the variolites of Mont Genèvre. One may say that the Great Crau is a complete mineralogical collection of all the rocks that form the chain of the Alps, whence flow the Rhone and its tributaries.

The aspect of the Crau is infinitely desolate, but it is no longer as barren as it was formerly. It is in fact, undergoing gradual but sure transformation. This is due to a gentleman of Provence, named Adam de Craponne, born in 1525 at Salon, who conceived the idea of bringing some of the waters of the Durance through the gap where some of its overspill had flowed in the diluvial epoch, by a canal, into the Great Crau, so that it might deposit its rich alluvium over this desert of stones. He spent his life and his entire fortune in carrying out his scheme, and it is due to this that year by year the barren desert shrinks, and cultivation advances. There are to-day other canals, those of Les Alpines, of Langlade, and d'Istres, besides that of Craponne that assist in fertilising the waste. Wherever the water reaches, the soil is covered with trees, with pasture-land, with fields of corn; and in another century probably the sterility of the Crau will have been completely conquered.

In its present condition, the Crau may be divided into two parts, that which is watered, and which has been converted into a garden, and that which is not as yet reached by the rich loamy waters of the Durance, and is therefore parched and desolate, overrun by herds of sheep and cattle, driven down in winter from the Alps, when a certain amount of herbage is found on the desert, which in summer is utterly dry and barren. These migrations date back to a remote epoch, for they are mentioned by Pliny.

Previous to the construction of the canal by Craponne, who began it in 1554, the desert reached to Arles; the whole of the plain south of the chain of the Alpines was either marsh lagoon, or a waste of stones, where now grow and luxuriate mulberries, olives, almond trees and vines. The canal of Craponne was carried by the originator for thirty-three miles, sending out branches at Salon, Eyguières, and elsewhere. In winter the meadows are green as those of Devon in spring, and the fields yield heavy crops. Indeed, the Durance acts to this region in the same way as does the Nile to Egypt. "The meadows I viewed," says Young, "are among the most extraordinary spectacles the world can afford in respect to the amazing contrast between the soil in its natural and in its watered state, covered richly and luxuriantly with clover, chicory, rib-grass, and *Avena elatior.*"

The climate of the Crau presents contrasts most extreme. In winter the thermometer falls and remains below zero for many nights in succession, and the glacial *bise* sweeps over the face of the desert, curdling the blood; the flocks and herds seek shelter from this blast behind the long walls of dry stones, which sometimes the violence of the wind throws down upon them.

During the summer the phenomenon of the mirage is almost continuous. The bed of air in contact with the surface of stones scorched by the blazing sun becomes rarified and dilated, so that the horizon appears to be fringed on all sides with lakes of rippling water, most deceptive and tantalising to the eye of the traveller.

The troops of wandering bulls and wild horses, flights of rose-coloured flamingoes, of partridges and wild ducks give this region a pronounced oriental physiognomy, and however painful it may be at such a time to traverse this burning plain, it affords a curious picture of the Sahara in miniature nowhere else to be seen in Europe.

The great scourge of the Crau is the north-west wind, the *bise*, the black boreas of the ancients, so violent as to roll over the pebbles, and to blow away the roofs of houses, and tear up trees by the roots. In fact, the Crau may be regarded as the Home of the Winds.

It is easy to explain the origin of these furious gales, *bise* and *mistral*. The low sandy regions at the mouth of the Rhone, denuded of all vegetation, and the great stony plain of the Crau, heated by the direct rays of the sun, rarify the air over the surface of the soil, and this rises, to be at once replaced by the cold air from the Alps and Cevennes; the air off the snow pours down with headlong violence to occupy the vacuum. formed by the heated ascending column of air off the plain, sweeping the valley of the Rhone, and reaching its maximum of intensity between Avignon and the sea, where it meets, and is blunted in its force by the equable atmosphere that covers the surface of the Mediterranean.

The violence of the wind is consequently due to the difference of temperature between the hot air of the plain and the cold air of the mountain.

An old saying was to this effect:—

> "Parlement, Mistral et Durance
> Sont les trois fléaux de Provence."

Parlement exists no longer, or rather is expanded into a National Assembly that is a discredit to all France, and not Provence alone; the Durance has become, thanks to Adam de Craponne, an agent of fertilisation and wealth. But the *mistral* (*magistral*, the master-wind) remains, and still scourges the delta of the Rhone. In 1845 it carried away the suspension bridge between Beaucaire and Tarascon; the passage of the Rhone is often rendered impossible for days, through its violence. It has been found necessary to plant rows of cypress on each side of the line that crosses the Crau, to break the force of the wind upon the trains. Indeed, throughout the district, the fields will, in many places, be found walled up on all sides by plantations of cypresses from thirty to fifty feet high, as screens against this terrible blast, to protect the crops from being literally blown out of the ground.

When I was a child of five years my father's carriage with post horses was crossing the Crau. It was in summer. I sat on the box with my father and looked at the postilions. Presently I saw a number of little figures of men with peaked caps running about the horses and making attempts to scramble up them. I said something about what I saw, whereupon my father stopped the carriage and put me inside with my mother. The heat of the sun on my head, he concluded, had produced these illusions. For some time I continued to see these dwarfs running among the pebbles of the Crau, jumping over tufts of grass, or careering along the road by the carriage side, making faces at me. But gradually their number decreased, and I failed finally to see any more.

One June day in the year 1884, one of my boys, then aged eight, was picking gooseberries in the fruit garden at home, when, standing between the bushes, he saw a little man of his own height, with a brown peaked cap, a red jacket, and green breeches. He had black hair and whiskers and beard. He looked angrily at the boy and said something. The child was frightened, ran indoors and told his elder brother and sister. They brought him to me, and his elder brother repeated the story, but purposely varied the description of the apparition, so as to see whether the lad held to the same account, but the child at once corrected him, and told me his story, which his brother informed me agreed exactly with what in his alarm he had first told. The little boy was looking white and frightened. Again a case of sun on the head.

Now for another. A lady whom I know very well

F

indeed, and who never deviated from the truth in her life—save when she swore at the altar to honour and obey me—was walking one day, when a girl of thirteen, beside a quickset hedge; her brother was on the other side. I believe they were looking for birds' nests. All at once she saw a little man dressed entirely in green, with jacket, breeches, and high peaked hat, seated in the hedge, staring at her. She was paralysed with terror for a moment, then recovering herself, she called to her brother to come round and see the little green man. When he arrived the dwarf had disappeared.

Now these are funny stories, and are to be explained by the fact that the sun was hot on the head. But it does not strike me that the explanation is wholly satisfactory. *Why* should the sun on the head superinduce visions of kobolds? Is it because other people have suffered from a hot sun, and that the hot sun reproduces year after year the same phenomenon, that the fable of little men, pixies, gnomes, brownies, fairies, leprechauns is to be found everywhere? Or— is it possible that there is such a little creation only visible to man when he is subject to certain influences?

Sir Charles Isham, of Lamport, has collected a good deal of evidence of a similar nature. I do not venture to express an opinion one way or another. I can remember still, with vividness, the impression produced on me by what I saw that hot day on the Crau, when but a child of five years; but I cannot for the life of me explain it satisfactorily to myself.

CHAPTER VI.

LES ALYSCAMPS.

Difficulty of finding one's way about in Arles—The two inns—The *mistral*—The charm of Arles is in the past—A dead city—Situation of Arles on a nodule of limestone—The Elysian Fields—A burial-place for the submerged neighbourhood—The Alyscamp now in process of destruction—Expropriation of ancient tombs—Avenue of tombs—Old church of S. Honoré—S. Trophimus—S. Virgilius—Augustine, apostle of the English, consecrated by him—The Flying Dutchman—Tomb of Ælia—Of Julia Tyranna—Her musical instruments—Monument of Calpurnia—Her probable story—Mathematical *versus* classic studies—Tombs of *utriculares*—Christian sarcophagi—Probably older than the date usually attributed to them—A French author on the wreckage of the Elysian Fields.

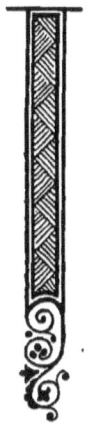

I do not know a more perplexing place anywhere to find one's way in and out of than Arles. During a fortnight spent there I never could hit my inn aright once on coming from the railway station. The place is like a labyrinth; but one of those labyrinths that our forefathers delighted to construct of pleached alleys of box or lime were always to be traversed when you possessed the key. There is no key, no principle whatever upon which Arles has been built. Every public edifice seems to be dodging round the corner, like Chevy Slyme, hiding from some other public edifice with which it is on dubious terms, or not quite on social equality, and wishes to avoid the difficulties of an encounter.

Arles streets are about the worst paved in Europe. They are floored with the cobble-stones rolled down by the diluvium, and torture the feet that walk over them and rick the ankles. There are two melancholy inns in the Place du Forum, and it is hard to choose between them, probably it does not much matter. I was given a bed-chamber in one where neither the door nor the window would shut, and where there were besides two locked doors that did not fit, and as the *mistral* was blowing, my hours in that room were spent in a swirl of draughts. Moreover, an old party with bronchitis was in the adjoining room, also suffering from the draughts, and in despair of recovering his health in such a situation. I complained, and was given another room where the draughts were the same, but I was without my coughing and hawking neighbour. No wonder that I was charged half a franc per night for my candle. It guttered itself in no time into the tray of the candlestick, as it was blown upon from four distinct directions simultaneously.

Arles—when not in a *mistral*—is charming, but the charm is in the past. There one must be a *laudator temporis acti*, for the present is wholly wretched and bad. The fact is, Arles had a glorious past, from which it has been falling throughout the Middle Ages till it reached a point approaching extinction, and it has not as yet realised that better days are shining before it, and that there is a future to which it may look up.

So depressed did Arles become some time ago, that its only lively trade was in old coffins. It had a vast cemetery outside its walls, crammed with memorials of the dead of all ages; and as the curators of the museums of Paris, Marseilles, Avignon, Aix, &c., thirsted after sarcophagi, the mournful Arelois went to their necropolis, dug up as many as were wanted, and forwarded coffins to those who had made requisition for them.

Arles is planted upon a nodule of limestone rock that rises out of the diluvium of rolled stones. In former times it was almost the sole dry spot to be found for miles round, and as the dead of Pagan and Christian times alike seem to have objected to wet beds, their bodies were transported from all the country round to the plateau east of Arles and there entombed. This plateau was called the Elysian Fields, now Alyscamp, and is so thick with tombs that you walk over them as you follow the road that runs along the plateau. You see the grass at the side dead in one place, there is a tomb there; you see a bit of white marble cropping up in another, that is a tomb. You see a great stack of stones heaped up by the side of a railway cutting, they are all tombs. You look at the cutting itself, and see that to a certain depth it is honeycombed with tombs, some cut through, some sticking out. In every farmyard the pigs eat out of old sarcophagi. The fountains squirt into them, the bacon is cured in them. The farrier dips his hot iron into a sarcophagus. In the churches the altars are made of them. The foundations of the houses are laid in them. The very air seems to be pervaded with the dust of the dead, and this dust lies heavy on the spirits and energies of the inhabitants.

But what an age we live in! Utilitarian and disrespectful of the past! The other day a cargo of mummied cat-deities arrived at Liverpool and was sold for manure. At Arles, the Paris, Lyons and Mediterranean Railway Company has bought up the Elysian Fields to convert them into a factory for their engines. The company are excavating Les Alyscamp for this purpose, throwing about the sarcophagi, Pagan or Christian, or using them for building materials— and sawn in half they make decent quoins for a brick-shed—and strewing the dust of the dead of ages under the wheels of the locomotives.

One undesecrated, unrifled headland remains above the factories, on which is a venerable but abandoned church. The company would grub that up too, but the proprietor will not sell, as he believes the tradition that an incalculable treasure is hidden somewhere among these tombs.

But the Arelois not only expropriate the tombs of their forefathers, they have given away or sold other things as well. On the Alyscamp is the venerable church of S. Honoré, half ruinous, in which, underground in the crypt is the ancient baptistery that had served the first Christians when the church was young. It was furnished with a large porphyry circular vessel for immersing adults. Louis XIV. saw it, coveted it for some water-works, and got the Arelois to give it him. Among the ruins of the theatre was found a Venus of Greek workmanship and of Parian marble. They sent it away also; it is in Paris.

The old church of S. Honoré is now reached by a long avenue of poplars lined with Pagan Roman tombs. The nave of the church is in ruins, but the choir is in tolerable condition, and is the most interesting portion. It consists in fact of an early Romanesque basilica with three aisles ending in three apses. The pillars separating nave from aisles, three on each side, are great drums ten feet in diameter. The later, ruinous nave contains the reputed chapel of S. Trophimus, apostle of Arles. When the fourteenth century church was added, this little chapel was left standing within, and though now crumbling, it is comparatively watertight. It has, however, undergone recasing in Renaissance times, and to understand its structure the chapel must be entered. It is then seen to have been an open porch of four semicircular arches, and may possibly have been erected over the tomb of S. Trophimus. The only ornament about it is a moulding, which may give its date.

S. Trophimus, reputed apostle of Aix, is now said to have been that Asiatic who was a companion of S. Paul mentioned in Acts xx. 4, xxi. 27–29, and 2 Tim. iv. 12, 20. But the very early diptychs of the church of Arles mention S. Dionysius as the first prelate, and the cathedral was built in 625 by S. Virgilius, and dedicated to S. Stephen. It did not take the title of S. Trophimus till the twelfth century, when the relics of this saint were brought to it from the little chapel just described. The exact date was 1152; the tradition of S. Trophimus having been one of the disciples of Christ and companion of S. Paul arose about this time. Not a trace of such a tradition appears in the Provençal poem composed by an eye-witness of the translation of the relics.

There was, no doubt, a bishop of this name at Arles, and probably early, but the first whose name is authenticated is Martianus, who followed the Novatian heresy in 254. Gregory of Tours—and his testimony is confirmed by a MS. of the fifth century—says that S. Trophimus was sent into Gaul in the consulship of Decius and Gratus, i.e., 250, and that he was the first bishop of Arles, and Gregory of Tours is the earliest and most reliable authority that we have on the beginnings of the Christian church in Gaul.

The church of S. Honoré was built by S. Virgilius, Archbishop of Arles A.D. 588–618, and the baptistery dates from his time. According to the legend, whilst he was erecting the basilica, the people toiled ineffectually to move the pillars to their destined place. At last they sent word to S. Virgil that the truck was fast, and the pillars could neither be taken on nor carried back. Then Virgil hurried to the spot, and saw a little devil, like a negro boy, sitting under the truck, obstructing its progress. Virgil drove him away, whereupon the columns were easily moved. He was buried in this church, but I do not fancy his tomb is known. A strange story is told of him, how one night, as he was pacing the walls of Arles, or possibly walking in the Alyscamp, he saw a mysterious ship come sailing over the meres. In the starlight he discerned forms of sailors. The ship drew up near where he stood, and a voice called to him: " Reverend father, we know who thou art. Now we are bound for Jerusalem, and are here to ask thee to come on board with us." " No, thank you," answered Virgilius, " not till you have shown me who you are." Then he made the sign of the cross, and suddenly the ship resolved itself into a drift of fog that rolled away before the wind along the surface of the mere. This is the *second* version of the world-wide-known myth of the Flying Dutchman. The earliest form comes to us in the legend of S. Adrian, a martyr in Asia Minor. As his widow Basilissa was sailing over the Black Sea with his body, to bury it at Byzantium, a phantom ship passed by, which also vanished when adjured in the sacred name.

What is, to us English, of interest in connection with S. Virgil of Arles is, that it was he who consecrated Augustine for his mission to Kent, at the command of Gregory the Great. So here, probably, in this ruinous, silent old church, our apostle of the English knelt and received his commission to go and preach the Gospel to us Angles. This same Virgil also built the cathedral, and dedicated it to S. Stephen. But of his work there not a trace remains. Another bishop of Arles of some note was Regulus, who when preaching one day was so troubled by the noise made by the frogs, that he interrupted his sermon to order them to be silent, and —they obeyed.

In a side chapel of the old church of S. Honoratus is a sarcophagus that contains the skull and bones and dust of a young girl. The coffin is of lead, and this perhaps accounts for the preservation. Along with it were found the gold ear-rings and other trinkets. On the ear-rings a cross, but the inscription on the tomb hardly leads one to believe the girl was a Christian. She was aged seventeen years, eight months, and eighteen days, when she died. Her name was Ælia. Here is the inscription in the lead, translated :—

ÆLIA, DAUGHTER OF ÆLIA.

Thou who can'st read these lines, read a sad mishap, and learn our plaintive lay.
Many call that a sarcophagus which contains bones,
But this has become the home of unhallowed bees.*
Shame it should be so! Here lies a damsel of exceeding beauty.
There's more than grief in this: a dearly loved wife has been snatched away.
She lived a virgin so long as Nature willed.
When she became a bride, the marriage vows were a joy to her parents.
She lived seventeen years, eight months, and eighteen days.
Happy the father who lived not to see such sorrow.
The wound rankles in the bosom of her mother, her precious jewel,
And her father, taken away in old age, still holds her clasped to his heart.

Here is the original with conjectural restorations. Would not old Dr. Keates have whipped the Eton boy who wrote such barbarous Latin verses! But it must be remembered the Arles folk were Græco-Gallic, and not masters of Latin. Some of the words are run together. It runs thus—

ÆLIA ÆLIÆ.

Littera. quinosti. lege. casum. et. d(*ice querelam.*)
Multi. sarcophagum. dicunt. quod. con(*tinet ossa :*)
Set. conclusa. decens. apibus. domus. ist(*a profanis :*)
Onefas. indignum. jacet. hic. præclara (*puella.*)
Hoc. plusquam. dolor. est. rapta. est. s(*uavissima conjux.*)
Pervixit. virgo. vbi. jam. natura. placebat.
Vixit. enim. ann. xvii. et. menses viii. diesque xviii.
O. felice. patrem. qui. non. vidit. tale. dolorem.
Hoeret. et. in fixo. pectore. volnus. dionysyadi matri.
Et junctam. secum. geron. pater. tenet. ipse. puellam.

---

* The ancients thought that bees were bred of dead bodies. See Virgil, Georgics. iv. 281–5.

This is an exact copy. I am not responsible for the grammatical blunders, they were made clearly by the sculptor of the inscription, who did not understand what he cut.

Among the tombs extracted from the Alyscamp and now in the Museum of Arles, is another of a girl, and a very accomplished young lady she must have been ; her name was Julia, and she was the daughter of Lucius Tyrannus. She died at the age of twenty ; the inscription on her tomb records that in her morals and in her schooling she was a pattern to all other girls.

MUSICAL INSTRUMENTS FROM THE TOMB OF JULIA.

What is particularly interesting about this monument is that it gives illustrations of all the musical instruments she was able to play, and it affords us I believe, the earliest known example of the organ.* But what is even more curious is that on it is represented a guitar, very much the same as is now manufactured.

* Nero on the night when he died was going to try a water-organ, when the news of the revolt of Galba and the defection of the troops reached him. I am puzzled about this organ on the tomb of Julia Tyranna. Sir George Grove, in his 'Dictionary of Music,' gives an illustration of this same organ copied from Dom. Bedos' 'L'Art du Facteur d'Orgues,' Paris, 1766. This represents two slaves crouched and blowing into the organ bellows. I could not see these figures. I made my sketch carefully, and can hardly suppose the figures have been chipped away since the monument was placed in the museum.

The instruments she could play were the organ, the guitar, the syrinx or panpipe, and the lyre, which she struck not with her fingers, but a plectrum represented beside it. Observe, between the lyre and the banjo her little satchel of music-books, and below the syrinx a lamb and palm. This is the only sign on the monument that could in the least lead to a supposition that Julia Tyranna was Christian. The inscription bears no trace of Christianity.

Another interesting monument found there is that to Calpurnia, daughter of Caius Marius. Probably she died from the exposure and roughness of life camping out, when the barbarian hordes rolled west, and all the inhabitants of the towns were obliged to fly before them to the hills. I shall in a future chapter tell the story of Caius Marius and his great victory at Pourrières over the Teutons, having first thrashed the Ambrons near Aix. Suffice it now to note that here is the tombstone of his poor little daughter. I must, however, state that the genuineness of this inscription has been called in question. It is also worthy of notice how that the victory of Marius and delivery from the barbarians impressed the people of the neighbourhood. In the museum the name of Marius occurs on other monuments. The name of Marius is even now a popular Christian name in Provence.

CALPURNIA'S MONUMENT.

But to return to Calpurnia. The place where the Arles inhabitants fled from the Teutons was the limestone range of Les Alpines, almost an island, so surrounded was it by lagoons and marshes.

Looking at Calpurnia's monument I fell into a dream, and saw her whole story unfolded before me. Caius Marius was a rough-mannered man, of peasant origin, but he had a wife Julia, of patrician rank, and who, I have not a shadow of doubt, flourished her noble origin before him, and talked very big of her grand relations. When little missie was born: "I'll have none of your plebeian names, if you please, for my baby," said Julia; "you will please note that my family derives from the immortal gods. I shall call the child Calpurnia."* Madame Julia was a good wife, and she followed her rough husband everywhere. At the beginning of windy March, tidings came that the Teutons and Ambrons were on the move. In April all the women and children of Arles, Glanum, Ernaginum, and Cabelio were clustered on the heights of Les Alpines, in extemporised cabins or in some of the prehistoric habitations they found scooped out of the limestone. Down came the rains. A gale and driving out-pour then as to-day, when M. Carnot comes into Provence. The roofs of the cabins let in water, the sides of the caves ran down with moisture. Then the wind changed, the sun shone out hot, but the *mistral* tore over the country cold and sharp as a double-edged sword. Poor Calpurnia could not stand it. She shivered and coughed, lost appetite and spirits. Next came the tidings of the battle at Les Milles, and

* See Appendix A. on this monument and the question of its genuineness; as well as for some other inscriptions in the Arles Museum.

a couple of days later of the extermination of the enemy at Pourrières. Now the refugees might in safety descend from their rocky refuges, and return to their homes.

Then Julia went with the sick girl to Arles. Meantime Marius on the battlefield had received the ovation of his officers and soldiers, and the salutations of the delegates from the senate proclaiming him consul. But at the same time there appeared—I doubt not, though Plutarch does not say so—a slave with a note from Julia :—

"I am sorry to tell you that Calpurnia is very unwell. That horrible *mistral* froze her, and she has done little else than cough night and day since. I have given her snail broth, but it has not relieved her much, and she is now spitting blood. Bother these Teutons, it is all their work. I always told you that you made a mistake in letting them come into Provence, and cross the Rhone. However, you were ever pigheaded, and now it serves you right. You will lose Calpurnia, who is the apple of your eye. Now if you had listened to me, etc., etc.

"Salve."

But there was something further to complicate matters, and superinduce sickness in a delicate girl. To escape to the hills the good people of Arles could not follow a road, for the whole district between them and the range of Les Alpines was covered with one vast lagoon. They could not travel in boats, for the lagoon was shallow, so they went on rafts supported on inflated skins, about which I shall have something to say presently. So Calpurnia, creeping close to her mother,

LES ALYSCAMPS. 79

wrapped in her *pallium*, was exposed for hours on a raft at the beginning of April to the cold winds, and to the water oozing up between the joints of the raft.

The whole story works out like an equation. I fancy—but am not sure—a quadratic equation, somehow thus :—

As I, in a 19th cent. hotel, and in Jäger underclothing :
Calpurnia, on a raft and in a pre-historic cave : : a cold in the head
I got : x
$x \times$ self in hotel and Jäger costume = Calpurnia on a raft and in a cave $\times$ cold in the head.
$x =$ pthysis.

I think this is right. I cannot be sure ; and I cannot be sure, though I was educated to be a mathematician by a senior wrangler.

The facts were these. My dear father thought, and thought perhaps justly, that a classical education was but a throwing back of the current of the mind into the past, whereas a mathematical education directed it to the future, and was the sole course which would prove Pactolean. So I was cut down in my classical studies, and drawn out in those which were mathematical. Likewise I was sent the year before entering the university to a senior wrangler to ripen me. I then learned that what as a boy I was wont to call the Rule of Three was more properly termed equations, and that equations might be complicated to the highest limits of muddledom, and when so complicated were termed quadratics. After a course of equations that flattened out my head like the Camargue, I was thrust into what are called surds, a sort of wood of errors, in which one spends hours in hewing one's way to get at nothing of the slightest profit to man or beast; finally, I believe my good tutor, now a bishop, got tired of me. I was stupefied by surds; and I entered the university. Now, after thirty-seven years, I find that every ode of Horace, every chapter of Cæsar, every line of Virgil I learned at school lies as a sprig of lavender in the folds of my memory—but I cannot even set and work out a common equation, or add up a sum in compound addition correctly.

I beg the pardon of the reader for this digression. I have made it because I think, should my reader be a father, this experience of mine may be of profit to him.

To return to the monuments of the Elysian Fields. A considerable number have been found here, also at Nimes, S. Gabriel, and Cavaillon, which are the memorials of *utriculares*.* There were guilds of these men. They appointed noble Romans as their patrons, and these patrons on their tombstones made mention of the fact. But what were these *utriculares?* They were raftsmen who carried on trade over the lagoons, sustaining their flat vessels upon distended skins. The lagoons were so shallow that no vessel of deep draught could travel over them, and all the merchandise of central Gaul for the Mediterranean—the tin from Britain for instance—and all the goods of the Mediterranean for Gaul, had to be transhipped at Arles from the river boats, unable to cross the bar, on to these barges sustained on inflated skins that conveyed them to Fos, at the mouth of the lagoons, where they were again

* See Appendix C.

shipped for the sea voyage. After Marius had cut a canal, matters were better. Ships could come up through the lagoons to Arles, but none at any time of deep draught, and the raftsmen, the *utriculares*, carried on their trade till the Middle Ages, when the mouths of the lagoons became choked, and the lagoons themselves turned into noxious morasses. Here is one of their monuments, in the museum of Arles :—

"To the manes. To Marcus Junius Messianus, of the guild of the utriculares of Arles, four times president of this corporation Junia Valeria raised this monument to him, her son, who died aged twenty-eight years, five months, and ten days."

Here is another, found near Lyons :—

"To the manes and eternal repose of Caius Victorinus .... urix, also called Quiguro, citizen of Lyons, one of the corporation of utriculares there, who lived twenty-eight years, ... months and five days, without giving offence to anyone. His mother, Castorina, raised this to the memory of her sole and very dear boy."

The navigation on distended skins is now everywhere extinct except on the Euphrates. On some of the Nineveh sculptures may be seen men swimming across rivers sustained on these primitive air-vessels.

In the museum at Arles are numerous sculptured Christian sarcophagi, with groups of the Raising of Lazarus, the Multiplication of Loaves, the Striking of the Rock by Moses, the Opening of the Eyes of the Blind, &c. These are attributed to the fourth and fifth centuries. For myself I am by no means satisfied that the Christian sarcophagi of rich and beautiful sculpture are as late as the dates generally given to them. I judge by the fashion of the hair worn by the ladies. Now there is a sarcophagus at Arles with the twelve apostles on it, six on each side of Christ, and a portrait of the deceased. This is set down to be a tomb of the fifth century, and yet the lady wears her hair in precisely the fashion, and it was a peculiar one, of the Faustinas, the wives of Antoninus Pius and Marcus Aurelius, A.D. 138-177. It must not be forgotten that the protection of the laws was extended to Christian sepulchres as well as Pagan till the edict of Valerian in A.D. 257, and although this was withdrawn by Gallienus in A.D. 260, yet after that edict, the cemeteries, the catacombs, were never quite secure; before that, the Christians made no concealment of their places of burial, they used the richest available decorations for them, in sculpture and in painting. Only after A.D. 257 do the ornamentations cease, or become hastily sketched and rude, and the inscriptions degenerate into scrawls. All the finest, costliest work in the Roman catacombs belongs to the first two centuries and the beginning of the third. When peace returned to the Church, art had fallen into decay, and there were not sculptors capable of performing such work as had been done before. No more convincing proof of this can be found than the two porphyry tombs of Constantia and Helena, daughter and mother of Constantine, now in the Vatican.

To what a depth of degeneracy sculpture fell may be judged by the lid of the sarcophagus of S. Hilary, Bishop of Arles, d. 449, now in the Arles museum. Beside the rude lettering, there are but a leaf and two birds on it, but they might have been scribbled by a child. It is to me inconceivable that some of the beautiful white marble sarcophagi both at Arles and at

Rome, sculptured with Scriptural scenes, can belong to the period when art was as degraded as it certainly was in the time of Constantine, and I think that antiquarians have been misled in dating them.

Before taking leave of the Elysian Fields, I must quote the words of a French author upon them :—" It has been a rich quarry only too easily worked, and we will not here enter on the painful story of its spoliation. All the museums of the south of France possess tombs stolen from the Alyscamp. As to the monolithic tombs, they were abandoned to any one who cared to have them, and for many centuries have been regarded as stones quarried ready for use. The city of Arles has on several occasions had the culpable condescension of giving up the tombs of its ancestors to the princes and great men of the world. Charles IX. laded several ships with them, which sank in the Rhone at Pont S. Esprit. The Duke of Savoy, the Prince of Lorraine, the Cardinal Richelieu, and a hundred others have taken away just what they liked, and Arles to-day has hardly more to show of this vast cemetery than an avenue—but a noble one—of sarcophagi and some fragments of fine Gothic or Romanesque chapels lost in the midst of a desert." *

* Lenthéric, ' La Grèce et l'Orient en Provence,' 1878.

CHAPTER VII.

PAGAN ARLES.

The Arles race a mixture of Greek and Gaulish—The colonisation by the Romans—The type of beauty in Arles—The amphitheatre—A bull-baiting—Provençal bull-baits different from Spanish bull-fights—The theatre—The ancient Greek stage—The destruction of the Arles theatre—Excavation of the orchestra—Discovery of the Venus of Arles—A sick girl—Palace of Constantine.

BEFORE describing Arles I began with the Elysian Fields, the great cemetery of Pagan and Christian Arles, for this seems to have affected the whole town, and with the dust of ages to have smothered the life out of it.

Now let us look at the remains of ancient Arles. But first of all let me observe that the Arles race prides itself on its singular purity of descent. There was, unquestionably, a Gaulish settlement there. The Keltic name Ar-lath, the "moist habitation," tells us as much. So does the legend of Protis and Gyptis, already related. But it was speedily occupied by a large Greek contingent, and the race was formed of

Greek and Gaulish blood united. In the year B.C. 46 a Roman colony was planted at Arles. Cæsar, desirous of paying off his debt of gratitude to the officers and soldiers who had served him in his wars, commissioned Claudius Tiberius Nero, one of his quæstors, father and grandfather of the emperors Tiberius, Claudius, and Caligula, to conduct two colonies into Southern Gaul, one was settled at Narbonne and the other at Arles, and this was one of the first military colonies planted beyond Italy.

The office of this Tiberius was to portion out the land among the veteran soldiers, six thousand men of the Sixth Legion occupied the town and country round —such of it, at all events, as was not under water—and thenceforth the city took the name of Arelate Sextanorum. Tacitus gives us a picture of the proceedings on such occasions. After the tribunes and the centurions came a cloud of officials called *agrimensores*, surveyors, charged with the duty of parcelling out the soil among the new comers. Then followed a hierarchy of civil officers, religious, judicial, administrative, all under the direction of an administrator-general, who was entitled *curator coloniæ*. From that moment the transformation of the colonial town into a little Rome was a matter of time only. The new comers constructed a capitol, a forum, temples, triumphal arches, aqueducts, markets; besides these, theatres, a circus, baths. In a very few years the aspect of Arles was completely changed. A mercantile city of Græco-Gauls had become Latinised, bureaucratic, and flattered itself that it was like its new parent on the Tiber. It called itself *Gallula Roma, Arelas*.

Consequently, we find in Arles a strong current of Roman blood mingled with the Greek and Gallic, and there has been practically no other admixture. Cut off from the country round by its marshes and lagoons, it has maintained its purity of blood and its characteristic stamp of face. The Arles women are said to be, believe themselves to be, and show to everyone that they believe themselves to be, the handsomest women in France. Their type is quite distinct from that of the inhabitants of Nimes, Marseilles, Aix, and even of the peasantry outside the gates of Arles. What is the more singular is that this peculiarity of type is not noticeable among the men. Among the women it is quite unmistakable. Their straight brows and noses are sometimes Greek, but the Roman arch appears as frequently as the straight nose; they have magnificent dark eyes; black hair which is curled up over their broad straight brows, brought forward about their faces so as to form a dark misty halo round the olive-complexioned features, then tied into a horn at the top of the head, which is bound round with black satin ribbon, that flows down at

AN ARELAISE.
(*From a Photograph.*)

the back. The face is haughty, noble, somewhat imperious. Queens these Arelaises feel themselves to be, down to the fishwives in the market-place; they walk as queens, as well as the cobble stones will permit, and bear themselves, their black mantillas cast over their arms, in a queen-like manner.

I had a fine opportunity of studying them, for I went to the first bull-fight of the season in the old Roman arena, and all Arles was there, male and female, down to the babies in arms. Between each *course* all the spectators promenaded under the galleries and on the terrace at the top of the amphitheatre, the women in gala dress of white lace bodices, black mantle, and dark silk skirts; and a very fine sight they were; it was worth the forty centimes I paid for admission to see these majestic women pace along and sweep the little men from their path as they careered round and round the amphitheatre, with cold, stern faces, full of pride of ancestry and conscious beauty.

I will quote the opinion on the Arles type of a very competent judge perfectly acquainted with the whole of Provence :—" It can be affirmed without contradiction that Greek beauty exists at Arles, and exists only among the women. The men are clumsy, small and vulgar, rude in form and rough in vocal intonation. The women, on the contrary, have preserved the ancestral delicacy. The face is that of a cameo, the nose is straight, the chin very Greek, the ear delicately modelled; the eyes, admirably shaped, have in them a sort of Attic grace, transmitted from their mothers, and to be handed on to the children.

" To get an idea of this characteristic type, one must

not study two or three subjects, but must observe the whole population *en bloc*, and especially compare it with the neighbouring populations. The result of such a comparison brings out with force the grand lines constituting in the Arelaise the character of a perfectly definite and distinct race."*

As I have already mentioned the amphitheatre, I will begin my account of the antiquities of Arles with that. In the Middle Ages it was turned into a fortified *bourg* in the heart of fortified Arles; it contained streets about as broad as a man could walk up and touch walls on both sides with arms akimbo, a crowd of houses, and two chapels or churches. Four great towers were erected at the cardinal points, and the vast galleries and arcades were a very warren of human habitations. Constructed of huge blocks of limestone, laid without cement, the amphitheatre forms an ellipse, whose axis measures four hundred and twenty feet by three

PART OF THE AMPHITHEATRE OF ARLES.

* Lenthéric, *op. cit.*

hundred and ten feet. It is said to be able to contain twenty-six thousand spectators, which is just two thousand five hundred more persons than the entire population of modern Arles.

Externally it presents two stages of sixty arcades, between the arches are engaged Doric pillars in the lower storey, those above are Corinthian, but only about six of the capitals of these latter remain. There are, within, three stages of seats, those for the senators, those for the knights, and the upper range for the common people, now much mutilated, and turned into a promenade. Fortunately the accumulation of earth over which the houses were built within the arena was so great, that when that was cleared away, the marble casing of the *podium* was disclosed in very tolerable perfection.

When I visited the amphitheatre, Les Arènes they are called, it was to see a *Course aux Taureaux*. The Provençals are passionately fond of these bull-baits, which take place weekly through the summer, beginning at Easter, but it is only at Arles and Nimes that they are carried out in the ancient Roman amphitheatres.

These *courses* are quite distinct from the Spanish bull-fights. There is no brutality, no torturing of the beast with arrows and crackers, no goring of horses. The bull is uninjured, and, though he gets furious, clearly relishes the fight, and in some cases cannot be induced to abandon it. The old proconsular seat was draped, and occupied by the *préfet* and madame, and the *sous-préfet*. The spectators went where they liked, men paid fourpence, women threepence for admission. The arena was enclosed within a screen of strong timber boards.

Five wild bulls from the Camargue were advertised to be baited. One, a strong black fellow, Nero, was clearly a favourite—his name was announced in very large letters. Every bull is given a rosette of coloured ribbons, fastened between his horns, and the sport consists in plucking away this rosette, and bearing it in safety beyond the barricades. Should a rosette fall to the ground, it does not count. A prize is given to whoever recovers a rosette. The blood-red rosette of Nero entitled the snatcher of it to one hundred francs. Another characteristic feature of the Provençal *courses* is that there are no professional toreadors. Any man or boy who likes enters the lists against the bull. Usually there are from a dozen to a score and a half in the arena, all endeavouring to pluck the bunch of ribbons from the brow of the enraged bull.

From practice, and acquaintance with the habits of bulls, the young men become very skilful, and fatal accidents are rare. The amateur runs up alongside of the bull, swings himself round in front of it, and makes his snatch. The bull at once goes at him, and he takes to his heels. When he is flying a second invariably runs across his path at right angles, and the bull can never resist the temptation of turning upon this second. If he also is hard pressed, a third crosses between him and the bull, and again diverts the angry beast. In one case a man's foot slipped as he was flying, and he fell. Then the bull was on him before another could intervene, but the brute rolled over the prostrate man, who got up, shook himself, and cleared the barricade.

One very nimble young fellow in a grey shirt had attracted general attention by his dexterity. He was resolved to have Nero's rosette. He managed to wrench it from between the bull's horns, but not completely to disengage it. The bull drove after him so close that it was impossible for another man to run between, the grey shirt reached the barrier and swung over, but the horns caught his nether garment and rent it, fortunately without really injuring the man, who, however, was not able to enter the arena again that day.

BACK OF A HOUSE AT ARLES.

When a *course* has been run the doors are opened, and one or two young bulls are sent into the arena; they run round, and the bull who has been baited adjoins them, and they all run out together. Nero, however, would not go. He was fagged, but his blood was up. Five bulls were sent in to lure him away, but he was resolved to gore his man before he left. His rosette he had dangling on his brow, uncaptured.

Then the keepers entered with a species of halbert, with half-moon shaped steels at the head, and one small spike in the midst. With this they caught the horns of Nero, and he was forced to retreat before the men, for if he resisted the spike entered his head and hurt him. Thus finally, by sheer force, he was driven, snorting, pawing the ground, and with arched tail from off the place of contest.

The sport is good. It is not cruel. It draws out the courage, provokes dexterity and nimbleness, and takes the place in Provence that cricket does in England and golf in Scotland.

The Romans loved the brutal and demoralising games of the amphitheatre. Wherever they went they erected these huge places for entertaining themselves with the spectacle of suffering. There never was an amphitheatre at Marseilles, for Marseilles was Greek and not Roman, and to the Greek such spectacles were abhorrent.

At Arles there are the equally interesting remains of a theatre. The stage is fairly perfect, with its customary scenery of Corinthian pillars grouped so as to form two doors for entrance and exit between them. The pillars of this permanent scene are not all in place. Two are standing, and the bases of others remain. At the proscenium may be noticed the grooves into which the beams fitted for the wooden small stage that stood forward in front of the curtain.

The ancient Greek theatre was composed, like that of our days, of a hemicycle for the spectators, and a rectangular portion that formed the place for dramatic performance. The pit was a semicircle, and was not fitted with seats, but constituted the orchestra. This orchestra among the Greeks formed an inferior stage, and, as its name implies, was reserved for the ballet. It was not till Roman times that specially privileged spectators were admitted into it, but it never had the musicians installed in it. These latter were placed in front of the stage, much where is our modern proscenium. The actors performed, as nowadays, on the boarded anterior portion, which was called the *pulpitum*. Finally, to facilitate communication between the stage and the orchestra, a pair of flights of steps descended laterally from the proscenium. In the centre of the pit or orchestra was usually placed an altar to Bacchus, around which the choirs executed their evolutions; and against this little altar sat the prompter, hidden by it, whilst some flute-players stood beside the altar, in flowing robes, acting as ballet masters, and giving the measure with the shrill notes of their pipes.

The Greek tragedy, therefore, had a double action, one on the stage proper and the other below, and all was graceful and refined. The purest taste, the most elevated sentiments, were the characteristics of the Greek drama, and the most beautiful and stirring effects were produced by means of the utmost simplicity. Thus, when the Tragedy of the Persæ of Æschylus was being performed, the depth of the stage opened, to show in the distance the blue sea on which a recent victory had taken place, with the rocky isle of Salamis bathed in the tints of the Eastern setting sun. A thrill of the most lively emotion ran instantly through the whole crowd of spectators. But with the Romans the theatre lost its dignity, and was degraded to low buffoonery, indecencies the most repulsive, and to gaudy spectacles. So bad was the moral result produced by the theatre, that the first Christian bishops who were able to do so, stirred their adherents to the destruction of this breeding-place of moral pestilence. The MS. chronicles of the church of Arles have preserved the name of the man who destroyed the theatre. He was a deacon, Cyril; acting under a strong moral impulse, filled with righteous indignation at the obscenities perpetrated on the boards, he roused the Christian populace of Arles to attack and wreck the theatre and expel the actors. The mob burst in—tore the marble from the proscenium, smashed the statues of admirable Greek sculpture, overthrew the altar and ground it to powder, upset the columns, and reduced it to a state of ruin very little better than that in which it is at present. Heads of statues were knocked off, bas-reliefs broken in half, cornices, capitals, were thrown into the pit and choked it to the level of the stage.

In 1651 the pick was set to work to clear out this orchestra, and almost the first stroke revealed one of the most admirable works of Greek sculpture that has descended to us, the Venus of Arles, an imitation or reproduction of the celebrated Venus of Praxiteles, now, unhappily, lost. This statue lay before the columns of the proscenium and had been saved from destruction by the ruins that had buried it. Head and body are almost intact, only the arms were gone.

The goddess is half naked, like the Venus of Milo. The bust is slightly turned. Head and coiffure are of the noblest and purest execution.

It was evening when I visited the theàtre, a balmy spring evening, where shelter could be obtained from a cold wind. The pink Judas trees were in full flower. The syringas scented the air. The golden sunlight filled the theatre with light and warmth. But two persons were present, except myself. Seated on one of the white marble steps for the audience, was an Arles mother with a royal face, in the quaintly beautiful costume the women of all classes still affect, and she had spread her mantle over the shoulders of a girl of fourteen, sick, with face of the purest alabaster, and of features as fine as were ever traced for Venus Anadyomene, with large, solemn, dreamy eyes, watching a robin that was perched on the proscenium and was twittering.

The pity, love, and sorrow of that mother's heart were not to be read in her calm disciplined countenance, but I could see the emotions flow in short wavelets from her heart, through the arm that encircled the sick girl, into the hand that rhythmically contracted and expanded on the sharp little shoulder, rocking the child in the warm sun, against her own heart, and with her dark eyes looking into the future, in which she would have no more the child at her side to sway. In that theatre!—the ebbing tide of a white and limpid life taking its last sunning, where the crowds had laughed and roared their applause at sights and songs of unspeakable foulness.

In the museum may be seen some of the treasures from the theatre, a head of Augustus, a so-called Livia, a bust of the

A BOAT WITH TWO RUDDERS AT ARLES.

young Marcellus, bas-reliefs, dancing women, a few inscriptions, and the seal of a Roman dentist, which I suppose he lost there one day when watching a play, and which has recently been found there.

PAGAN ARLES.

It is worth the visitor's while to walk by the broad muddy Rhone, and observe the clumsy picturesque vessels moored there, or gliding down the turgid stream. So clumsy is the construction that some are provided with two rudders, one being found insufficient to direct the course of these tubs.

At Arles, near the river, is a palace of Constantine the Great, now turned into cottages and sheds, and in a very ruinous condition, but sufficient of it is preserved to show what a falling off in architecture had ensued through the anarchy of rising and sinking emperors, and the destruction of the great families of the Patriciate. Employment for architects and sculptors was gone in times of proscription and military revolts, and apparently all at once the arts that had reached the utmost perfection fell into a condition of the most abject degradation.

CHAPTER VIII.

CHRISTIAN ARLES.

Sunday in France—Improved observance—The cathedral of Arles—West front—Interior—Tool-marks—A sermon on peace—The cloisters—Old Sacristan and his garden—Number of desecrated churches in Arles—Notre Dame de la Majeur—S. Cæsaire—The isles near Arles—Cordes—Montmajeur—A gipsy camp—The ruins—Tower—The chapel of S. Croix.

I SPENT the first Sunday after Easter at Arles. It was a bright and joyous spring day. I went to the cathedral at nine o'clock and found a good congregation there, listening to a sermon on the obligation of observing the Sunday. It was dull, and I left. But I may here observe what a great change has taken place in France of late years relative to this observance. I can remember when I was a boy how that every shop was open, and business went on much as on other days. But the Church has made great efforts to obtain a due recognition of the Lord's Day, and all who consider themselves to be good Catholics now shut their shops, and others, who find that there is now very little trade going on upon Sunday, shut their shops also because it is of no use having them open. It is only the polemical infidels who continue to keep their factories in full work and their places of merchandise open to invite purchasers.

Some few years ago I was talking with a Frenchman in Rome, a commercial man, about the phylloxera that was devastating the vines, and ruining the peasantry, and I asked him what was being done to correct the evil. "Bah!" said he. "Everything has been tried. Mon ami. We don't observe the Sunday. Voilà le vrai phylloxera."

Now this observation of his was only worth so much, that it showed how that the clergy had been going hammer and tongs at the consciences of their sheep, till they had impressed a conviction on them that if they neglected the commandment of God relative to the observance of one day in seven, He would chastise them till they realised that they had erred, acknowledged their error, and endeavoured to rectify it.

ON A HOUSE AT ARLES.

The cathedral of Arles is a very interesting church indeed. Externally the west front is rich in the bold rude style of the twelfth century, and consists of a deeply-recessed semicircular arch resting on a horizontal sculptured frieze which forms the lintel of the door, and is continued on each side upon pillars that rest on the backs of lions and have apostles and saints standing between them. The interior of the church is very solemn and striking. It has been cleaned, but judiciously, without sand-papering away the tool-marks on the ancient stone. Has the reader never been puzzled to note the difference between old

SAMSON AND THE LION, FROM THE WEST DOOR OF THE CATHEDRAL OF ARLES.

work and new, even when the new is a reproduction of the old? In the new there is an absence of something, but what we cannot tell. This something is very probably nothing more than the old tool-marks. The ancient workers left on the stone the tale of every stroke they dealt, and to ages on ages these marks tell us: here was a strong arm employed, here was dealt a vigorous blow; here Symon the hewer was tickled with a comical story that mason Peter told and he laughed, and the blow he dealt ran jagged with his laughter. These strokes were done in the morning, when the workers were fresh; those at even, when their arms were weary. But nowadays the stone is all gone over with a metal toothcomb, and scraped till not a toolmark remains, and wood is glass-papered till every particle of sharpness and character is taken out of the work.

The aisles of the cathedral of Arles are but five feet wide, the arches are round, the windows Romanesque; the church is barrel-vaulted, nothing could be plainer, and yet somehow that old church is full of poetry and charm. I went to High Mass at eleven. It was all very homely, quiet and reverent. Another congregation was gathered; a Gregorian simple service sung, which the congregation knew and joined in heartily. Then up into the pulpit got a canon, and gave out his text, from the Gospel, S. John xx., end of verse nineteen. My heart stood still. Why—you shall hear. Just twenty-two years ago, I was in Switzerland on Whit Sunday, and went to the little village church. The *curé* gave out these same words as his text, and preached a very good sermon on Peace, though perhaps not very appropriate to the day. Peace, he said, was an excellent thing, whether (1) in a country; (2) in a household; (3) in the conscience. There we had the three heads; on these he dilated. First we had a picture of the miseries of war in a country, and the converse picture of prosperity in peace. Then, secondly, we had a description of domestic discomfort, where husband and wife were at loggerheads, and—naturally, a charming family piece where both were in unity. Then came, thirdly, the special topic of his discourse, peace in

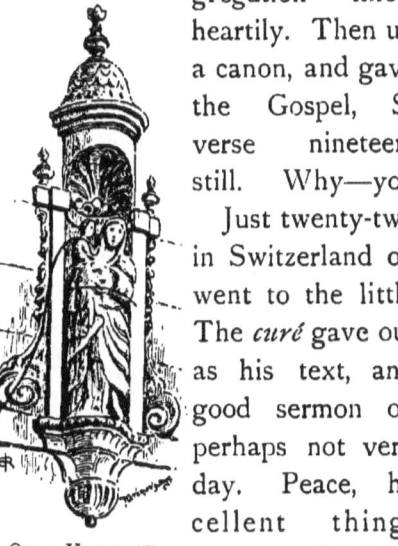

ON A HOUSE AT ARLES.

the conscience, and how it was to be obtained and secured.

I bottled up that sermon in my memory and have preached it since, myself, once or twice.

One day, some fifteen years ago, I was at Eichstädt in Bavaria, on a Saturday. The church of S. Michael there is reserved for the episcopal seminary; I wanted to see the interior and found it locked, but discovering a side door into the cloisters open, I, and my wife who was with me, entered. The church was empty, save that a sacristan with a feather brush was dusting the side altars, but to my surprise I heard a sermon being preached, and caught a glimpse of a priest in the pulpit haranguing and gesticulating to an empty church.

The sacristan, who saw us enter, went into convulsions of laughter. I did not understand the situation, and walked slowly down the aisle looking at the pictures, and listening to the discourse. I was very much surprised to hear the subject of Peace being chopped into three portions: peace in the country, peace in the family, peace in the conscience. It was my old friend the sermon on Peace again. Presently, my wife and I, having finished with the pictures in the north aisle, crossed the nave of the church to look at those in the south aisle, when, suddenly the preacher was aware of a strange gentleman and lady acting as his audience. His voice faltered, he broke down, searched for his MS., could not find his place, fell into complete confusion, turned tail, and bolted down the stairs and out of the church. He was a recently ordained seminarist rehearsing his first sermon.

Two years later I was in Brussels. A new dean had been appointed to S. Gudule, and was to preach his first sermon. I went there with a friend. He gave out his text. I pricked up my ears. Then he addressed himself to his subject, Peace; and showed how it naturally divided itself into three heads, peace in a country, peace in a household, peace in the conscience. It was my old friend again.

Now when I heard this text given out by a canon at Arles, I thought with a shock: Bless me! we shall have those three heads once more! But I was mistaken. The old man gave us a simple, crystal-pure discourse of ten minutes on the peace that passeth man's understanding.

SOUTH ENTRANCE TO THE CLOISTER, ARLES CATHEDRAL.

Now I do not mean to hint that the Swiss, the German, and the Belgian preachers all used literally the same discourse; but I suppose that in the seminaries there are supplied certain skeleton discourses for the whole year, and these skeletons are dressed up sometimes in homely fustian, sometimes in rhetorical tinsel: yet they never remain other than dressed-up skeletons.

There is very little of colour in the cathedral of Arles—only nine great pieces of Flemish tapestry, green and soft pale yellow, that are suspended in the aisles. All the rest is of unadorned limestone blocks, unadorned save for the chipping marks of the old masons seven hundred years ago.

On the south side of the church is a delightfully rich cloister, the arcade resting on double columns whose capitals are richly sculptured with sacred subjects, incidents from the Old and New Testament. In the cloister is a well, fed, I believe, originally by the old Roman aqueduct that supplied the town with pure water from the hills, but which was suffered in the Middle Ages to fall into complete ruin. This aqueduct was older than the amphitheatre, for it ran in a cut channel through the rock beneath it. One evening that I was in the cloister the aged sacristan was engaged drawing from this well and watering a little garden of flowers he had made in the sunny sheltered nook within the cloister, against the south wall.

It was a pretty little subject; the old man in his long black coat, with silvery hair, stooping over his anemones and tulips, tying up the white narcissus that a swirl of the *mistral* had broken; with the quaint sculptured capitals of the pillars above, and the deep shadows between the pillars before him; in the junctions

PART OF THE NORTH CLOISTER OF ARLES CATHEDRAL.

CHRISTIAN ARLES. 105

of the old blocks above the arcade were wild gillyflowers blooming, and under the tiles were swallows busy over their mud nests. And as the old man tied up the bruised narcissus, in a cracked voice he sang to himself one of the vesper psalms, and I caught the verse: "Hæc requies mea in sæculum sæculi: hic habitabo quoniam elegi eam." ("This shall be my rest for ever, here will I dwell, for I have a delight therein.")

Arles was at one time a city of churches, but the hurricane of the Revolution swept over

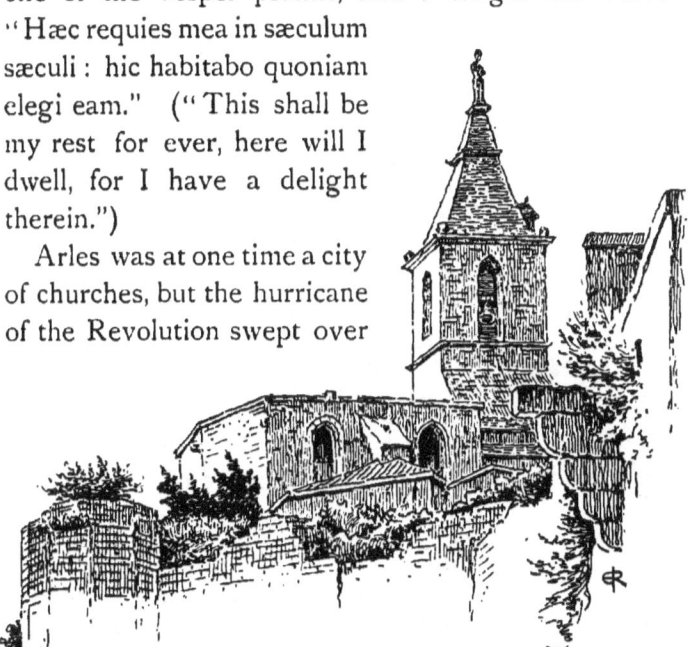

CHURCH OF NOTRE DAME DE LA MAJEUR, ARLES.

her, and now she has left but four. On the walls, is a very early Romanesque church, tottering to ruins, because the Society for the Promotion of Athletic Sports, to whom it has been surrendered up for tumbling, climbing, wrestling, are impecunious and cannot keep it watertight. Hard by is another church, still earlier, a temple adapted to Christian worship, now half swept away, half devoted to a cabaret. The church of the Cordeliers is turned into a school, and the octagonal tower rises out of the roof of the dormitory. The beautiful fourteenth-century church of the Dominicans is a stable for the horses of the omnibuses that ply between the train and the town. S. Martin is desecrated, so is S. Isidore. The earliest church in Arles is Notre Dame de la Majeur, near the Arènes, but it does not look its age. It was in that church that the Council assembled in 475 on the doctrine of Grace, when the Gallican prelates were by no means disposed to admit S. Augustine's predestinarian teaching. Outside the church in the open space are traces of walls that are level with the earth; and if I am not mistaken, they are the foundations of an early basilica, with apse to the west. The church was rebuilt in the Middle Ages, and made to orientate, and was thrown further east than the earlier church. That is my impression, but nothing can be determined without pick and spade.

TOWER OF THE DESECRATED CHURCH OF S. CROIX, ARLES.

In the church of S. Antonine is a metal font, made to resemble the laver of Solomon, resting on the backs of oxen.

PART OF THE COURTYARD OF THE CONVENT OF S. CÆSARIUS, ARLES.

The old Grand Priory has a charming Renaissance front to the river, and some late rich flamboyant work in a street at the back. It is now turned into a gallery of indifferent pictures. The Church of S. Cæsaire is modernised, and has, alas! nothing of interest remaining in it, only its historic memories to hallow it.

S. Cæsarius, son of a count of Chalons, born in 470, had been educated at Lerins, but thence he was drawn in 501, to succeed the first fathers of that holy isle, Honoratus and Hilary, upon the archiepiscopal throne of Arles. He was engaged in erecting a great monastery for women outside the walls, when the Ostrogoths and the Franks met in a furious conflict

CHURCH OF THE PENITENTS GRIS, ARLES.

beneath them. His monastery was reduced to a ruin. A priest, a relative of Cæsarius, had the meanness to let himself down the walls at night, escape to Theodoric the Ostrogoth king, and denounce him as engaged in secret communication with Clovis, king of the Franks. As soon as Arles was taken, Cæsarius was led under custody to Theodoric, but was speedily set at liberty by that great-minded prince. Another and similar charge was made against him later, and Cæsarius was forced to travel to Ravenna to exculpate himself. On his return to Arles he set to work to rebuild his monastery, not this time without the walls. He made his own sister, Cæsaria, the abbess, and she governed it for thirty years, and gathered about her a community of two hundred nuns. This brave Christian woman caused to be prepared, and ranged symmetrically round the church, stone coffins for herself and for each of the sisters. They sang day and night the praises of God in the presence of the new tombs that awaited them. When each sister was dead, she was placed in one of these stone coffins and carried off to the Elysian Fields, and most likely some of them are among those there strewn about or being now broken up. It was into this church that Cæsarius himself, feeling his end approach, had himself conveyed, that with feeble uplifted hands he might bestow his final blessing on that band of faithful women who were labouring to bring a higher ideal of womanhood before the Arles folk, corrupted by the vices of the decayed civilisation of Rome.

As already said, Arles was formerly surrounded by water, river on one side, meres on the other. Out of the lagoons, however, rose islets of limestone rock; of these there are two, Cordes and Montmajeur, but there were also formerly a number of smaller tofts standing above the water, but not always rocky, forming an archipelago, and were covered with the cottages of fishermen and *utriculares*, and farmers who cultivated vines and olives on the slopes above the reach of the water. Such were Castelet, Mont d'Argent, Pierre-Feu, and Trébonsitte. Nowadays we can go by road to all these spots, formerly they could be reached only by boat or raft. The isle of Cordes is about five miles from Arles, it was evidently at one period fortified, and is believed to have formed for some time the camp of the Saracen invaders who scourged and swept Provence with sword and flame. In the rocks of Cordes is a very curious cave, called the Trou des Fées, formed exactly in the shape of a sword, with lateral galleries to answer to the cross-piece at the hilt. It was undoubtedly a prehistoric habitation, probably enlarged by the Saracens and used by them as a storehouse for their spoils. It is entered through an oval antechamber which resembles the hilt of the sword; and which most likely was the original prehistoric dwelling. But the largest of the islands was Montmajeur, that now rises abruptly from the plain, crowned with ruins. I walked to it in driving rain and *mistral*. As I approached, I saw a gipsy woman bringing water in a pail to the camp, but the wind literally scooped the water out of the pail as with a spoon, and when she reached her destination very little remained. I stopped and had a little chat with the gipsies. They had tried to set up their tent, but it had been blown down over their heads, and had been rolled along with them in it, as they said, like a bag of potatoes. They were now squatted in the lee of a wall, an old ruined wall, and were endeavouring to boil a kettle, but the flames were carried by the wind in horizontal flashes, and would not touch the bottom of the vessel. They wanted me to have a cup of coffee with them when I returned from seeing the ruins, and I promised to do so, but, on my return, I found that rain and wind had blown and soused out their little fire, and they had not been able to get the water to boil, so were drinking it lukewarm. Good-natured, merry folk, they laughed over their troubles as though it were a sovereign joke, and yet they were drenched to the skin.

Montmajeur was a great Benedictine abbey, with a glorious church founded in the sixth century, that was rebuilt in the eleventh and thirteenth centuries, over a large and interesting crypt, and with cloisters at the side like those of Arles, but by no means as rich. Beneath the abbey are the chapel and the reputed cell of S. Trophimus, who probably never lived there—a charming specimen of early Romanesque. Part of this chapel is scooped and sculptured out of the living rock. But what is one of the grandest portions of the abbey is the machicolated tower that commands the plain for miles to the sea, a noble specimen of a donjon, and in excellent preser-

IN THE CLOISTERS, MONTMAJEUR.

vation. The abbey buildings adjoining the church were erected about fifty years before the Revolution, when the monastery was in the plenitude of its wealth. They form the wreckage of a palace for princes rather than of an abbey for the sons of S. Benedict, who I am quite sure would have been one of the first, had it been possible for him to be there, to lay his hand to destroy it, along with the mob of Arles' republicans, as utterly out of accord with the spirit of his rule. Indeed, on looking up at these sumptuous halls and stately galleries, one cannot but feel that the time was past in which the monastic orders, wealthy and luxurious and idle, could be endured. The church is no longer in use, and is ruinous.

Below the rock is a spit of land that stood anciently dry above the meres, and on that is a very singular old church dedicated to the Holy Cross, round which has been discovered a minor Alyscamp, a place of sepulture utilised from the earliest times. Sainte Croix is now regarded as a national monument, and is preserved carefully. It consists of a central square tower, from which project four equal semicircular apses, that to the west having a porch attached. It was consecrated in 1019. It is lighted by three little windows, only one to the east and two to the S. and S.E. Internally it is entirely deficient in sculpture, and was probably decorated with paintings. This was a funeral chapel in the midst of the cemetery, and was never used as a church. "The monks brought their dead hither," says Viollet le Duc, " processionally ; the body was placed in the porch ; the brethren remained outside. When Mass was said, the body was blessed, and it was conveyed through the chapel and out at the little S. door, to lay it in the grave. The only windows which lighted this chapel looked into the walled cemetery. At night, a lamp burned in the centre of this monument, and, in conformity with the use of the first centuries of the Middle Ages, these three little windows let the gleam of the lamp fall upon the graves. During the office for the dead a brother tolled the bell hung in the turret, by means of a hole reserved for the purpose in the centre of the dome." A similar but earlier mortuary chapel is at Planès, in Roussillon.

IN THE CLOISTER AT ARLES.

CHAPTER IX.

LES BAUX.

The chain of the Alpines—The promontory of Les Baux—The railway from Arles to Salon—First sight of Les Baux—The churches of S. Victor, S. Claude, and S. Andrew—The lords of Les Baux claimed descent from one of the Magi—The fair maid with golden locks—The chapel of the White Penitents—The *deïmo*—History of the House of Les Baux—The barony passes to the Grimaldi.—The ladies of Les Baux and the troubadours—Fouquet—William de Cabestaing—The morality of the loves of the troubadours—The Porcelets—Story of a siege—Les Baux a place of refuge for the citizens of Arles—*Glanum Liviæ*—Its Roman remains—In the train—Jäger garments.

From east to west runs the chain of Les Alpines, for just twenty miles, separating the Durance from the plain of the Great Crau. It is of limestone, and rises to the height of about eight hundred or a thousand feet, but is remarkable from the abruptness with which it springs out of the plain, and the fantastic shapes assumed by its crest.

This chain dies into the plain to the west at S. Gabriel, and its extreme limits to the east are the crags of Orgon, which rise sheer above the Durance, and the Mont du Defends farther to the south To the north is the broad flat valley of the Durance stretching away to Tarascon, to the south the vast desert of the Crau reaching to the sea.

About twelve miles from S. Gabriel, the chain of the Alpines thrusts forth an arm to the south that rises sheer from the plain some five hundred feet, and forms a plateau at the top encrusted with white crags, two thousand seven hundred feet long, by six hundred feet wide. It is detached from the main chain by a dip, and on every other side stands up in precipices. This is Les Baux, the name in Provençal signifies *cliffs*.

There is a little railway from Arles to Salon, by which one travels at a snail's pace to the station of Paradou, whence a walk of five miles takes one into a crater-like valley surrounded by bald white limestone crags, and there, towering overhead, are the walls and towers of Les Baux, in a position apparently inaccessible. This valley struck me as very much like one of the Lunar craters, as I had seen it through the Northumberland telescope, just as white, ghastly and barren. In the bottom were, indeed, a few patches of green field and a cluster of poplars, but the sides of the crater were almost wholly devoid of vegetation; and the white stone where quarried, and it was quarried extensively, glistened like sugar, with a greenish white lustre. In coming from Arles I had travelled third class, in a compartment on top of the second and first class carriages; for on these little lines the carriages are of two storeys; the upper storey commands the best view; and in the compartment with me was an intelligent postman. We got into conversation about Les Baux. He told me that he had lived there, and had found there a considerable number of flint and bronze weapons. He was now stationed at Tarascon, and he invited me to pay him a visit, when he would show me the weapons he had found on these hills. He also strongly urged me not to return by the same route, but to strike across the chain, reach S. Remy, see the Roman remains there,

LES BAUX.

catch the evening train, and so return to Arles by Tarascon.

And now for Les Baux, which is certainly one of the most astounding places I have ever seen.

Let the reader conceive of a rocky plateau standing up on abrupt precipices above the plain, with its top not altogether level, but inclined to the west, and the eastern side fringed with white crags. Let him imagine a little town clustered on the slope to the west, clinging to the inclined surface to prevent itself from slipping over the edge and shooting down the precipice. Then let him imagine the white limestone fringe that rises to the east some ninety feet above the town, adapted to serve the purpose of a castle, natural cliffs sculptured and perforated to form window and door, and vault and hall, and where living rock did not avail, masonry added, and the whole thrown into ruin. This is what he sees looking up from the valley. Then let him climb the steep ascent, anciently the only way by which the town and castle could be approached, and his amazement will grow with every step he takes. After having passed under a gateway well defended, he will find himself in the street of a Mediæval Pompeii : houses—not cottages, but the mansions of nobles—all, or nearly all, in ruins and uninhabited, some with architectural pretensions ; a church, still in use, dedicated to S. Vincent ; another still larger, S. Claude, half sculptured out of the living rock, half of masonry, beautifully vaulted, with no glass in the windows, and the doors fallen in ; a chapel of S. Anne, without a roof, and some trees growing out of the floor. Another church, the second parish church of Les Baux, S. Andrew, crumbled to its foundations. Further up the ascent, bedded in the ruins of the castle, a beautiful Gothic chapel with delicate ribbed vaulting of the thirteenth century, also in ruins. On one portion of the platform to the south the remains of a great hospital, with the recesses for the beds of the patients round it. A cemetery enclosed within walls ; guard rooms, halls, a mighty dove-cot hewn out of the rock ; galleries and the windows of banqueting halls cut in the rock ; high up, unapproachable, as the masonry has been blown up and thrown down that formed the western side of the castle. And to the north, where was the only approach to the castle by the neck of land, a curved ridge of limestone rock was hewn into a wall of defence. Now a road has been engineered along this *col*, and the rock wall has been cut through; not only so, but it has been carried through a nobleman's mansion, and the sculptured fireplaces overhang the carriage road.

Such, briefly, is the general aspect of Les Baux. Now we will enter into details. We will begin with the only parish church still in use. This church consists of nave and side aisles, with lateral chapels. The floor of the church is honeycombed with graves scooped out of the rock. In one of these before the high altar, a few years ago, when the slab that covered it was raised, the body of a man in rich garments was disclosed holding a book in his hand, that seemed to have escaped the ravages of time. However, on the first touch, it fell to dust. In another sepulchre was found the body of a young lady. Singularly enough, her hair, which was of a golden straw colour, was uninjured, though the rest of her body crumbled to dust in the air. The innkeeper of the little place managed to possess himself of it, and at once dubbed his tavern "A la Chevelure d'Or." He was wont to exhibit the mass of golden locks to the visitor for a consideration. Recently the tavern has changed hands, and the old innkeeper has carried off with him the golden locks. Consequently, the inn has changed its name, and is now the Hotel Monaco.

LES BAUX.

In front of the church is a small platform that overhangs the precipice. On it is the ruined chapel of the White Penitents, erected in 1659. Over the door may be read with difficulty the inscription in Latin, "At the name of Jesus every knee shall bow." Hard by is a cistern, semicircular, dug out of the living rock; this goes by the name of the *deïmo*—that is to say, the place of tithe. Into this cistern the farmers of the manor were bound to pour the tenth of all the wine they made, as the due of the Lord of Les Baux.

The ruined church of S. Claude has in the bosses of the vaulting the arms of the Princes of Les Baux, and of other noble families who lived in the little town and were feudatories of the princes, as well as of some of the guilds which had chapels in this church. The arms of the princes represented a star, for these princes claimed descent from Balthazar, one of the Magi who came from the East to bring gifts to the infant Saviour.

The tomb of Raymond des Baux, grand chamberlain of Queen Jeanne of Naples, at Casaluccio, bears the inscription, "To the illustrious family of the Baux, which is held to derive its origin from the ancient kings of Armenia, to whom, under the guidance of a star, the Saviour of the world manifested Himself."

The Barony of Les Baux consisted of seventy-nine towns or bourgs, which formed the territory called La Baussenique. It was confiscated by Louis III., Duke of Anjou, and Count of Provence in 1414, after having been governed by one family from Pons des Baux, the first who appears in history, and who died in 970. The last male representative died in 1374, and his sister and heiress, Alice, married Conrad, Count of Freiburg, who died in 1414. She bequeathed the principality to her kinsman, William, Duke of Andria, but on account of his attachment to the opposed party, Louis III. seized on Les Baux. In 1642, Louis XIII. erected it into a marquisate, and gave it to Honoré Grimaldi, Prince of Monaco, and it remained in the possession of the House of Monaco till the revolution of 1789.

The princes of Baux were podestas of Milan, consul-podestas of Arles, where they had a castle, were seneschals of Piedmont, grand justiciaries of the kingdom of Naples, princes of Orange, and viscounts of Marseilles. They bore also the titles of counts of Provence, kings of Arles and Vienne, princes of Achaia, counts of Cephalonia, and finally assumed that of emperors of Constantinople.

The castle was thrice besieged, twice destroyed, and again rebuilt; it lasted over eleven centuries. The most complete restoration of the castle and of the town-walls took place in 1444 by Louis III. of Provence; but when it passed to the Crown of France in 1630, by order of Cardinal Richelieu, it was destroyed. The strength of the position was such that he feared it.

In the old days, when the Princes and Princesses des Baux held court in this eagle's nest, it was a great resort of the troubadours, who came to it from all quarters. Fouquet, the Provençal poet, celebrated in his verses Adelasia, wife of Berald, Prince of Baux. He was filled with a romantic love for this exalted lady, and on her death, in a fit of sorrow, became monk of Citeaux. Afterwards he became abbot of Thoronêt, bishop of Marseilles, and finally archbishop of Toulouse.

He was born between 1160 and 1170, and was the son of a merchant of Venice who had retired from business and settled at Marseilles. When Richard Cœur de Lion was on his way to Syria, he made some stay at Marseilles before going on to Genoa, where he was to embark, and there Fouquet insinuated himself into his good graces. He was married, but his wife was sorely neglected, and all his devotion was paid to the lady Adelasia des Baux.

Provençal traditions diverge as to the result of his suit. According to one account, he could "jamais trouver merci, ni obtenir aucun bien en droit d'amour," from the object of his passion, and, in disgust, he turned to make love to Laura de S. Jorlan, sister of Berald des Baux. But the other account is that he made love to both ladies at once, and that Adelasia cast him off because she found that his fickle heart was turning to the fresher charms of Laura. Anyhow, he made his rejection by Adelasia the subject of poetical laments, and prosecuted with vigour his siege of the heart and virtue of his patron's sister. And then he pursued with the same ardour the conquest of Eudoxia, wife of William, Count of Montpellier.

As already said, after the death of Adelasia, he assumed the cowl. As Bishop of Toulouse, he exercised the ferocity of a wolf in his dealings with the Albigenses. "There is no act of treachery or cruelty throughout the war," says Dean Milman, "in which the Bishop of Toulouse was not the most forward, sanguinary, and unscrupulous." The historian of his life, in the 'Histoire Littéraire de la France,' says of him : " After having given half his life to gallantry, he gave up, without restraint, the remainder of his life to the cause of tyranny, murder, and spoliation, and unhappily he profited by it. . . . Loving women passionately, a ferocious apostle of the Inquisition, he did not give up the composition of verses which bore the impress of his successive passions."

Another troubadour, William de Cabestaing, sang the praises of Berengaria des Baux. Afterwards he lost his heart to Sermonda, wife of Raymond de Roussillon, who, not seeing the fun of this romantic spooning of his wife, waylaid and slew him, then plucked out his heart and had it served up at table in the evening. After his wife had partaken of the dish he informed her that what she had tasted was the heart of her admirer. She, full of horror, threw herself from a window of the castle and was dashed to pieces. This outrage was the occasion of civil war. The relatives of the lady and of William de Cabestaing persuaded Alphonso I., King of Aragon, to ravage the territories of the Count of Roussillon and to destroy his castle.

Again, another troubadour, Sordel, sang the praises of Rambaude des Baux, but in such enigmatical fashion that his verses may be read as a satire upon her charms.

The princely family, moreover, had among its members two troubadours, Berard des Baux in the twelfth century, and in the next Rambaud des Baux, who in 1236 distinguished himself by his songs in honour of Marie de Chateauvert and of the Countess of Argeuil.

In 1244 the troubadours vied with each other in lauding Cecilia des Baux, who was called Passe-Rose, on account of her beauty. Other ladies of the same family sung by the poets were Clairette in 1270 and 1275 by Pierre d'Auvergne, and Etiennette de Ganteaume—who shone in the Court of Love in 1332 at Romanil, and Baussette, daughter of Hugh des Baux in 1323, sung by Roger of Arles. So the family must have been one that in its alliances and daughters was distinguished by its beauty, or else paid liberally for flattery.

Vernon Lee, in her Euphorion, passes a severe sentence on the romantic affection professed by the minstrels of the Middle Ages for noble ladies. She says it was rank adultery and nothing short. I do not think so. There may have been cases, there no doubt were instances of criminal passion, but in nine cases out of ten these troubadours sang for their bread and butter. They lauded the seigneurs to the skies for their *gestes* of valour, and their ladies for their transcendent beauty; they laid on their colours with a trowel, and were paid for so doing. That some of them burnt their fingers in playing with fire one cannot doubt, but I hardly think that they set to work in their trifling with the intent of provoking blisters. The husbands of the much-lauded ladies were hardly likely to suffer this sort of fun to proceed beyond romancing. There was always a chance of a minstrel who went too far with his heart into the flames, getting it roasted on a spit and served up à la William de Cabestaing.

Besides, a good many of these much-besung ladies were no young brides, but mature and withering matrons. A troubadour attached himself to a lady as he attached himself to a seigneur, and, as a client of both, fawned on and flattered both. I cannot refer to Petrarch, for I believe his Laura was not a married woman, and the Platonism of his affection is more than questionable. He was not an acknowledged troubabour, but an exile, whom the haughty family of Sade would not suffer Laura to marry. But there is the case of Dante and Beatrice, and of Wolfram of Eschenbach, one of the noblest and purest of singers, who idealised his lady Elizabeth, wife of the Baron of Hartenstein, and with him most undoubtedly the devotion was without tincture of grossness. It is precisely this unreal love, or playing at love-making, that is scoffed at by Cervantes in Don Quixote and the peerless Dulcinea del Toboso.

Why, that unfortunate William de Cabestaing, whose heart was offered to his mistress, sang of her as cold to his suit:—

> "Since Adam gathered from the tree
> The apple, cause of all our woe,
> Christ ne'er inspired so fair a she.
> A graceful form, not high nor low,
> A model of just symmetry,
> A skin whose purity and glow
> The rarest amethyst surpass;
> So fair is she for whom I sigh.
> But vain are all my sighs, alas!
> She heeds me not, nor deigns reply."

The Courts of Love held by ladies of high rank were

originally courts in which the rules of minstrelsy were laid down, they pronounced on the qualifications of a candidate, they polished and cherished the Langue d'oc in its purity, dictated the subjects upon which the troubadours were to compose their lays, judged their pretensions, settled their controversies, recompensed their merits, and punished by disgrace or exclusion those who violated the laws. In the twelfth century these Courts of Ladies drew up Provençal grammars, in which the rules of the dialect were laid down. One of these is the "Donatus provincialis," another was composed by Raimond Vidal. But these Courts of Love went further. They laid down rules for love; they allowed married women to receive the homage of lovers, and even nicely directed all the symptoms they were to exhibit of reciprocation. But it is quite possible that this was all solemn fooling, and meant no harm.

I wonder whether those golden locks carried off by the taverner had belonged to one of those queens of beauty sung by the troubadours! Probably so, for the church of S. Vincent was their mausoleum.

One of the noble families that owed feudal duty to the Lords of Les Baux was that of Porcelet, and their mansion is one of the very few that is not deserted and ruinous in the little town. It is now occupied by some Sisters of Mercy who keep in it an orphanage. The Porcelets were the first nobles of Arles. King René of Anjou, who was fond of giving nicknames, sometimes flattering, sometimes the reverse to this, entitled the family Grandeur des Porcelets. Other of his designations were Inconstance des Baux, Déloyauté de Beaufort, Envie de Candole, Dissolution de Castelane, Sottise de Grasse, and Opiniâtreté de Sade.

A story is told of one of the sieges of Les Baux which is found elsewhere. The garrison of the castle and the inhabitants of the town were reduced to great straits for food, when orders were issued that everyone should surrender what he had into a common fund, to be doled out in equal portions to all. As none complied with this order, a domiciliary visit was made to every house, when an old woman was found to have a pig, likewise a sack of barley meal. The Sieur des Baux ordered the pig to be given a feed and then to be thrown over the precipice. When the besiegers found that the besieged had a pig so well nourished they thought it was hopeless to reduce the place, and raised the siege.

In the thirteenth century the little eagle's nest of a town numbered three thousand six hundred inhabitants. At the present time it cannot count four hundred. Every two or three years sees another house deserted, and the tenants migrate to the valley or plain.

The houses are, like the castle, partly scooped out of the rock, and partly constructed. Whole chambers, kitchens, cellars are veritable caverns. There can be no doubt that the place has been colonised from prehistoric times, and that many of these caves are the dwellings of a primitive population in the Stone period. Vast quantities of Greek Marseilles medals and of coins of the Empire have been found here, as well as fragments of pottery of every age. A few years ago a beautiful bronze helmet of Greek shape was here discovered.

The place has served as a refuge for the inhabitants of Arles at various periods. ' Hither they fled before the Teutons and Ambrons in B.C. 102, when these invaders swept across the south of Gaul on their return from Spain; and opposite Les Baux, on the heights of Costa Pera, may be traced the walled camp and cisterns, where they took refuge and remained till the danger was overpast. Again, in A.D. 480, when Earic, king of the Visigoths, took possession of Arles, the inhabitants fled to the heights of Les Baux and constructed dwellings for themselves there in the rock. These chambers, scooped out of the limestone crag, are locally called Baumes.

Anciently the roofs of the castle caught the rains, and shoots conveyed the water into great reservoirs that remain, but since the destruction of the castle the inhabitants have had to pave one whole sweep of the plateau so as to catch the showers, and convey them away into a subterranean cistern where the water purifies itself for use.

After the Hôtel Dieu ceased to be used as an hospital, it was converted into an arena for bull-fights, but as on several occasions the bulls escaped and fell over the precipices, the utilisation of the great hall for this purpose was abandoned.

I had a charming walk across the hills to S. Remy, near which are the remains of the Roman city of Glanum Liviæ. These remains consist of a triumphal arch, and a lovely monument about fifty feet high, quadrangular at the base, adorned with well-preserved bas-reliefs representing a skirmish of cavalry, a combat of infantry, and a sacrifice after a battle. Above this basement rises a circular temple with Corinthian pillars, containing in the midst two statues. The triumphal arch is not in equally good condition. The bas-reliefs on it represent captive barbarians and their wives. I caught the evening train at S. Remy, and again ascended to the third-class compartment in the upper storey. Presently after me came the guard: "Would not Monsieur like to descend? There is female society downstairs." "But, assuredly—only I have a third-class ticket." "Ça ne fait rien," replied the guard, "so have the ladies below, but we never send them up into the attics. Come, monsieur!" Accordingly I descended to a carriage-load of cheery Arles damsels and matrons in the quaint and picturesque costume of that town, and to a little French doctor and a couple of good-natured Zouaves.

"But—this is very remarkable," said the doctor. "Only an hour ago I saw a monsieur in the same hat and boots as yourself—only the face was not the same." "Very possibly. Are you a doctor, and do not recognise Jäger garments? I am not, it is true, in coat and continuations of that sanitary reformer, because I had to discard them. The fact is, I had a complete suit, but having been out in the rain in them, they shrank on me to such an extent that I entered the house contracted like a trussed fowl, and had to be cut out of the suit with a penknife."

"What countryman are you?" asked the doctor.

When I told him he shook his head. "You have not an English pronunciation. Are you German?" I also shook my head. Then he attempted some words in English. I was obliged to laugh: he was un-

intelligible. As I could not understand his English—
"Mais, Monsieur!" said the Arles women, "you must be a Swiss."

It was not complimentary, I must admit, to be thought to speak French with a German accent. It has come about thus, I suppose, that, though as a boy I lived in France for many years, yet of late I have been, almost annually, a visitor to Germany.

I only mention this incident, because I got into trouble later through a similar misapprehension as to my nationality.

RANGE OF THE ALPINES FROM GLANUM LIVIÆ.

K

CHAPTER X.

THE CAMPAIGN OF MARIUS.

The Trémaïé—Representation of C. Marius, Martha, and Julia—The Gaïé—The Teutons and Ambrons and Cimbri threaten Italy—C. Marius sent against them—His camp at S. Gabriel—The canal he cut—The barbarians cross the Rhone—First brush with them—They defile before him at Orgon—The rout of the Ambrons at Les Milles—He follows the Teutons—The plain of Pourrières—Position of Marius—The battle—Slaughter of the Teutons—Position of their camp—Monument of Marius—Venus Victrix—Annual commemoration.

RUINS S. GABRIEL.

THE two oldest and most interesting monuments of Les Baux have been unnoticed in the last chapter. These are the sculptured stones of Trémaïé and Gaïé. They are two limestone blocks fallen from the precipices above, lying on the flounce of rubble near the bottom of the promontory of Les Baux, the one on the east the other on the south. That on the east, La Trémaïé, consists of a block of shell-limestone about twenty-five feet high, in which, twelve feet from the soil, is sculptured a semicircular headed niche, five and a half feet high by four and a half feet wide, that contains a group of three personages, a bearded man on the left of the observer, a tall woman in the centre wearing a mitre, and on the right another woman. At first glance, I confess I supposed this was a bit of sculpture of the eleventh century, but on climbing to the roof of the chapel erected beneath the niche, some forty-five years ago, I was able to examine the group minutely, and satisfied myself that the work is of the Classic period.

What gave me the first impression that it was of later date was the use of the honey-suckle ornament at the crown of the arch, and at the capitals of the pillars supporting it, which was adopted by architects of the eleventh century from Classic work. But on close examination I found that, not only were the figures dressed in pure Classic tunics and togas, but that the drapery is modelled in conformity with that of the same epoch, and is quite distinct from the modelling by the Mediæval artists. This is specially noticeable where the statues have been protected by the sides from weathering.

LA TRÉMAÏÉ.

Moreover, below the figures is an inscription in letters, the date of which is unmistakable, though unfortunately it can be only partially deciphered. It runs :—

.   .   .   . F. CALDVS
.   .   .   .   . AE POSVIT. P. . .

The three figures are life-size. The central one is very peculiar, owing to the mitre or diadem it wears, which, however, is utterly unlike the episcopal mitre of the eleventh century. Moreover, there is no doubt about the person wearing it being a female.

Popular belief, also, does not err as to her sex; it has made a mistake relative to that of the man on her right, and when some forty-five years ago the curé of Les Baux erected the chapel under the rock, he believed that these figures represented the Three Marys.

The man is in consular habit, the toga, *neque fusa neque restricta*, worn till the time of Augustus. His feet appear beneath the tunic. Unfortunately the face is too much weathered to present any features. Not so the tall, mitred central figure, whose right hand is raised, as is thought, to hold a staff wreathed with chaplets. Her mantle, the ἱμάτιον, is clasped on the shoulder of her right arm. The third figure is that of a Roman matron.

Now it has been supposed, with a great degree of probability, that these three figures represent C. Marius, his wife Julia, and the prophetess Martha, who attended him in his campaign against the Teutons and Ambrons. Plutarch says: "He had with him a Syrian woman named Martha, who was said to have the gift of prophecy. She was carried about in a litter with great solemnity, and the sacrifices which he offered were all by her direction. When she went to sacrifice she wore a purple robe, lined with the same, and buttoned up, and held in her hand a spear adorned with ribands and garlands."

I confess that the staff with ribands and chaplets seen by some in this sculpture, were not distinguishable by myself. At the same time I was puzzled with certain ornaments below the raised hand of the diademed lady, which I could not explain. It is said that the staff is only visible when the morning sun strikes the weathered surface. It may be there—but I think that a fold of drapery has been mistaken for a staff. Yet—the wreath or buckle below her hand in such a case remains unaccounted for.

If these three figures represent Caius Marius, Martha, and Julia, then we can understand the name given the group—Les Trémaïés—the three Marii ; Caius Marius, Martha Marii, and Julia Marii, which has since been altered into Les Trois'Maries, and the figures assumed to be those of Mary the wife of Salome, Mary Magdalen, and Martha the sister of Mary. In the belief that such is the case, Mass is said in the chapel on the 25th of May, and there is a concourse of devotees assembled from the neighbourhood around the little chapel and memorial stone.

The second sculptured block lies about three hundred paces to the south, and is called Les Gaïé, i.e., *Caii imagines*. It resembles hundreds of similar Roman monuments to a husband and wife, found in the museums of Rome, Arles, Nimes, and Avignon.

Here also there is a niche, four feet wide by two

feet four inches high. On the right of the observer is a bearded man holding a roll in his left hand, and with his right he clasps the right hand of his wife. He is in consular habit; unfortunately both heads have been damaged. At some time or other a Vandal thought that the upper portion of the block would serve his purpose as a step or threshold, and drove a crowbar into the face of the stone between the two heads, and split off the cap, thus exposing the sculpture to the ash of the rain.

Beneath the figures is an inscription no longer legible. It is *possible* that this monument may represent Caius Marius and his wife Julia. A somewhat lively French imagination has taken the figure of the man to be Martha with her staff and mitre, but I examined the sculpture under a favourable light, and satisfied myself that this figure is that of a man. The face was apparently struck by the crowbar, which has broken off a film of the limestone, and destroyed the nose.

Les Gaïé.

The Caldus whose name appears on the Trémaïé is probably Caius Cælius Caldus, who belonged to the party of Marius, was created tribune B.C. 107, and who was one of the lieutenants of Marius in the war against the Cimbri, and signed a disgraceful treaty with the Ligurians to save the remnant of the army, after the

THE CAMPAIGN OF MARIUS.

death of the consul Cassius. He was named consul B.C. 97, and some medals struck by him exist. Possibly Caldus erected this monument in honour of Marius, who had made the platform of Les Baux and the range of the Alpines the vantage ground whence he watched the march of the Teutons and whence he swooped down to destroy them.

The great figure of Caius Marius overshadows the whole of Provence, and it is not possible for one who has any interest in the past not to feel its influence and be inspired by it. Stirred by the sight of these sculptures at Les Baux, I resolved to go over all the ground of his campaign, Plutarch in hand, and I venture to think that what I saw and discovered will not only interest the reader, but help to elucidate the history of that memorable struggle.

In the year B.C. 113, there appeared to the north of the Adriatic, on the right bank of the Danube, a vast horde of barbarians ravaging Noricum—the present Austria, and threatening Italy. Two nations prevailed, the Cimbri, Kaempir, *i.e.*, warriors, perhaps Scandinavian, and the Teutons, pure Germans. They had come from afar, from the Cimbric peninsula, now Jutland and Holstein, driven from their homes by an irruption of the sea. For a while they roamed over Germany. The consul Papirius Carbo was despatched in all haste to defend the menaced frontier of Italy. The barbarians pleaded to be given lands on which to settle. Carbo treacherously attacked them, but was defeated. However, the hordes did not yet venture to cross the Alps. They inundated the Swiss valleys, and as they flowed west swept along with them other races, amongst which was that of the Ambrons, a German race, whose name meets us again as Sicambrians, of which stock later was Chlodovig (Clovis). When Clovis was about to enter the font, S. Remigius thus addressed him: "Bow thy head, haughty Sicambrian; adore what thou hast burned; burn what thou didst adore."

In the year B.C. 110 all together entered Gaul, and then, continuing their wanderings and ravages in central Gaul, at last reached the Rhone and menaced the Roman province. There, however, the fear of Rome arrested their progress; they applied anew for lands, but Silanus, the governor, answered them haughtily, that the commonwealth had neither lands to give nor services to accept from barbarians. He attacked them and was defeated. Three consuls, L. Cassius, C. Servilius Cæpio, and Cn. Manlius, sent in all haste against them, successively experienced the same fate. With the barbarians victory bred presumption. Their chieftains met, and deliberated whether they should not forthwith cross into Italy and exterminate or enslave the Romans. Scaurus, a prisoner, was present at this deliberation. He laughed at the threat, and cried to his captors, "Go, but the Romans you will find are invincible." In a transport of fury one of the chiefs present ran him through with his sword. Howbeit the warning of Scaurus had its effect. The barbarians scoured the Roman province, but did not as yet dare to invade the sacred soil of the peninsula.

Then the Cimbri broke off from their comrades and

passed into Spain, as an overswollen torrent divides, and disperses its waters in all directions.

After ravaging Spain, the Cimbri returned, and the re-united hordes resolved no longer to spare Italy. The Cimbri were to invade it by way of the Brenner pass and the Adige, the Teutons and Ambrons by the Maritime Alps.

The utmost terror prevailed in Rome, and throughout Italy. There was but one man, it was said, who could avert the danger. It was Marius, low-born, but already illustrious, esteemed by the senate for his military genius and successes; swaying at his will the people, who saw in him one of themselves; beloved and feared by the army for his bravery, his rigorous discipline, and for his readiness to share with his soldiers all toils, and dangers; stern and rugged, lacking education, eloquence, and riches, but resolute and dexterous in the field. His father had been a farmer, and his hands had been hardened in youth at the plough. But as a free-born Latin he had been called to serve in war, and his skill and genius had advanced him, from step to step. He was consul in Africa at the time when

CAIUS MARIUS.
(*From a bust in the Vatican.*)

summoned to save his country from the danger threatening it from the barbarian hordes.

On reaching Provence, he found the soldiers demoralised by disaster, and with discipline relaxed. The barbarians had not as yet reached the Rhone, they were moving east slowly, and during the winter remained stationary. He had therefore time to organise his troops and choose his positions.

Now the old Græco-Phœnician road along the coast, that had been restored by the consul Cn. Domitius,

ORGON AND THE DURANCE.

and thenceforth bore his name, deserted the coast as it approached the mouths of the Rhone, the region of morasses, stony deserts, lagoons, and broad streams; kept to the heights, and reached Nimes, whence, still skirting lagoons, it ran along the high ground of limestone to Beaucaire. The Rhone was crossed to Tarascon, and thence the road followed the Durance up to Orgon, where it branched; one road to the left went to Apt, and crossed the Alps into Italy by Pont Genèvre, the other turned south to Aix and Marseilles. The road, afterwards called the Aurelian way, led from Aix up the river Are, over a low *col* to S. Maximin, and reached the coast by the valley of the Argens, that flows into the sea at Fréjus. It was a little doubtful to Marius which course the barbarians would pursue. Accordingly he formed a strong camp at Ernaginum, now S. Gabriel, at the extreme limit of the chain of the Alpines, to the west.

Almost certainly all the inhabitants of Arles, Tarascon, Glanum, and Cavaillon, all Græco-Gaulish towns, took refuge on the plateau of the limestone hills. The barbarians could not go south of the Alpines, because the whole region was desert, or was covered with lagoons. In order to victual his camp, Marius set his soldiers to work to convey a branch of the Durance* past Ernaginum into the lagoons below, and he cut a channel of communication between these lagoons, and opened a mouth into the sea through the Etang de Galéjon. By this means vessels from Rome or Marseilles could reach the walls of his camp with supplies.

In the spring of 102 B.C. the Teutons and Ambrons packed their tents and began to move east. The grass had grown sufficiently to feed their horses and oxen. Marius allowed them to traverse the Rhone without offering resistance; and they began their march along the road that ran at the foot of the precipitous Alpines.

* Plutarch says the Rhone, but he is almost certainly mistaken. The canal was afterwards probably that called Les Lonnes (lagunes), the dried-up bed of which can be distinguished in places still. The line from Tarascon to Arles runs beside it for a little way. See Appendix B.

They soon appeared, "in immense numbers," says Plutarch, "with their hideous looks and their wild cries," drawing up their chariots, and planting their tents in front of the Roman camp. They showered upon Marius and his soldiers continual insult and defiance. The Romans, in their irritation, would fain have rushed out of their camp, but Marius restrained them. "It is no question," said he, with his simple and convincing common sense, "of gaining triumphs and trophies, but of averting this storm of war and of saving Italy."

A Teuton chief came one day up to the very gates of the camp, and challenged him to fight. Marius had him informed that if he were weary of life, he could go and hang himself. As the barbarian still persisted, Marius sent him a gladiator.

However, he made his soldiers, in regular succession, mount guard on the ramparts, to get them familiarised with the cries, appearance, and weapons of the barbarians. The most distinguished of his officers, young Sertorius, a man whose tragic story is, itself, a romance, and who understood and spoke Gallic well, penetrated in the disguise of a Gaul into the camp of the Ambrons, and informed Marius of what was going on there.

At last, the barbarians, in their impatience, having vainly attempted to storm the Roman camp at Ernaginum, struck their own, and put themselves in motion towards the Alps.

Marius followed them along the heights, out of reach, ready to rush down on their rear, observant of their every movement. They reached Orgon. There the limestone precipices rise as walls sheer above the plain, now crowned by a church and a couple of ruined castles. It was probably from this point that Marius watched the hordes defile past. For six whole days, it is said, their bands flowed before the Roman position. The Teutons looked up at the military on the cliffs and flung at them the insolent question: "Have you any messages for your wives in Italy? We shall soon be with them."

The soldiers, still restrained by Marius, waited till all had passed, and then the general struck his camp, and crossing the dip at Lamanon, where the overspill of the Durance had once carried its rolled stones into the Crau, he regained the heights on the farther side of the Touloubre, at Pelissanne, the ancient Pisavis.

Still keeping to the heights, now of red sandstone, Marius again came on the barbarians at Les Milles, four miles to the south of Aix. He had observed all their movements, and had seen that the Ambrons had detached themselves from the Teutons at Aix, so as to make a descent on Marseilles. Possibly Aix had been given up to ravage by the Teutons, and the Ambrons were bidden find their spoil in Marseilles. At Les Milles the red sandstone cliff stands above the Are, which makes here a sweep, leaving a green meadow in the loop. Here, from under the rocks ooze forth countless streams; some were, like those at Aix, hot;[*] now I will again quote Plutarch. "Here Marius

---

[*] Whether so at present I am unable to state, not having been able to test them. All the hot springs have been reduced in temperature considerably since Roman times.

pitched on a place for his camp, unexceptionable in point of strength, but affording little water; and when his soldiers complained of thirst, he pointed to the river that flowed by the enemy's camp, and told them, 'that they must thence purchase water with their blood.' 'Why then,' said they, 'do you not immediately lead us thither, before our blood is quite parched?' To which he replied, in a milder tone, 'So I will; but first of all let us fortify our camp.'

"The soldiers, though with some reluctance, obeyed. But the camp-followers, being in great want of water for themselves and their cattle, ran in crowds to the stream, some with pick-axes, some with hatchets, and some with swords and javelins, along with their pitchers; for they were resolved to have water, even if forced to fight for it. These were, at first, encountered by only a small party of the enemy; for of the main body, some, having bathed, were engaged at dinner, and others were still bathing, the country there abounding in hot wells. This gave the Romans a chance of cutting off a number of them, while they were indulging themselves in these delightful baths. Their cry brought others to their assistance, so that now it was no longer possible for Marius to restrain the impetuosity of his soldiers, who were uneasy for the fate of their servants. Besides, these were the Ambrons, who had defeated Manlius and Cæpio, that they saw before them." The contest became general. The Ambrons rushed across the river, yelling "Ambra! Ambra!" their war-cry, which was at once retorted on them by a body of auxiliaries in the Roman camp, who heard their own cry and name. After a furious engagement, the Romans remained victors, the little river Are being choked with the bodies of the barbarians.

Those who retreated to their camp were pursued by the Romans. There the women, with loud cries, armed themselves, and made a desperate resistance, catching at the swords with their naked hands, and suffering themselves to be hacked to pieces.

The night was spent by the Romans in some alarm, for though they had defeated their foes and penetrated to their camp, yet they had not time to fortify their own position; and they dreaded lest the Ambrons should make head during the night, call the Teutons to their assistance, and charge up the hill. "A cry was heard from the defeated Ambrons all through the night, not like the sighs and groans of men, but like the howling and bellowing of wild beasts."

Two days after this a second and decisive battle ensued. The narrative in Plutarch is a little confused, and it is only by familiarity with the sites that the whole story becomes unfolded clearly before us. Thus, it is only on the spot that one sees how it was that Marius, striking from the chain of the Alpines, came up over against the Ambrons on the hill above Les Milles, and how he pursued his course thence. Plutarch, though he speaks of the two battles, does not distinguish the sites effectually.

The Teutons, as already said, were making their way east from Aix. The road ran through the broad basin of the Are; to the north rise, precipitously, the bald white precipices of the limestone Mont Victoire, to the height of 3,000 feet, with not a ledge on the sides where a shrub can find root. Between these cliffs and the plain are, however, two low sandstone ridges, the higher of which forms an arc, and dives into the wall of Mont Victoire, about half way through the plain. On the southern side of the river are low hills; at the extreme north-east is a conical green hill named Pain de Munition, which is fortified much like the Hereford Beacon, with walls in

MONT VICTOIRE AND THE PLAIN OF POURRIÈRES.

concentric rings. To the south-east is the chain of Mont Aurelien, and there, on the Mont Olympe, is another fortified position, beneath which is the town of Trets, an ancient Roman settlement.

Now the barbarians followed the road on the north side of the river Are, to the Roman station on it named Tegulata, the first station out of Aix, their numbers swelled by the discomfited Ambrons. Marius, however, being at Les Milles, crossed the river, and kept to the south side of it till he reached Trets. Then he had a fortified position in his rear, the camp of Mont Olympe; moreover, the barbarians were encamped on three tofts of red sandstone on the north side of the river, at the station Tegulata, with, at their back, the Roman fortified position of *Panis Annonæ*, now called Pain de Munition, where one may conjecture Marius had his stores and reserves. They were probably unaware of the trap into which they had walked. Marius, however, had despatched on the day before Claudius Marcellus, with three thousand men, up the long valley of the Infernet, to the north side of Mont Victoire, so as to reach and strengthen the fortress of Panis Annonæ, and secure his stores, and next day to descend the height and fall on the rear of the enemy.

The slopes along which Marius marched were probably well-wooded, and he was unobserved by the Teutons.

They had spent one whole day in pacing along the straight flat Roman road under Mont Victoire. As they approached the station Tegulata, a singular blood-red splash on the white sides of Mont Victoire emerged from behind the lower wooded sandstone road, a signal of warning to them that they were approaching a place of peril. Moreover, the sandstone deepened in colour, till at Tegulata the little streams that oozed from under the sandstone ran like blood about their feet. Of these they could not drink, therefore they halted at Tegulata, where they again reached the river, and where there was a bridge; they there encamped on the three tofts already mentioned, the surfaces of which are of hard, dry, yellow sandstone, superposed on beds of friable red sand. Here the river flowed sparkling and clear, and supplied them with what water they required. Everything points to

L

this spot as their camp. It is one day's march from Aix. It is the first point at which drinkable water is reached. The sandstone tofts stand up above the plain, then undrained and marshy, as a dry base for their tents. Finally, the monument of Marius is opposite them, on the farther side of the river.

In the meantime the Romans had approached from the south, from Trets, making a slight détour, following the tactics of Marius as before, to keep to the south of the horde, and with now a river between

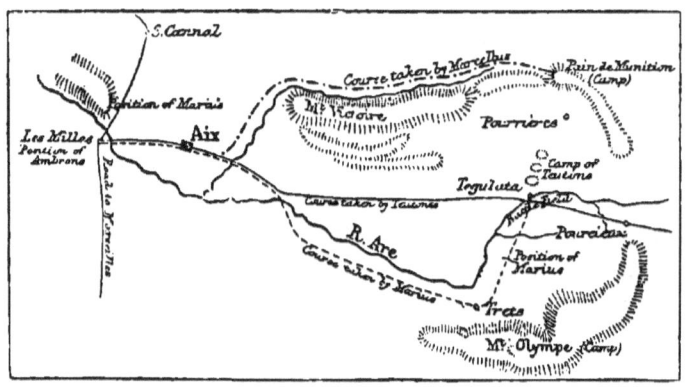

SKETCH PLAN OF THE BATTLE FIELDS.

him and them. At Trets the ground inclines from south to north, with a broken edge of sandstone—invisible from the river, serving as a screen behind which troops could be massed unperceived. Here it was, I suspect, that Marius passed that spring night, the second after the defeat of the Ambrons. The broken edge of sandstone is not eighteen feet high. From the top the ground slopes down for a mile, and then ensues a gully cut in the sandstone by a small blood-red confluent of the Are. Another mile, or mile and a half beyond, is the river, and close to the river, on the farther bank, was the camp of the Teutons.

On the morning of the 23rd March* the Roman cavalry were discovered by the Teutons drawn up on the slope.

"On seeing this, unable to contain themselves," says Plutarch, "nor stay till the Romans were come down into the plain, they armed themselves hastily and advanced up the hill. Marius sent officers throughout the army, with orders that they should await the onslaught of the enemy. When the barbarians were within reach, the Romans were to hurl their javelins, then draw their swords, and advance, pressing the enemy back by their shields. For the place was so slippery that the enemy's blows could have little weight, nor could they preserve close order, where the declivity of the ground made them lose their balance." One can see exactly where this took place, it was where the confluent of the Are formed a natural protection to the position of the Romans; the hollow cut in the greasy red marl was too insignificant to prevent the Teutons from attempting to pass it, but was sufficient to break their order, and to give the Romans the first advantage over them.

Having driven back the assailants, the Romans now crossed the natural moat and bore down on the Teutons. At the same moment the well-designed manœuvre of Marius, in despatching Marcellus to the fort on Panis Annonæ, produced its result. Marcellus had descended the hill, screened by the trees, and had

* My reason for fixing the day I shall give in the sequel.

suddenly fallen on the rear of the camp of the Teutons.

Thus attacked, both in front and in the rear, the barbarians were seized with panic. A frightful carnage ensued. No quarter was given. Women and children were mown down; the dogs furiously defending their masters' bodies were also slaughtered.

"After the battle, Marius selected from among the arms and other spoils such as were elegant and entire, and likely to make the most brilliant show in his triumph. The rest he piled together, and offered

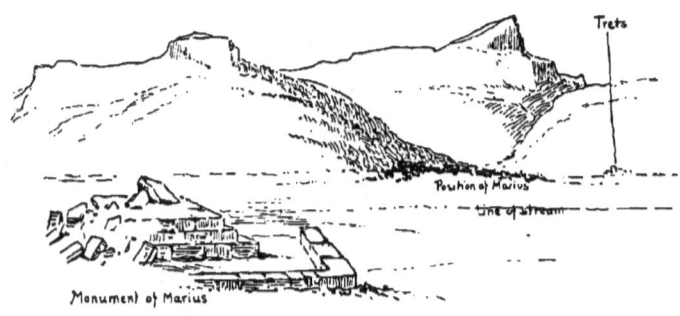

them as a splendid sacrifice to the gods. The army stood around the hill crowned with laurel; and he himself, arrayed in a purple robe, girt after the manner of the Romans, held a lighted torch. He had just raised it with both hands towards heaven, and was about to set fire to the pyre, when some men were seen approaching at a gallop. Great silence and expectation followed. On their coming up, they leaped from their horses and saluted him with the title of Consul for the fifth time, and presented letters to the same purport. This added joy to the solemnity, which the soldiers expressed by acclamations and by clanking of arms; and, while the officers were presenting Marius with new crowns of laurel, he set fire to the pile, and finished the sacrifice."

According to some accounts the number of Teutons slain numbered two hundred thousand, and that of the prisoners is stated to have been eighty thousand. The most moderate computation of the slain is fixed at one hundred thousand. In any case the carnage was great, for the battle-field, where all the corpses rested without burial, rotting in the sun and rain, got the name of *Campi Putridi*, the Fields of Putrefaction, a name still traceable in that of Pourrières, the neighbouring village.

VENUS VICTRIX.

On the site of the battle, on the south bank of the river, over against the camp of the enemy, where also was the pyre in which the waggons, chariots, arms and vesture of the invaders was consumed, a monument to Marius was erected, which was tolerably perfect before the French Revolution, but which now presents a mass of ruins. It consists of a quadrangular block of masonry, measuring fifteen feet on each side, within an enclosing wall fourteen feet distant. This quadrangular block sustained a pyramid, with statues at the angles, as it still figures upon the arms of the Commune and on some Renaissance tapestry in a neighbouring château. Here, three or four years ago, was found a beautiful statue in Parian marble of Venus Victrix, unfortunately without head and arms, but quite of the best Greek workmanship. The city of Avignon bought it of the proprietor of the field for one thousand eight hundred francs, and it is now one of the principal ornaments of the Avignon Museum. The statue, to my mind, proves that this monument was raised by Julius Cæsar ; there is an indirect compliment to his own family in it. Venus was the ancestress of the Julian race, and Cæsar perhaps insinuated, if he erected the statue, that the success of Marius was due to the patronage of the divine ancestress and protectress of the Julian race, and of Julius Cæsar's aunt, the wife of Marius, quite as much as to the genius in war of Marius himself.

We know, moreover, that the trophies erected to Marius for his Cimbric and Teutonic victories were overthrown by Sulla, and that they were re-erected by Julius Cæsar in A.D. 65.

The anniversary of the battle was annually celebrated in a little temple dedicated to Venus Victrix on the apex of Mont Victoire, that overhangs the plain.

When Provence became Christian the temple was converted into a chapel, Venus Victrix became transformed into S. Victoria ; and the procession remained unaltered, the inhabitants of the neighbouring villages ascended the mountain bearing boughs of box, which they waved and shouted "Victoire ! Victoire !" On reaching the chapel, Mass was celebrated. This took place annually on March 23rd till the Revolution, when the chapel was suffered to fall into ruin. I was on the battlefield on the day which is traditionally held to have been that when this decisive battle took place. A brilliant day. The frogs were croaking in the marshes and dykes, the tones of some like the cawing of young rooks. The ground was strewn with grape-hyacinth, and white star of Bethlehem, the rocks were covered with rosemary in pale grey bloom, the golden chains of the broom waving over the blood-red sandstone rocks.

That the tradition is correct, or approximately so, I think probable, for towards the end of March would be the suitable time for the barbarians to set themselves in motion for the invasion of Italy. Sufficient grass could be had for their horses and cattle, and they would desire to reach the plains of Italy before the great summer heats.

I talked a good deal to peasants working in the fields. They were all of one mind as to where the battle had raged—from north to south, they said, between Trets and Pourrières. The tradition is only worth anything in that it is based on the fact that along this line the greatest amount of weapons has been turned up by the spade, and pick, and plough.* A French writer, referred to in the footnote, says that

* M. Gilles, "Campagne de Marius dans la Gaule," Paris, 1870, thinks that Marius pursued the Teutons along the Aurelian road, and that the battle was fought on the north side of the river. I do not hold this. The monument of Marius is on the south side, and I think he would naturally secure a fortified camp in his rear.

MARCH OF S. VICTOIRE (23rd March).

Harmonised by F. W. Bussell, Esq., M.A.

THE MARCH OF S. VICTOIRE.

if a little rill trickling into the Are be examined where it flows in, opposite the monument of Marius, the banks will be found at first to be full of broken Roman pottery, but if the course of the stream be pursued a little farther up it will be found to flow through beds of charcoal and molten masses of metal—clearly the site of the pyre raised by Marius. I accordingly searched the locality. I found the pottery, and picked out fragments of Samian ware; the bank is from three to nine feet deep in them. Farther on, I came, as M. Gilles said, to remains of charcoal and cinder. I was perplexed. I followed the stream farther up, and found that it crossed a road that was metalled for half a mile with cinder, and that the cinder lay on the road and on the road only. I instituted inquiries and ascertained that this was all brought from a steam mill a mile and a half off along this road. But though these remains of charcoal and scoria are not ancient, yet the little rill does ooze from the plateau on which I believe Marius raised the pyre. It is exactly opposite his monument, between his position and the Panis Annonæ, whence swept down Marcellus with his cavalry. It was the site at once of the camp and of the pyre. No remains could possibly be found on it of camp or pyre, as the sandstone is in constant disintegration, and the whole surface has been many times washed bare and renewed during the nineteen hundred and ninety-two years that have elapsed since the battle.

The story how Marius, having destroyed the hordes of Ambrons and Teutons, and secured Italy on the west, returned to the Peninsula, and finding that the

Cimbri were streaming down from the north-east, met them near Vercellæ, and there defeated and slaughtered them also, I leave for other pens to describe. That battle took place on July 30th.

I have given (*ante*, pp. 152, 153) what may interest the musical reader, the traditional march performed on the day of the battle of Pourrières, when the pilgrims ascended the mountain to return thanks for the victory of Marius.

CHAPTER XI.

TRETS AND GARDANNE.

The fortifications of Trets—The streets—The church—Roman sarcophagus—Château of Trets—Visit to a self-educated archæologist—His collection made on the battle-field — Dispute over a pot of burnt bones—One magpie —Gardanne —The church—A vielle — Trouble with it—Story of an executioner's sword.

is an odd little place, surrounded by its ancient walls and towers, and with its gates—but, oh! if anyone would know what a cramped, unwholesome place one of these old mediæval burghs was, let him visit Trets. The streets are some four and some five feet across; in threading them you pass under a succession of archways, for every house desiring more space has thrust forth a couple of storeys over the street, sustained by an arch. The exhalations from the dirt-heaps, the foulness of every house, the general condition of tumble-down, compose a something to make a sanitary officer's hair stand on end. But it is very wonderful. Carcassonne is marvellous, but this is Carcassonne seen through a diminishing glass.

Trets has an ancient church, but that has a tower in ruins, and it is a marvel to the visitor how that the rain does not enter and souse the interior and congregation, so dilapidated is the whole structure. In the basement of the tower is a white marble sculptured Roman sarcophagus; on it are the heads of husband and wife, supported by genii. Within the church is a slab bearing record of the consecration, A.D. 1051.

The town has a stately château, now abandoned to the poor and cut up into small habitations. There is in it a grand stone staircase with ornamental plaster ceilings on the several landings; one represents a boar hunt, the other an ostrich chase.

In the château lives a miner, a M. Maneil, who is an enthusiastic archæologist. The publican of the little inn at Trets told me of him : of how, when his work is over, and other labouring men come to the cabaret or the café, he spends his time in prowling over the battle-field of Pourrières, searching for antiquities, and how he hoards up his little savings to buy books that deal with archæological subjects.

It was to see M. Maneil that I visited the château. He has a rich collection of objects. I counted twenty-four stone hatchets, and something like three hundred beads strung for necklaces, flint arrow-heads in large numbers, also many bronze implements, a quern, pierced shells, several sculptured stones found in Dolmens, and a great many Roman coins. It is the collection of a life, made by an enthusiast, and ought to be acquired by the museum of Aix. In the mairie at Trets is an urn full of calcined bones, in very good condition. It was found by two boys some little while ago in a tumulus on the side of the road to Puyloubier. The farmer whose land it was on, hearing of the discovery, and concluding that something precious had been found, brought an action against the youthful archæologists, and strove to recover the treasure. After a hard-fought battle he obtained his rights. They were forced to surrender their acquisition—a crock—and, to the disgust of the farmer, it contained not a coin of any sort, only bones. So he has left it in the mairie, in the hopes that some one will be induced to buy it, and so contribute a trifle towards the heavy expenses of the trial.

GARDANNE.

Now, as I was walking from the field of Pourrières to Trets, one solitary magpie appeared on my left, flew a little way, lighted, and flew on farther, and accompanied me thus for half the journey. "One is for sorrow." My mind immediately recurred to home—to wife and children. What had or would happen? Influenza—would that decimate the flock? or a fire—would that consume my books and pictures? Nothing happens but the unexpected. Never for one moment did I obtain a glimpse, no, not half a glimpse, into the trouble in store for me, which was to arise, not from the loss of anything, but out of an acquisition.

From Trets I went on by train to Gardanne,

watching the evening lights die upon the silver-grey precipices of Mont Victoire. At Gardanne I had to change, and kick my heels for two hours. Gardanne is a picturesque little town, built on a hill round a castle in ruins and a church very much restored. So restored did the church seem to be from the bottom of the hill that I doubted whether it would be worth a visit. Gardanne is surrounded by broad boulevards planted with trees. Now, no sooner has one passed inward, from this boulevard, than one finds a condition of affairs only a little less dreadful than that at Trets.

Gardanne was a walled town, but all the walls have been transformed into the faces of houses, inns and cafés, plastered and painted and so disguised as not to reveal their origin till one passes behind them. Then one is involved in a labyrinth of narrow, dark lanes scrambling up the hill, running in and out among the houses, paved with cobble stones in some places, in others resolving themselves into flights of broken steps.

On scrambling to the terrace on which the church stands on the apex of the hill, I saw that it was of very remarkable width, all under one low gable—certainly extraordinarily ugly, and newly plastered, marked out in sham blocks of stone, and made as hideous as the ingenuity of man could well achieve. However, I entered the west door, and passed into almost complete darkness, only relieved by the paschal candle that was burning at a side altar and the red lamp in the choir.

As my eyes became accustomed to the gloom, I discovered to my surprise that I had entered a very interesting eleventh-century church, of five aisles, all under one roof, without clerestory. But the evening light through the small stained windows did not suffer me to make out any details. The east end of the church rises from the crag on which it is built, without any window in it.

On leaving the top of the hill and descending into the town I met my fate in the form of a woman who was playing a hurdy-gurdy, and singing to its strains a Provençal ballad. I stopped at once, and asked her to let me investigate the instrument. I have a fancy for ancient musical instruments. A handle is turned that grates on one catgut string, and the fingers of the left hand, passed under the hurdy-gurdy, touch notes that stop the string at various lengths, and so vary the tone.

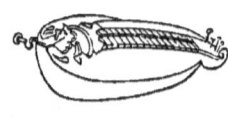

THE VIELLE.

She told me the instrument was called the vielle, in fact—our old English viol; a very ancient instrument, which is represented as being played by one of the minstrels sculptured on the east front of Launceston Parish Church, circ. 1525. On a capital at S. Georges de Boscherville, in Normandy, is an eleventh-century representation of a huge hurdy-gurdy resting on the knees of two performers. One turns the handle, the other plays on the keys. Mr. Chappell at one time believed it was the old English *Rote*, from *rota*, a wheel, but changed his mind later, and showed that the rote had a hole through it, which enabled it to be played with both hands like a lyre or harp, and derived its name from the Anglo-Saxon "rott"—cheerful.

This branch of archæology being one in which I was particularly interested, nothing would suffice me but buying the viol of the woman; and having acquired it, I slung it round my neck by a very dirty blue ribbon, and hastened to the station to catch my train to Aix.

Now only did I discover what the magpie portended, for with the acquisition of that hurdy-gurdy my life became a burden to me. I could not pack it into my Gladstone bag. I could not fold it up with my rugs. I was forced to travel with it slung round my neck. Naturally, in a railway carriage I was asked to perform on the singular instrument—but I was incapable of doing this. Fellow travellers disbelieved in my statement. Why did I wander through Provence, the land of troubadours, if I were no troubadour? Surely I was sulky—not incapable; unwilling to oblige—not unable to do so. When I arrived at an hotel—especially late in the evening—I found the host doubtful about receiving me. He looked at my bag, then at my hurdy-gurdy, then scrutinised my boots; wanted to know what priced rooms I required; must consult madam. On the railway platform again, I found myself an object of attention to certain men in plain clothes, with keen searching eyes—and, as I shall relate in the sequel, brought one of them down on me.

Vexed that I was unable to pass the tedious time in the train with a tune on my vielle, and entertain my fellow travellers, I began to practise on it in my room at night. Then the fellow inmates complained: they sent their compliments and desired to know whether

M.

there were wild beasts next door—they objected to be lodged near a menagerie.

My experiences with the hurdy-gurdy recall to my memory some others I went through a few years ago.

On one occasion I spent a winter in a city in the south of Germany, where I made the acquaintance of an antiquary who was very old and bedridden, and had no relations, no one to care for him but an old housekeeper. The man had belonged to the town-council, and had spent his life in collecting curiosities connected with the history of his town. Among his treasures above his bed, was the city executioner's sword, much notched. This sword was six feet long, with a huge handle, to be grasped with two hands, and with an iron ornamented knob as counterpoise at the end of the handle.

How life is made up of lost opportunities! How much of the criminal history of the city might I not have learned, if I had paid longer visits to Herr Schreiber, and listened to his account of the notches in the blade, to each of which a ghastly history attached. But the antiquary's bedroom measured fifteen feet by seven, and the window was hermetically sealed; moreover, there was a stove in the room, and —Herr Schreiber himself, always.

"Ach, mein Herr! do you see dis great piece broken out of de blade? Dat vas caused by a voman's neck. De executioner could not cut it drough; her neck vas harder dan his sword. She vas a very vicked voman; she poisoned her fader.— Do you see dis littel nick? Dis vas made by a great trater to the Kaiser and Vaterland. I vill tell you all about it."

I never heard all the stories : I should have been suffocated had I stayed to listen ; but I found, whenever I called on my friend, that my eyes invariably turned to the sword—it was so huge, it was so notched, and had such a gruesome history. Poor old Schreiber, I knew, would have to bow his neck before long under the scythe of Time. How he hung on in that stuffy room under the great sword so long was a marvel to me, and would be pronounced impossible by sanitary authorities in England. Nevertheless, he did live on for a twelvemonth after I left the town. When about to depart, I said to the English chaplain : "Old Schreiber can't last long ; he must smother shortly. Keep an eye on the sword for me, there's a good fellow. He has left everything to the housekeeper."

A twelvemonth after, as I was about to leave England for a run into Bohemia, I got a letter from the chaplain : "Schreiber is dead. I have the sword." I wired at once to him : "Send it me to my inn at Aix-la-Chapelle. Will pick it up on my way home."

So I went on my way rejoicing, ascended the Rhine to Mainz, trained to Nuremberg, and passed through the gap of the Bohemian mountain-chain to Pilsen, and on to Prague. After six weeks in Bohemia and Silesia, I descended the Rhine to Aix-la-Chapelle, and arrived at my inn.

"Dere is vun vunderful chest come for you," said the landlord. "Ve vas not very comfortable to take him in. Ve keep him, dough."

And no wonder. The chest was shaped somewhat like the coffin of a very tall man.

"Vat ish he? He have been here four veek and doe days.—Dere is no schmell."

"I cannot take that thing—I really cannot. It is preposterous. How could the chaplain have put my sword into the hands of an undertaker?—Get me a hammer; I will knock the case to pieces."

Now, there was a reason why the chest should assume the shape of a coffin—that was, because of the crosspiece between the handle and the blade. My name and address were on the lid, at the place where usually goes the so-called "breast-plate."

The host of my inn, the waiters, the porter, the boots, all stood in breathless curiosity to see the box opened, and when the sword was exposed—"Ach!" exclaimed the host gravely, "I vas right—dere vas no schmell, because dere could be no schmell."

I could not see the force of this reasoning, remembering Herr Schreiber's room, and how long the sword had been in it; and allowing that there is no porosity in tempered steel, still, the black velvet casing of the handle might have absorbed a considerable amount of Schreiberian bacteria, bacilli, or whatever it is that physiologists assert to be so nasty and so ubiquitous, and so set on finding out our weak places and hitting us there, as swordfish "go" at whales.

I had got my sword out of its coffin, but had not considered what to do with it next, and I found myself in as great a difficulty as before. I got a porter to convey it for me to the station, and he placed it in the first-class waiting-room with the iron counterpoise on the floor, beside a divan, and leaned the tip of the blade against the wall. There it was allowed to remain; and I walked about, pretending that it did not belong to me. Presently, a well-dressed, very stately lady—she was a *Gräfin* (countess)—came in, stalked to the divan, and seated herself on it, very upright, without observing the sword. She opened a reticule and produced a lace-edged handkerchief, with which she proceeded to dust the velvet of her dress, and in so doing, with the end of her delicately-shod foot, touched the counterpoise. At once the sword-blade began to grate against the wall. She looked up suddenly, saw the huge notched executioner's sword descending upon her bowed neck, uttered a little scream, sprang to her feet and ran, fleet as a rabbit, across the waiting-room; whilst down its full length after her with a clang fell the weapon—followed by a burst of laughter from everyone in the room but the countess.

After this, I took the sword up and marched on the platform with it at my side. This I will say for it—that, considering its size and weight, it is easily carried; for not only is there the crosspiece as handguard, but above this is a crescent worked in the iron, the horns extending with the convexity towards the point of the blade. By putting a couple of fingers under these horns, the sword is carried at the side, pommel downwards, blade up, with perfect ease, the balance is so true. Some difficulty attended the getting into the carriage with the sword; I had to enter backwards and bring my sword in after me, passengers keeping judiciously out of its reach till it was safely brought within.

Not the Douvres-Calais that day! only that horrible little narrow boat that always upsets me—and I—such an heroic being, bearing the mighty mediæval sword, an object of wonder and questioning to sailors, *douaniers*, passengers alike. As it happened, I was the sole individual on board whose inner organs had not their sea-legs on this occasion. I lay on a bench upon deck, hugging my executioner's sword, and faintly calling: "A basin please!" Two ruffians—I can call them nothing else—paced the deck, smoking, and passed me every forty seconds. If there is a thing which tumbles a human being of a highly-strung nervous temperament over when he feels squeamish, it is the occasional whiff of a cigar. Then, added to the occasional whiff, were occasional catches of derogatory remarks, which came home to me as unpleasantly as did the tobacco: "A chap with a sword like that should live up to it, and not grovel over a basin."—And a quotation from the Burial of Sir John Moore: "He lay like a warrior taking his rest."

My spine, with the pitching and vibration of the vessel, felt not like a spinal column, but like a loose string of beads. If by swallowing the sword I could have acquired stamina, I should have tried it; but I did not think I could keep it down. At length, with a pasty face, blear-eyes, liver-coloured lips, a battered hat, a dripping and torn waterproof, reeling, holding my ticket in my teeth, the sword in one hand and my portmanteau in the other, looking like a dynamitard every inch, and at once pounced on and overhauled by the police and customs-officers, I staggered ashore. Having that sword was as much as proclaiming that I had infernal machines about me somewhere, and even my pockets were not sacred. Having turned out all my insides at sea, I had to turn out my exterior pockets and portmanteau now. It was monstrous. That was not all. I am sure a detective followed me to town. When I got into a hansom at Charing Cross, the sword would go nowhere except between my knees, with the blade shooting up between the reins of the driver, high above the top of the conveyance. I caused great amusement as I drove through the streets of London thus.

The sword is at rest now, lodged on my staircase, and of one thing I am sure: no one is likely to run away with it. I have lost curiosities too tempting for specialists to keep their fingers from ; but no one will carry away my sword. I shall go, but the sword will remain.

CHAPTER XII.

AIX.

Dooll, but the mutton good—Les Bains de Sextius—Ironwork caps to towers—S. Jean de Malthe—Museum—Cathedral—Tapestries and tombs—The cloisters—View from S. Eutrope—King René of Anjou—His misfortunes—His cheeriness—His statue at Aix—Introduces the Muscat grape.

HAD a friend, a parson, a good fellow, who was some years ago in Cumberland, where he was concerned about the spiritual condition of the neighbouring parsons. Among these latter was one, very bucolic, with a heavy red face. My friend urged him to take advantage of a "retreat," that is a gathering of clergy for devotion and meditation, that was to take place in Carlisle. After some persuasion the heavy-souled parson agreed to go, and my dear good friend hoped that some spark of spiritual zeal might be thus kindled in him.

When the retreat was at an end he button-holed him, and asked, "Well, how did you get on?"

"Dooll, varry dooll!" replied the heavy soul, "I shud ha' left long ago, but—the mutton was good."

I had gone for a couple of weeks to commercial inns, and now that I visited Aix I thought I would like to see another aspect of Gallic life, so I went to the Hôtel des Bain de Sextius, and took a plunge into the society of patients drinking waters and taking baths. I may say of that social phase in the Bain, that it was "dooll, varry dooll, but the mutton was good." I was a fool to go there ; of course one cannot expect people with their livers and their spleens, and their entire internal tubular mechanism out of order, to be chirpy and frolicsome. There were a good many ladies there, pale, I could not quite make out whether from ill-health or from violet-powder ; but I think the latter had something to do with their pallor, for, after drinking, when they wiped their lips, roses began to bloom, wherever the napkin touched. They lived up to their appearance, natural or applied, they were "mild-eyed, melancholy, lotus-eaters," to whom it was "always afternoon." The gentlemen were equally sad, still and forlorn. But the mutton was good. The feeding left little to be wished for.

Aix lies in a green basin of hills, at a little distance from the river Are, clustered about the hot springs that rise at the junction of the porphyry and the limestone. They were certainly hotter when Aix was founded by Caius Sextius Calvinus, B.C. 123, to serve as a protection to the Greeks of Marseilles against the attacks of the Salyes. Roman colonists were planted there, consequently in race distinct from the Massalliotes. I cannot say that the Greek type lingers in Marseilles, certainly the women who hover about the Vieux port are as ugly as women can well be, nor have the natives of Aix a peculiarly Roman character of face and head. The only people who retain any distinguishing features of their ancestry are those of Arles, of whom I have already told.

Aix has lost its old walls and towers within the last twenty years. It has good boulevards and shaded walks, and in the old parts of the town many charming bits. Most charming perhaps are the iron crowns to two of the towers, one by the Hotel de Ville, which is conical, the other opposite the church of La Sainte Esprit, which is like a papal tiara. When I saw in Baedeker that "en face de cette église—une tour de 1494, qui a un beau campanile en fer," my mind turned at once to that horrible iron spire at Rouen, and I felt disposed to look at the pavement when approaching the church. However, it is not modern, and not hideous; it is quite the reverse, a study in fine ironwork. That the ancients could, however, do very villainous things, may be seen on a visit paid to the church of S. Jean de Malthe. It has a square east end, is an edifice of the thirteenth century, with a tower of the fourteenth and fifteenth. The original architect in the thirteenth century was a fool, and those who desired to complete the church a century later probably advertised for the greatest fool then in the profession, and secured him. Within the church is a monument that pretends to be the tomb of Alphonso II., Count of Provence, in 1209, and to be adorned not only with his statue, but also with those of his son Raymond Berengarius IV., and of Beatrix, Queen of Naples, the wife of the latter. The monument is, however, a hoax. The statues are there, but are modern, of the namby-pamby school, and of the original tomb possibly a crocket and a cusp may remain.

Hard by this odious church, with its horrible modern garish windows, is the museum, containing some Greek inscriptions, a Christian sarcophagus or two, not grown on the spot, but imported from Arles, and some fragments of statues.

The Cathedral of S. Sauveur is the great attraction in Aix, and it is, indeed, a very fascinating church. The west front contains à recessed gateway with ranges of saints in the outer member, and a legion of cherubim with their wings, some spread, some folded, in the inner member. The lower portion of the doorway was encased by a hoarding, and I could not see it. It is undergoing restoration. The saints' figures thereon had their heads knocked off at the Revolution, and these were restored in bad taste later, and now fresh heads—we will hope more successful—are being adjusted.

Oh that we also could change our heads!

The octagonal tower, which formerly had a somewhat bóld appearance, has been successfully completed with an open traceried parapet and pinnacles.

On the right hand of the church is a very interesting doorway, clearly Classic. Two fluted Corinthian pillars are let into the wall, and support an entablature. Between these a Romanesque doorway has been inserted, with a twisted pillar on one side, and another fluted, opposite it.

The interior of the cathedral is full of surprises, The baptistery on the right is supported on Classic columns of grey polished granite. The S. aisle of the church is Romanesque of the twelfth century, and was the original nave of the minster. In the fourteenth or fifteenth century the present nave and N. aisle were added, and then the S. aisle of the Romanesque church was destroyed. Consequently the cloister of the twelfth century, which originally abutted on the S. wall of the church, now stands detached from it by the width of the destroyed aisle.

In some chapels is soft old glowing marigold-yellow cinque-cento glass. The choir of the cathedral is hung with tapestries, said to be by Quentin Matsys, gorgeous in colour, of, however, beauteous harmony of tone. There are quaint old paintings on gold grounds in the nave. In the N. aisle lovely tombs that served as memorials of the dead, and likewise as altar-pieces.*

The church is rich in picturesque features, not to be sketched with pencil, but laid in with the brush and colour.

Moreover, the cloister is charming in its rich quaintness. The sculptors have revelled in the foliage with which they have adorned the capitals. Here we have twisted pillars, there they are sculptured over with scales, lozenges, and other ornamental fancies. In the capitals, groups of figures alternate with bursting fronds of ferns, unfolding vine leaves, and fantastic playing monsters. In the centre of the quadrangle stands an old column, on which is S. Mary Magdalen with her ointment-pot, and doves were fluttering and cooing as an old canon scattered crumbs to them about his feet.

Aix lacks one thing greatly, a terrace above the town

* Christ on the cross is between kneeling figures of a knight and a lady; S. Anne and the B. V. Mary are also represented. This reredos is so excellent, so beautiful, that of course it did not suit the taste for tawdriness that sprang up in the eighteenth century, and a vulgar reredos has been erected, and the altar moved before that.

whence the valley may be seen, the towers of Aix, and the crags of Mont Victoire. But a walk should on no account be omitted up the heights of S. Eutrope to an old windmill that stands on a crest of limestone.

The view thence is charming. To the right the green valley of L' Infernet, up which marched Marcellus on the eve of the great battle of Pourrières. Towering overhead, catching the evening sun on its glistening bald peaks is to be seen Mont Victoire. A little to the S. E. the cleft in the wooded hills through which the Arc breaks its way, a cleft up which the Teutons trudged with their wives and children and the spoil of Gaul, to their destruction. To the south-east also a quaint chain of hills that rise above Gardanne, with a boss like a great snuff-box on the top, the Pillon du Roi. At one's feet is Aix, with its many towers, surrounded by silvery olive orchards, and away to the south is the red hill above Les Milles where Marius was encamped the night after the fight with the Ambrons.

Aix is closely associated with that delightful old Mark Tapley of kings, René of Anjou, whose character has been hit off with such masterly fidelity by Sir Walter Scott in " Anne of Geierstein." René was born at Angers in 1409, and was the second son of Duke Louis II., of the junior house of Anjou, and of Iolanthe, daughter of king John of Aragon. He bore the title of Duke of Guise till his father's death. Louis II. had been adopted by Joanna of Naples, as her heir, and had been crowned king of Naples at Avignon by Clement VII., but was never able to obtain possession of his inheritance. After his death, in 1417, René's eldest brother, Louis III., succeeded to his titles and rights, and when he died without issue, in 1434, Anjou, Provence, and claims to Naples, Sicily and Jerusalem devolved on René, who had in the meantime acquired, by the death of an uncle, the Duchy of Bar, and, by right of his wife, laid claim to the Duchy of Lorraine.

When he desired to make these latter claims good, he was involved in war with his wife's kinsmen, and was taken prisoner and locked up at Dijon. Finally, the question of the right to the Duchy of Lorraine was referred to the decision of the Emperor Sigismund, who gave it in favour of René. His opponent, however, appealed to Philip of Burgundy, who summoned René to appear before him, and when he did not appear, ordered him to return to his prison, from which he had been released on parole. René at once submitted. Whilst he was in prison at Dijon, delegates from Naples arrived offering him the crown; but Duke Philip would not release him. Thereupon René transferred his rights provisionally to his wife, the Duchess Isabella, and she became regent of Naples, Sicily, Anjou, and Provence. She, however, soon found herself involved in war with the king of Aragon. In the meantime René managed to ransom himself for the sum of 400,000 gold florins (1437) and at once hasted to Naples. There, however, he found himself unable to make head against Alphonso of Aragon, and he was finally driven out, and obliged to return to Provence. He died at Aix on July 10, 1480.

Sir Walter well says of him: "Born of royal parentage, and with high pretensions, René had at no period of his life been able to match his fortunes to his claims. Of the kingdoms to which he asserted right, nothing remained in his possession but the county of Provence, itself a fair and friendly principality, but diminished by the many claims which France had acquired upon portions of it by advances of money to supply the personal expenses of its master, and by other portions, which Burgundy, to whom René had been a prisoner, held in pledge for his ransom. . . . René was a prince of very moderate parts, endowed with a love of the fine arts, which he carried to extremity, and with a degree of good humour, which never permitted him to repine at fortune, but rendered its possessor happy, when a prince of keener feelings would have died of despair. This *insouciant*, light-tempered, gay and thoughtless disposition conducted René, free from all the passions which embitter life, to a hale and mirthful old age. Even domestic losses made no deep impression on the feelings of this cheerful old monarch. Most of his children had died young; René took it not to heart. His daughter Margaret's marriage with the powerful Henry of England was considered a connection above the fortunes of the king of Troubadours. But in the issue, instead of René deriving any splendour from the match, he was involved in the misfortunes of his daughter, and repeatedly obliged to impoverish himself to supply her ransom. . . . Among all his distresses, René feasted and received guests, danced, sang, composed poetry, used the pencil or brush with no small skill, devised and conducted festivals and processions, and studied to promote the mirth and good humour of his subjects."

In the cathedral is his portrait along with that of his second wife, Jeanne de Laval. In the *place* is his statue, a mediocre work, holding a bunch of Muscat grapes, a species he first introduced to Europe. I sought in vain at Aix for a photograph of the Merry Monarch taken from the authentic picture, and was offered one from the characterless statue, which I declined. Poor king René's poems have found an editor and a publisher—in four volumes (Paris, 1845-6, edited by Quatrebarbes), but, I fear, not many readers. No; it will not be through his laboured poetic compositions, nor through the daubs which he painted, that René will be known and will have earned the gratitude of posterity, but through the introduction of the Muscat grape. Henceforth, let my readers, whenever they enjoy their muscatels out of the grape-house at home, or sip Moscada Toscana in Italy, or Muscat in La Vallais, give a kindly thought to that much-tried but never downcast monarch.

CHAPTER XIII.

THE CAMARGUE.

Formation of the delta of the Rhone—The diluvial wash—The alluvium spread over this—The three stages the river pursues—The zone of erosion—The zone of compensation—The zone of deposit—River mouths—Estuaries and deltas—The formation of bars—Of lagoons—The lagoons of the Gulf of Lyons—The ancient position of Arles between the river and the lagoons—Neglect of the lagoons in the Middle Ages—They become morasses—Attempt at remedy—Embankments and drains—A mistake made—The Camargue now a desert—Les Saintes Maries—No evidence to support the legend—Based on a misapprehension.

AS I said when speaking of the Crau, the whole delta of the Rhone, which extended in the diluvial epoch from Cette to Fos, consists of a vast sloping plain of rolled stones from the Alps. What is now a great convexity thrust into the Mediterranean, perpetually gaining ground on the sea, was at the commencement of the present geologic epoch a great bay, and the waves of the Mediterranean broke against the cliffs of les Monts Garrigues, at Lodève, the heights of Nimes and Beaucaire, against the limestone crags of the Alpines, and swirled against that calcareous spur that now separates the lagoon of Berre from the desert of la Crau.

But, at an epoch which it is impossible to fix, which, however, is posterior to the last geologic dislocations of the soil, two formidable deluges swept from the Alps down the troughs of the Rhone and the Durance, carrying with them vast masses of stone torn from the flanks of the mountains. They were veritable avalanches of water, mud and rubble, that filled the entire bay and covered the land, wherever they poured, with the wreckage of the Alps. The stones were broken into a thousand pieces in their course, their angles rubbed down, and their surfaces polished by friction, and this vast bed of rubble measures near the mouth of the Rhone some sixty feet in depth, and extends under the blue surface of the sea to the distance of many miles.

But, when the diluvium ceased, and the rivers Rhone and Durance assumed approximately their present character, a change of procedure took place. The volume of water rolled down was by no means so great, the inclination of the fall was vastly lessened, consequently the rivers were enabled to do what they had not been able to do in the diluvial period, chew up their food of stone, and reduce it to the condition of mud. This is what the two rivers are engaged upon now, and instead of strewing their *embouchures* with pebbles, they distribute over them, or would do so, if permitted, a film of fertilising mud.

Through many ages the Rhone has rambled at its sweet will over the vast tract of rubble that formed its delta in the diluvial age, changing its course capriciously, and always, wherever it went, covering up the pebble bed with a deposit of fertile soil. Other streams helped in the good work—the Hérault, rich with red mud, the Ley, that flows past Montpellier, and the Vidourle from Lunel: consequently a very large portion of the rubble bed is covered with rich soil, that grows vines, mulberries, and olives. The plough and spade, however, speedily reach the boulders that lie but slightly buried beneath the surface. The canal of Craponne, that conveys the charged waters of the Durance over the Crau of Arles, is effecting artificially over that portion of the rubbly desert, the work that was done by Nature herself in past ages over the whole region from Cette to Aiguesmortes.

Now let us examine very shortly the stages through which every mountain-born river runs.

When young, sprung from eternal snows, gushing from under glaciers, it cuts its way through mountain gorges, receiving the rocks that fall from above, and carrying them along in its course, tearing its way round rocky spurs, and breaking them in its fury, and, as it travels down into the lower ground, it carries with it a vast mass of stone. Every tributary does the same. This first stage is called the *zone of erosion*.

But, as the river leaves the Alps, its course becomes less rapid, and the fall is not so abrupt. The bed widens, and what was a boiling torrent becomes a rapid river. As it rolls along, it carries down with it the stones that it has brought from the mountains, turning them over and over in its course, rubbing down all rough points, and becoming itself discoloured with the particles it has rubbed off the pebbles. All this matter thus produced has a tendency to fall to the bottom and form banks of gravel; but the violence of the stream is constantly altering the shape and position of these beds, carrying the gravel farther, and throwing down in their place half-triturated deposits of the same character.

This is called the *zone of compensation*.

Any traveller who has visited the Vallais may see the Rhone at work in its first stage. In the second he can trace the river from below Lyons, and see the thousand gravel-banks formed, swept away, and reformed, at every flood, that mark the course of the river in its second stage.

By the time the Rhone has reached Arles all its gravel has been champed up and reduced to impalpable mud. That blue crystalline flood that gushed from the Lake of Leman, unsullied by a particle of earth, is now a river of brown mud—thick as pea-soup, and as nutritious. The stones that would have killed all vegetation have been pounded into a condition so attenuated, that they form rich alluvial matter. The river now seeks to deposit all this mud. On reaching the sea, the difference in gravity between the meeting waters, and their variation in temperature, produces rapid precipitation of all the earthy matter held in suspense by the stream. This last stage in the river's course is called the *zone of deposit*.

The inclination of the bed of the Rhone between Tarascon and Arles is four feet three inches in the mile; but at Arles the elevation of the bank is but three feet six inches above the level of the sea; and the river has to run sixty-two miles before it reaches salt waves. Consequently the bed widens, the river branches, and the rapidity of its movement diminishes progressively. The alluvium is deposited, banks multiply, the mouths are encumbered with submarine islets, locally called *theys*, which the waves and currents of the sea displace and remodel continuously, and render the entrance to the river impracticable.*

River mouths vary greatly; they are either estuaries, like those of the Thames, the Seine, and the S. Lawrence, or they are deltas, like those of the Nile, the Po, and the Rhone. Very generally in tidal seas we have estuaries; but in those that are tideless, as the Mediterranean and the Black Sea, they are deltas. Where there is a tide, the mouth of the river is washed out and kept open by the flux and reflux of the sea; but where there is no tide there is nothing to interfere with the river choking its mouth with its deposits. In such a case, after a while, the mass of deposit becomes so great as to interfere with the course of the river. The sea beating against this bar throws up sand and gravel upon it, and at every storm raises it higher. Then the river divides into two or more branches, and forms for itself new beds, which are destined in turn to undergo the same process.

Now, when a river has formed its bar choking its mouth, and is then forced to make a fresh mouth, it leaves a lagoon behind this bar. At every flood its waters overflow, and are unable to escape to the sea when left behind the bar. Sometimes, in like

* Lenthéric: 'Les Villes Mortes du Golfe de Lyon,' Paris, 1883.

manner, in a gale of wind on shore, the waves are carried over the bar, and there are left as a brackish pool, unable to return to the sea.

Thus the whole of the Bay of the Gulf of Lyons is masked by a false coastline of old bars, behind which lie lagoons all formed in the way indicated. Between Rousillon and Leucate is the Etang de Salses; Narbonne anciently was seated in the lap of another great inland lake or lagoon. The vast Etang de Tau has a barrier between it and the sea on which is planted Cette. Lagoons behind bars extend thence the whole way to Aiguesmortes; and between the mouths of the Rhone, as they flow at present, is the Etang de Valcarès.

After the river has deserted its old bed, and the lagoon has been formed behind the bar, or littoral cord, wave and storm working upon this long line of mud and sand succeed in breaking through; then, as the inclination of the land is but 0^m, 01 in the metre—almost nothing, the sweet and salt water mingle in these lakes, they never run dry, though in many cases not three feet deep.

A look at the map of the Gulf of Lyons will show the reader that its special characteristic is the chain of lagoons separated from the sea by a narrow ribbon of sand. It may have caused perplexity in the mind of many that the Gulf should bear the name it does. It cannot take its name from the city of Lyons—the ancient Lugdunum—which is two hundred and twenty miles inland. It certainly cannot derive it from the wild beasts—lions—for there are none nearer than Africa.

The fact is, that the Gulf takes its title from the

Keltic word for a lagoon, lôn or lyn, a name that recurs in Maguelonne—the Dwelling on the Pool—in the Canal des Lonnes, a channel connecting the ponds and lagoons of the Durance and Rhone, and, indeed, in our own London (Londinium) the Dinas, Castle on the Lon, or pool of the Thames and the Essex marshes.

Anciently, in historic times, Arles, that lies near the apex of the triangle formed by the branches of the Rhone, was bathed on one side by the river, by which she received merchandise from the north; and, on the other side by the *lones*, or submerged land, that extended to the sea; and after Marius had connected these lones with his canal, she exported and imported merchandise over the Mediterranean through the lagoons, as the sea could not be reached by the river on account of its bars.

Moreover, the Greek and Roman cities along the coast are not found on the actual coast, on the bars, but were planted on the lagoons, which afforded them perfect harbourage for their merchant vessels. These lagoons, through which flowed salt and fresh water, were always healthy, and remained healthy as long as communication was maintained with the sea and the river. But wind and wave and alluvium working together choke these communications, and directly the mouth seawards of a lagoon is closed it is converted into a stagnating marsh that exhales malaria.

During the Middle Ages no attention was paid to this fact, and those stations which had been perfectly wholesome in the Classic Epoch were rendered pestilential, and dwindled from populous cities to a cluster of fever-smitten peasants' hovels. In later times this desperate condition of affairs called for remedy. Louis XIV. sent engineers to examine and report on the state of this region, and works were begun which have been maintained and extended annually, the raising of dykes against overflow by the Rhone and by the sea. Drains have been cut in all directions to carry off the stagnant water, opening by traps into the sea. The extent of dyke now reaches two hundred and thirty miles. The banks of the two main branches of the Rhone are protected, as well as the sea-face of the Camargue, the triangle between them, and the annual cost to the country to keep them in repair is one hundred and twenty thousand francs. A flood, however, often breaks through the banks, and submerges a large district. On such occasions the additional expense is heavy.

Now, what is the result of all this outlay? The engineers and scientific authorities of the coast-works and dykes are pretty unanimous in saying that a great mistake was made in the beginning by Louis XIV. The Rhone ought never to have been embanked. What should have been done was to keep open the mouths of the lagoons, to preserve them from festering.

Formerly, the large island of the Camargue, occupying nearly twenty thousand acres, was periodically inundated by the Rhone, and when the waters fell, a film of the richest deposit was left behind, just as in Egypt the Nile overflows and fertilises its delta. At every overflow eighteen thousand cubic yards of alluvium was deposited over this district, all of which is now carried into the Mediterranean and thrown down in the construction of new bars; utterly wasted.

In the time of the Roman domination the Camargue was a second Egypt, and was called "The granary of the Roman army;" and Arles was given the designation of "The Breasts," so flowing with plenty was it held to be. At the initial cost of millions of pounds, and an annual outlay of five thousand pounds, the Camargue has been reduced to absolute sterility.

The protected lands, deprived of the sweet water which would have washed from them the salt that now spoils their fertility, and of the natural dressing that Providence sends down to them every spring and autumn, are now productive of only a little coarse wiry grass and thistles, and the dried soil is white with saline efflorescence. At the present day the value of land in the neighbourhood of Arles that is subject to periodic inundation is three times that of the land guarded by costly embankments against the bounties of the river.

On descending the sinuous course of the lesser Rhone the hills disappear, the horizon is level as the sea, and all around is desert. Then the current of the Rhone seems to fail wholly, the waters of the river and of the lagoons on both sides of its bed mingle, and become confounded in one sheet. All nature is dead. The dull and sluggish water, streaked with lines of ooze, extend on all sides as far as the eye can reach. The effects of the mirage add bewilderment. One can hardly distinguish water from sky. Nothing can be more dreary than this naked surface, hushed into silence, where vegetation is reduced to a few tufts of rushes and tamarisks.

But, suddenly, out of the marshy, submerged plain, a strange pile of buildings is seen cutting the horizon, half a castle, half a cathedral, imposing in a mass as it towers above the fragile and squalid hovels crouched at the feet. This building is *Les Saintes Maries.*

Probably nowhere in the world is to be seen a spot so desolate and so wretched. The village is planted

LES SAINTES MARIES.

at the extreme west angle of the Camargue. It can be reached by one road only, rough to travel over, and impracticable in winter. This road leaves Arles, or rather Trinquetailles, opposite Arles, traverses the marsh of the Gránd Mar, follows the dyke of the river, and then threads its way among morasses, and over soil white with salt, and burning under the rays of the sun. Once in the year this route is crowded with pilgrims, who come to pay their devotions at the spot where it is supposed that the Three Marys,

Mary, the mother of James, Mary Salome, and their servant Sara, landed. The legend is somewhat mixed. According to one version, those who came to Provence, flying from the persecution raised by the Jews, were Lazarus, Mary Magdalene, and Martha. Lazarus, as we have seen, has been appropriated by Marseilles as its apostle; Martha has been settled at Tarascon, and Mary Magdalene has been given a cell in La Sainte Baume. Here, at Les Saintes Maries, however, the apostolic three are said to be Mary, mother of James, Mary, wife of Cleopas, and Sara, their servant; but a concession to the other tradition is made, in that it is allowed that these three brought with them Lazarus and Martha.

Nothing was known of all this till the time of good King René. The church at this point was called in the sixth century S. Maria de Ratis, S. Mary of the Boats, by S. Cæsarius, Bishop of Arles. William, Count of Provence, in his will, A.D. 992, gives it the same designation; so Raimbald, Archbishop of Arles in A.D. 1061, "The Church of the Ever Virgin Mother of God, Mary of the Boats." So also Bertrand II., Count of Provence, at the same date. Two bulls of popes in 1123 and 1200 speak of the church as that of S. Mary on the Sea. So does Gervais of Tilbury. In 1241 Raymond Berengarius, Count of Provence, entitles it Notre Dame de la Mer. And so it continued to be called in documents down to 1395. If not Our Lady of the Sea, it was S. Maria de la Mar, of the Mere, the Lagoon.

However, in 1448, King René took it into his head that Mary and the Mere were distinct persons, that

Mary was not, could not be, the Virgin, she must be one of the other Marys; so with a little putting together of heads and puzzlement, he and his advisers decided that the two Marys were Mary, the mother of James, and Mary Salome. The next thing to be done was to find their bodies there, but that naturally presented no difficulty. There were bones there—from Pagan times. Since that date a great pilgrimage has taken place annually to Les Saintes Maries; and the curé of Les Baux, being very satisfied that the Trémaïé in his parish must be the Three Marys, erected a chapel under the rock sculptured with the figures of Marius, Martha, and Julia.

The Magdalen is probably a personation of the perished city of Maguelonne, as one of the Marys is the Mar or Mere; and Martha, there can hardly be a question, is the Syrian prophetess who accompanied Marius, but who in her place inherited the attributes and cult of Martis, the Phœnician goddess, venerated, doubtless, at all the settlements of these mercantile adventurers along the coast.

CHAPTER XIV.

TARASCON.

Position of Tarascon and Beaucaire opposite each other—Church of S. Martha—Crypt—Ancient paintings—Catechising—Ancient altar—The festival of the Tarasque—The Phœnician goddess Martha—Story of S. Fronto—Discussion at *déjeuner* over the entry of M. Carnot into Marseilles—The change in the French character—Pessimism—Beaucaire—Font—Castle—Siege by Raymond VII.—Story of Aucassin and Nicolette.

ARASCON and Beaucaire stand frowning at each other across the Rhone, each with its castle; Beaucaire a grand pile on a crag, Tarascon dipping its feet in the water, and sulkily showing to its enemy a plain face, reserving all its picturesqueness for its side towards the town. This castle of Tarascon was one in which King René resided, as well as in that at Aix, but the Aix castle is gone, and that at Tarascon remains. Beaucaire belonged to the counts of Toulouse, whereas Tarascon, as already said, belonged to Provence. I do not like to venture on an explanation of the name, but the *Tar* with which it begins is

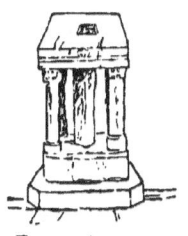
EARLY ALTAR, TARASCON.

most probably the Keltic *Daur*, water.* But the Tarasconese will not hear of this. To them the name is taken from the Tarasc, a monster that devastated the whole country round, but whom S. Martha bridled and slew. S. Martha, as we have already seen, is the very prophetess who directed Caius Marius in his campaign against the Teutons and Ambrons, the devastating horde that has in the popular imagination been represented as a dragon. The body of S. Martha is supposed to lie in the crypt, in an early Christian marble sarcophagus, probably brought from the Alyscamp at Arles, representing Moses striking the rock, and the miraculous feeding of the multitude, the miracle of Cana, and the resurrection of Lazarus.

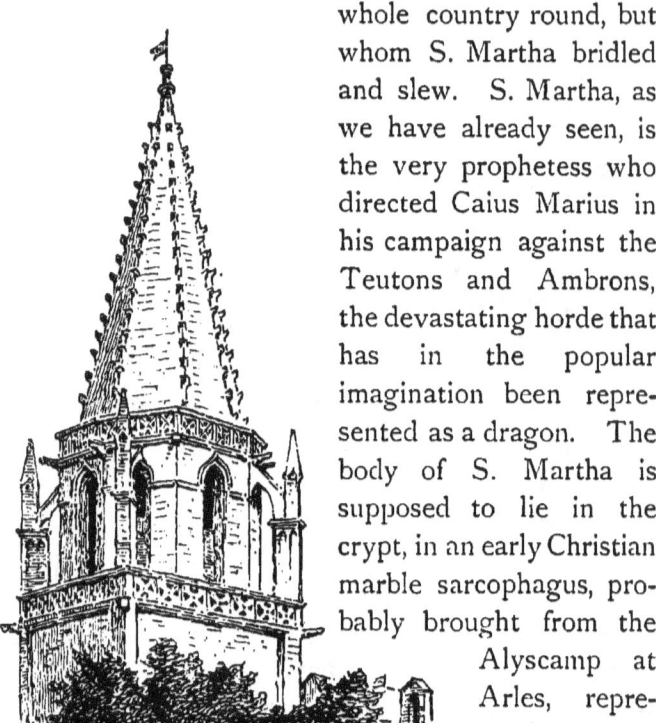

SPIRE OF S. MARTHA'S CHURCH, TARASCON.

* *Gwask*, in Breton, is *contraction*, and at Tarascon the river is drawn together by the opposed points of Beaucaire and Tarascon. This may perhaps form the second syllable.

In this crypt is a Corinthian capital turned upside down and converted into a holy water stoup; also a very early and curious altar, the slab of which is just two feet square, and has in the midst a square hole cut, probably of later date, for the reception of relics; the height of the altar is three feet three and a-half inches, it is of a porous stone that has become greatly corroded with weather. It is probably the earliest Christian altar in France.

In the crypt is a life-size representation of the entombment of S. Martha, with figures standing round, Chr st at the head, and S. Fronto at the feet.

The church of S. Martha is of the fourteenth century, with the exception of the south portal, which dates from 1187, and is rich in its deeply-recessed mouldings filled with sculpture, but has been sadly mutilated. Within the church is some very fine ironwork, a grille dividing the choir from the side aisles, and a charming iron safe let into the wall on the north side, of iron-work painted and gilt. There are moreover some quaint paintings; an ancient altarpiece representing S. Rocque, between S. John and S. Laurence, on a gold ground; a S. Mary Magdalen with the portrait of a canon kneeling at her feet; the finest painting is S. Michael, also with a canon kneeling below. The armour of the archangel is very rich, and heightened

IRON DOOR TO SAFE IN S. MARTHA'S CHURCH.

with gold. The date of these pictures is 1513. There is another of the Nativity that is inferior. Whilst looking round the church, I heard singing muffled and distant, and presently, on reaching the steps that descended to the crypt, found that a young priest was

KING RENÉ'S CASTLE, TARASCON.

there cate- chising a class of little girls. After some instructions they sang a hymn, which a Sister of Mercy was accom- panying on the harmonium. The air was taking. It puzzled me at first. It was familiar and yet strange, and not till the children had reached the last verse did I recognise a wonderfully distorted form of the mermaid's song in *Oberon*, all the accents being altered. In this crypt is the tomb of a Neapolitan knight attached to the court of king René; and in the floor a well the water of which rises and falls with the river. In all probability this crypt was originally the baptistery of the first basilica erected in Tarascon.

The castle of King René is wonderfully picturesque on the landside. It was begun in 1400; he is said to have instituted the festival of the Tarasque, that used to be conducted with great merriment annually on July 29th.

A procession of mummers attended by the clergy paraded the town, escorting the figure of a dragon, made of canvas, and wielding a heavy beam of wood for a tail, to the imminent danger of the legs of all who approached. The dragon was conducted by a girl in white and blue, who led it by her girdle of blue silk, and when the dragon was especially frolicsome and unruly dashed holy water over it.

The ceremony was attended by numerous practical jokes, and led to acts of violence, in consequence of which it has been suppressed.

S. Martha has inherited the symbols of the Phœnician goddess of her own name, the ship and the dragon; there can be little doubt that the first Phœnician settlers in Provence introduced her worship as the patroness of sailors, and that this worship acquired a fresh impulse after the destruction of the Teutons who had overrun the land, when the prophetess Martha was regarded as one with the earlier goddess. When Christianity came in, the name of the hostess of Bethany was given to the churches erected where

O

Martha the moon goddess had been venerated before, so as gradually to wean the heathen from their old faith. They came over into the Church, but brought with them their myth of the pagan goddess.

An odd legend is told of her death.

On a Sunday morning, S. Fronto, bishop of Perigeux was about to say Mass, and whilst waiting for the congregation to assemble, fell asleep in his chair, when he saw Christ appear, who bade him come and assist at the obsequies of Martha. Instantly he found himself translated to Tarascon, in the church with our Lord, he at the feet and Christ at the head of the body, and the Saviour sang the burial office. In the meantime at Perigeux, the deacon wondered at the heavy sleep of the bishop, and had much ado to rouse him. At length Fronto opened his eyes, when the deacon whispered that the people were impatient with long waiting.

A BIT IN TARASCON.

"Do not be troubled," said Fronto, "you do not understand what I have been about."

Now it fell out that whilst at Tarascon Fronto was engaged in burying Martha, he had taken off his glove and ring, and had put them into the hands of the sacristan. When Fronto informed the congregation at Perigeux what he had been about, they disbelieved. However, messengers were sent to Tarascon, and his glove and ring were identified. These were preserved as relics in the church till the Revolution. Unfortunately for the story, Fronto of Perigeux belongs to the fourth century, so that the lapse in dream was not merely a skip over half France, but also through four centuries.

Tarascon has some picturesque bits in the town, arcades with shops underneath, and quaint doorways of Renaissance work ; but its chief charm after the castle is certainly the view across the river to the heights of Beaucaire with its grand ruins.

I lunched at an hotel where, nearly opposite me, was a gentleman who had been at Marseilles on the arrival of the President, and was very full of what he had seen. At the table were half-a-dozen beside myself, and he held forth to them on the spectacle. Opposite him sat a bullet-headed commercial traveller.

" But," said the latter, " I would not have crossed the Rhone by the bridge of Tarascon to have seen him. What is M. Sadi-Carnot ? He is naught."

" No, but he represents the nation. Give us a pump as president, and we must garland that pump with flowers. And believe me, c'est un vilain métier cet de président. If he leans a little too much on this side he goes down into the mud, a little too much on the other he rolls in the dust. One must feel some respect for the man who undertakes such a thankless office. And, again, when a man rides in an open landau in pelting rain, when il lui pleut dans le nez, without an umbrella, with his hat off, saluting right and left, he deserves recognition."

"It was not worth the cost of his entertainment. I am surprised that Marseilles did it."

"I beg pardon. It was worth while doing it. Had the weather been fine, it would have brought money into the town."

"What! Would any English and American travellers desert Montecarlo for a day to see a Sadi-Carnot?"

"No, but every woman in Marseilles would have bought a new kerchief or a trinket to make herself smart, just because it was a fête. As it was, money circulated."

"How so?"

"One thousand and ninety-seven umbrellas were sold that day at prices ranging from five to fifteen francs, which on other occasions sell for two francs twenty-five centimes, and ten francs."

I do not know whether I have been peculiarly unfortunate in lighting on only one class of men under the present *régime*, but whether it be in France, Switzerland, Belgium, or Italy, that I have come across Frenchmen and had a talk with them of late years, I have noticed a prevailing discouragement, a pessimism, that certainly was absent in former days. The very character of a French *table d'hôte* is changed. Instead of Gallic vivacity, merriment, and general conversation, such as one was wont to find there, one encounters silence, reserve, and a marked absence of self-assertion. It is the Germans who are now boisterous and self-assertive at table. The French are quiet and subdued.

As I have already said, I may be mistaken; I may have hit on exceptional cases, but it is a fact that those Frenchmen I have conversed with during the last two or three years have been oppressed with a conviction that France has lost caste among the nations, that her future is menaced, and they say that they see no way out of their present condition.

As one said to me last winter in Rome: " The idea of France is an abstraction. We range ourselves now under parties, our devotion is no longer to our country but to our party. Have you ever been at a stag hunt? When the noble beast is down the huntsman slices it open and throws the heart and liver and entrails to the hounds. Then ensues a battle. Every dog snatches at what he desires, and envies the other the piece of offal he has secured. All are filled with hatred of each other, and selfish greed as to who can eat most and the best morsels of the fallen beast. And that is a picture of France. If war came upon us, we must infallibly be overthrown, for each general would be seeking out of the accidents of warfare to steal an advantage for himself or the party he favours."

The town of Beaucaire, on the farther side of the Rhone, is fuller of picturesque points than is Tarascon. Seated at the head of the Beaucaire Canal, that communicates with the sea, it has that commercial prosperity which is lacking at Tarascon. The old church is an exact reproduction of that of S. Martha, but has in addition a most remarkable font, a structure rising in stages like a tower, and with a spire to cap it, resembling somewhat the sacramental tabernacles in the German churches. The Hôtel de Ville is a picturesque Renaissance building with bold open staircase on pillars. The castle of Beaucaire crowns the ridge of limestone that extends across the country from Nimes and is cut through by the Rhone, again emerging, in a low eminence, at Tarascon. This noble castle was taken by Simon de Montfort in the Albigensian War from the Count of Toulouse, but the youthful Raymond VII., though only nineteen years old, laid siege to it in 1216, and succeeded in recovering it. In this siege, the inhabitants of the town, under the young count, assailed the castle. Simon de Montfort collected an army and attacked Raymond in the rear. There is a very curious account of this siege in a Provençal poem on the Albigensian War, from which I will quote a few lines, only premising that in the original the castle is called the Capitol :—

"The townsmen set up their engines against the Crusaders in the castle, and so battered it that castle and watch-tower were broken, beams and lead and stone. At Holy Easter the battering-ram was made ready, long, iron-headed, sharp, which so struck and cut that the wall was injured, and the stones began to fall out. But the besieged were not discouraged ; they made a loop of cords attached to a wooden beam, and with that they caught the head of the ram and held it fast. This troubled those of Beaucaire sore ; till the master engineer came, and he set the ram in motion once more. Then several of the assailants got up the rock, and began to detach portions of the wall with their picks. This the besieged were ware of, and they let down upon them sulphur and pitch and fire in sackcloth by a chain along the wall, and when it blazed it broke forth and was spilt over the workmen, and suffocated them so that not one could there continue. Then they went to their machines for casting stones, and they threw them with such effect into the castle as to break all the beams thereof."

Beaucaire castle is now in ruins, but the Romanesque chapel remains in tolerable condition. In it Louis IX.

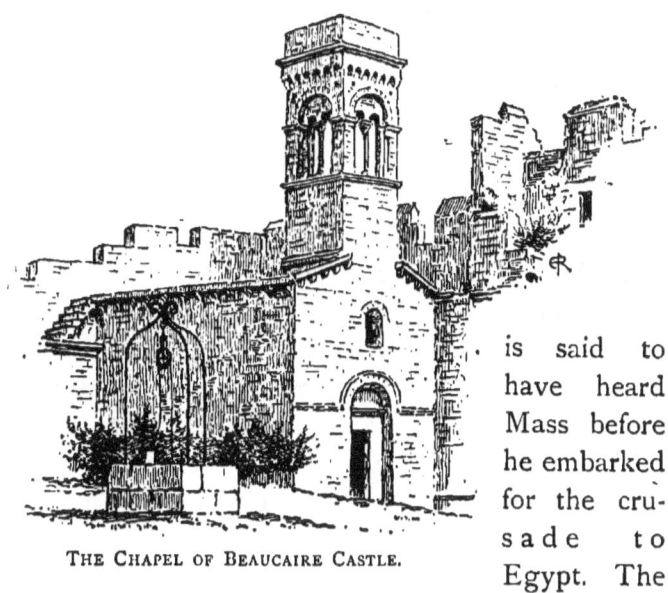

THE CHAPEL OF BEAUCAIRE CASTLE.

is said to have heard Mass before he embarked for the crusade to Egypt. The pretty old Provençal poem of Aucassin and Nicolette, which has been recently translated into English by Mr. Andrew Lang and daintily published, has its scene laid at Beaucaire. Tieck gave a version of it in his "Phantasus."

As we are on the very scene of this graceful little tale, I must give the essence of it. The romance, which dates from the second half of the thirteenth century, is in prose, mingled with scraps of rhyme, destined to be sung, and with their musical notation given. At the head of each scrap of verse comes the rubric "Now is to be sung," and the prose passages are headed, "Now is to be said."

Aucassin was the son of the Count of Beaucaire. He was fair of face, with light curled hair and grey eyes. Now there was a viscount in the town who had bought of the Saracens a little maid, and he taught her the Christian faith, and had her baptised and called Nicolette.

Then said the Count of Beaucaire to his son Aucassin that he should go to battle and win his spurs and be dubbed a knight. Aucassin replied that he had no wish to be a knight, unless his father would give him Nicolette "ma douce mie" to wife. The count is indignant. He says that his son must marry the daughter of a king or of a count; but Aucassin replies that were an empress offered him he would refuse her for Nicolette. Thereat the count goes to the viscount and bids him give up the little maid that he may burn her as a witch. The viscount hesitates, and promises he will put her out of reach of Aucassin. Thereupon he shuts her up in a tower, along with her nurse, where there is but a single window. And the count promises his son that he shall have his "douce mie" if he will go to fight against the mortal enemy of their house, the Count of Vallence. Aucassin believes his father; goes and captures the count. Then the father refuses to fulfil his promise. Aucassin in a rage releases the Count of Vallence, and the Count of Beaucaire imprisons his son in a tower of the castle.

One moonlight night, when her nurse is asleep, Nicolette ties the bedclothes together and lets herself down out of the window, escapes from the town, and goes under the castle, where she hears Aucassin lamenting in his prison. She speaks to him and he replies.

But (as it is ascertained that she has escaped) the guard are sent forth in search of her, with orders to run her through the body if found. However, the chief officer of the guard is a merciful man, and so, as he goes about, he sings a song to warn her, and she hides in the shadow of the tower till the watch is gone by and then flies away into the forest land. There she builds herself a hut. When no tidings of Nicolette are heard, the Count of Beaucaire lets his son forth from prison. One day, as Aucassin rides in the forest, he lights on the cabin of his dear Nicolette, and they resolve to fly together. So they take a boat on the Rhone and they are washed down towards the sea, captured by Saracen pirates and separated. Aucassin is ransomed and returns home. Nicolette stains her face, makes her escape, obtains a *vielle*, and travels about Provence, singing ballads. She comes to Beaucaire, where Aucassin is now count, his father having died, and sings to her hurdy-gurdy the song of her adventures. The tears run down his cheeks, and he promises her rich gifts if she will tell him more. Then she goes to the vicountess—the viscount is dead—washes off the walnut juice, dresses in best array, is seen and recognised by Aucassin, they are married with great pomp, and are happy ever after. A dear little innocent story, fresh and sweet with the springtime bloom of early literature, withal full of curious pictures of the feelings of the time relative to chivalry, monachism, and religion.

BEAUCAIRE CASTLE FROM TARASCON.—SUNSET.

CHAPTER XV.

NIMES.

The right spelling of Nimes—Derivation of name—The fountain—Throwing coins into springs—Collecting coins—Symbol of Agrippa—Character of Agrippa—What he did for Nimes—The Maison Carrée—Different idea of worship in the Heathen world from what prevails in Christendom—S. Baudille—Vespers—Activity of the Church in France—Behaviour of the Clergy in Italy to the King and Queen—The Revolution a blessing to the Church in France—Church services in Italy and in France—The Tourmagne—Uncertainty as to its use—Cathedral of Nimes—Other churches—A canary lottery—Altars to the Sun—The sun-wheel—The Cross of Constantine—Anecdote of Fléchier.

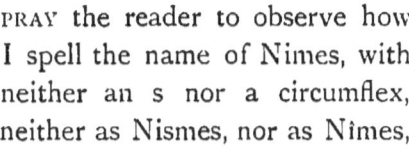

I PRAY the reader to observe how I spell the name of Nimes, with neither an s nor a circumflex, neither as Nismes, nor as Nîmes, for both are wrong. Nimes is Nemausus, and there is no s to be sounded or suppressed in the ancient name of the place, which comes from the Keltic *naimh*, a fountain or spring. And in very truth no other name could better suit it, for here under a limestone hill wells up the river in one large flood sufficient for boats to go on it at once. This great green spring, ever flowing, mysterious even nowadays, is the great feature of Nimes, and this fountain certainly awoke the veneration of the old Gauls, who believed it to be a direct gift of the gods. One follows up a canal between streets planted with trees, and looks down into the pure water like liquid green glass, then suddenly reaches a garden. Above rises a wooded hill, thick with pines, syringa, Judas tree of brilliant pink lake, laburnum with its chains of gold, forming an arc of flowers, and sees before one a wide enclosed pool, walled round, of the shape of the figure 8, heaving with cold pure water that flows away under the terrace and falls with a roar to the lower level of the canal. On one side are ruins—of a temple to the Nymphs; but one cannot at first look at that, the volume of water engages one—a lake lifting itself up by its own strength out of the earth, always, night and day, inexhaustible, hardly varying in volume, coming no one knows whence, deep and green, with no visible bottom, without a bubble, without a ruffle—it is indeed wonderful. I have seen the spring of the Danube at Donaueschingen: it is nothing to this; the fountain of Vaucluse one can understand—it breaks out from a cave in the mountainside, like scores of others; this is otherwise—a river rising with no fuss, no display, no noise, without even a ripple.

It does not gush, it does not boil up. It is simply one glassy surface, and looking at it you cannot conceive that it is a river rising vertically and sliding away under your feet. Pliny says of the source of the Clitumnus: "At the foot of a little hill covered with venerable and shady trees, a spring issues which, gushing out in different and unequal streams, forms itself, after several windings, into a spacious basin, so extremely clear that you may see the pebbles, and the little pieces of money that are thrown into it, as they lie at the bottom." I have quoted this passage, not because the source of the Clitumnus at all resembles that of the river at Nimes, but because of the mention of the coins thrown in. Suetonius speaks of this same practice in his life of Augustus. Now this fountain at Nimes has yielded, and yields still, an almost inexhaustible supply of Roman and Gaulish and Gallo-Greek coins that have been thus thrown in as oblations to the nymphs in remote times; and these coins are now in the museums of Nimes and Paris, and in those of private collectors. The same custom still remains, but instead of coins, pins are now cast into springs.

IN THE PUBLIC GARDEN, NIMES.

At the entrance to the public gardens, over the

iron gate is a medallion representing a crocodile and a palm-tree. The moment I saw it I stood still and stared. I knew that symbol, had known it from a boy. And this is how I came to know it. Living much in the south of France, and having always a hankering after old things, I collected coins, and I got them from the priests. The peasants were wont to drop old Roman coins which they found in their fields into the offertory bags and plates, and as these were of no use to the *curés*, they were very glad to give or sell them to me for small current sous. By this means I succeeded in making a very tolerable collection of Roman coins at an incredibly small cost. Now among these, one of the very first I got, and most curious, represented Octavius and Agrippa on one side, and on the reverse this identical symbol of a crocodile under a palm tree. Often enough did I turn that coin over and wonder what it meant, and highly delighted was I to discover its signification at length. It was symbolical of the subjugation of Egypt, and was struck in compliment to Agrippa. Then most assuredly Agrippa had something to do with Nimes. I turned to a little history of the place that I had, and to my delight found that he it was who is held to have been the great benefactor, indeed maker, of this little town.

I have the greatest possible respect for Agrippa. His stern, yet noble face, once seen in this bust is never to be forgotten, and infinitely sad—sad beyond comparison in history is the story of his family.

He was a man of obscure, plebeian birth, Marcus Vipsanius Agrippa, belonging to a family, the Vipsanian, of which the gentlemen of Rome professed never to have heard, or not to have found it necessary to trouble their heads to learn anything. He was a fine soldier, a man of plain manners, good morals, upright, faithful, unambitious. Octavius Augustus was warmly attached to him, and valued his good qualities and his admirable military genius; and Agrippa on his side was tenderly devoted to his noble friend. Their characters were as unlike as their faces and as their manners. When Octavius became the supreme ruler of the destinies of Rome, he heaped honours on his friend. He made him put away his wife and marry his own daughter Julia. He had children by her, Caius and Lucius, who grew to man's estate and then died, one from a wound, the other of decline, and another son, an ill-conditioned boy, Agrippa Posthumus, put to death, probably by order of Octavius, a commission given on his own death-bed, to save Rome from internecine war.

His daughter, Agrippina, starved herself to death, heartbroken at the murder of her two sons by Tiberius, and despairing at the thought that her other son, the crazy, debauched, cruel Caligula was alone left to represent her family. The other daughter of Agrippa, Julia, was infamous for her debaucheries, and died in banishment. The family was then represented by the second Agrippina, daughter of the first Agrippina, who became the mother of Nero—that son who was his mother's and his brother's murderer, and died finally by his own hand, amidst the execrations of the Roman world.

The sad shadow that lies on the brow of Agrippa almost seems to be cast there by the destiny awaiting his family. Not one drop of his blood mingled with the sacred *ichor* of the Julian race remains on earth. But other remnants of Agrippa abide. The Pantheon of Rome, and the Pont du Gard near Nimes, aye—and the baths he made for the washerwomen in the water he led into this town, that they might not sully the sacred spring that welled up before the temple of the Nymphs.

Agrippa in his various offices and governorships accumulated great wealth, but he was not a grasping man, nor one who spent his wealth upon himself. Wherever he was, he expended his fortune on improving and embellishing the cities under his sway. Thus it was that for quite an inconsiderable little town, which the classic authors pass over without notice, he lavished very large sums to provide it with excellent water from two springs twenty-five miles distant, not that the river that rises at Nimes is impure, but that a certain awe felt for it withheld the natives from desecrating the sacred waters to common use.

The Pont du Gard which carried the waters by three tiers of arches across the valley of the Gurdon, at a height of one hundred and eighty feet, is one of the most striking and perfect of the monuments left by the Romans in Gaul, or anywhere; and it is certainly remarkable that the two most complete relics of this great people that remain, should have been the work of Agrippa, the Pantheon and the Pont du Gard. This latter is a colossal work. Its length is 873 feet at top, and may well be compared to its advantage with the modern aqueduct that conveys water to the Prado of Montpellier, a more lengthy, but a feeble structure.

The Pont du Gard.

The Roman remains in Nimes are held famous everywhere. Nowhere, least of all in Rome, are the relics of that great people of builders to be seen in such perfection. There is the amphitheatre, smaller, but more perfect even, than that at Arles. There is the *Maison Carrée*, a temple almost quite perfect, and of surpassing proportional perfection. Small this temple is: it consists of thirty elegant Corinthian columns, ten of which are disengaged, and form the portico, whereas the remainder are engaged in the *naos* or sanctuary.

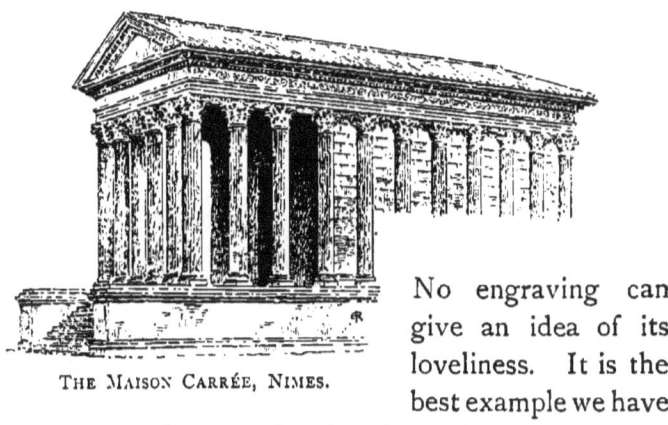

THE MAISON CARRÉE, NIMES.

No engraving can give an idea of its loveliness. It is the best example we have in Europe, of a temple that is perfectly intact. It is mignon, it is cheerful, it is charming. I found myself unable at any time to pass it without looking round over my shoulder, again and again, and uttering some exclamation of pleasure at the sight of it.

That temple is instructive in a way the ordinary traveller would hardly suspect. It is a valuable example to us of the complete and radical difference that existed between the Pagan and the Christian ideas of worship. The Pagan world had no idea of gathering a congrega-

P

tion together, any more than I may say have the old canons of Florence, or of S. Peter's, Rome, who shut themselves into glass boxes, of bringing all men into one building to unite in prayer and praise. The sanctuaries of the Pagan gods were quite small and dark. Worship was simply an individual matter, a bringing of a sacrifice to an altar. There was nothing like congregational worship in the Jewish temple either. The priest alone went within to offer the incense, whilst the people stood without. But in the Christian church the condition of affairs was completely reversed. The worship of God was to be for all the people, all together, with one heart and one voice. That is why the early Christians in the fourth century never adapted a temple to a church. A temple could not be adapted. The pillars were all outside, and within was a little dark box—the sanctuary—that would not hold more than a couple of score of persons. They could not use the temples; what they wanted were temples turned outside-in, the pillars within forming great halls in which a crowd might be gathered.

I had been looking at this delightful little temple and considering this, and it was a Sunday. I sauntered on, this still on my mind, when I fell in with trains of school children, all drifting in one direction. I followed them, and found myself in the great new church of S. Baudille. The time was afternoon. The church, quite a cathedral in size, was crowded, boys' schools, girls' schools, men, women, of all sorts and ranks were there. Then I heard such a service as did the heart good to hear. It was only vespers—just five psalms, a hymn, and the Magnificat; nothing more. But the psalms were sung in alternate verses between the choir and the congregation, who knew every word and every note, and sang lustily from their hearts' depths, the plain old Gregorian tones with which many of us are so familiar at home. I found the words welling up in my mind : " The voice of a great multitude, and as the voice of many waters, and as the voice of mighty thunderings, saying, Alleluia : for the Lord God Omnipotent reigneth." I was glad there was no one with me as we dispersed, to speak to me. I could not have answered, my heart was too full. But I went back to the Maison Carrée, and looked again at it for long, and then realised, in a way I had never realised before, how that the Carpenter of Nazareth had transformed the whole idea of worship into something of which the world previously had no conception.

To the ordinary English traveller the services in a foreign Roman Catholic church are so unintelligible that I may be excused if I say a word on vespers that may enable him to understand it. Usually—always on week days—two evening services, vespers and compline are said together, or rather one immediately after the other. Each consists of confession and absolution, a short Scriptural lesson, psalms, a canticle, a hymn and collects. The canticle for vespers is the Magnificat; for compline is the Nunc Dimittis.

Now as the two services were practically united, what our Reformers did was to weld them together. They cut out the second confession and absolution and the second batch of psalms, but retained the second lesson and the second canticle. The English even-song is therefore simply the Latin vespers and compline pressed into a single service. The Reformers, by putting a psalm as alternative for each canticle, perhaps intended the English even-song to serve as either vespers (when Magnificat was sung) or as compline (when Nunc Dimittis was sung).

When I was in Rome during the winter, I was very much astonished, one day, as the King of Italy passed, to see a whole school of little boys under the direction of three Christian Brothers, strut by with their little noses in the air, and without raising their hats. At the same pension with myself was a young Swiss Benedictine monk, who sat by me at *table d'hôte*, and with whom I struck up a warm friendship. I commented to him on what I had seen. "Oh!" he replied, "we make a point of never saluting the king. Why," he continued, "only yesterday I was walking down the Corso with Cardinal U——, when we saw the queen's carriage approaching. I asked what was to be done. His eminence replied, 'Keep your hat on, don't notice her.'"

I confess that my English blood boiled up, and for the first and last time I spoke sharply to my friend. I believe I made a certain allusion to an injunction of S. Paul, and told him plainly that I thought such conduct unbecoming in a gentleman and a Christian, and a priest.

On entering France ones sees what devastation the Revolution wrought on the Church, and one compares the condition there with the very light and easy

way in which she has been taken out of her temporal
throne and seated on the ground in Italy. She has been
treated there too easily, so easily that she pouts, and
frets, and sulks; whereas in France she has been an
Antæus who rose from the ground stronger than
when cast down. In Rome, the Church shuffles along
in her old slouching, hands-in-the-pockets, half-asleep,
don't-care style, letting every opportunity slip away,
neglected by the people, because she neglects them.
In France, the Church is tingling with fresh life-blood
to her fingers' ends, full of energy, activity, zeal.
Why, there is not to be found in Rome, or Florence, or
Naples, a church where a tolerable service is to be
heard sung. In Rome one gets sick of and angry with
the squalling of eunuchs, and longs for a scourge of
small cords to drive them out of the temple. No one
cares for the Church services in Rome. No attempt is
made to attract the people to them. At Florence the
service is like the bleating of a flock of sheep driven
into a pen to be shorn, and the old canons who baa
are enclosed within glass against draughts, and to the
exclusion of all congregational worship. But in France,
the people who have any religion in them love their
services—love them and have made them their own,
sing in them and follow them with eager interest. I
remember, when I was a youth in France, that few
men were seen in church, and the ladies lounged
through the service. It is not so now, you see as
many men in church as you will in England, and the
women are attentive and devout. The Italian Church
must suffer deeper humiliation, and learn to touch
her cap to "the powers that be, ordained of God,"

before the people will rally to her and show her reverence.

On the summit of the hill above the fountain and temple of the Nymphs is a most puzzling building, the *Tourmagne*. It is of Roman construction, a great tower like that of Babel, in stages, the upper stage with semicircular recesses that sustained the external wall, now in part fallen. No one can tell its purpose. It has clearly been utilised since its first construction by the Romans, by making it an angle tower of some other building, the foundations of which have been quite recently exposed. The tower is octagonal. It resembles the structure of the lighthouse at Ostia, already mentioned as in the Torlonia gallery. But why a lighthouse here? It is true that to the south of Nimes was lagoon and marsh, with islets and strips of dry land scattered about among the tracts of water, all the way to the sea, but one hardly supposes such a lighthouse would have been raised to guide the *utriculares* on their skin-sustained rafts. Yet for what other purpose it can have been raised it is hard to imagine. It stands on very high ground, and commands a most extensive prospect. It has long been, and is likely to remain, a hard nut for antiquaries to break their teeth upon.

The cathedral of Nimes has been, not so much restored as transformed internally, so as to void it of much interest, but it must have been a curious church at one time. Externally, at the west end, is a most wonderful frieze, a band of rich sculpture representing the story of man from the Creation to the drunkenness of Noah. In one chapel within is an old

Christian sarcophagus utilised as an altar, on it our Lord is represented as teacher surrounded by the apostles. S. Paul is a modern church good in proportion, with an admirable central octagonal tower and spire. The only fault to be found with the church is in the details. S. Baudille is a pretentious Gothic church, with two asparagus shoots as western towers, it has a square east end, with a really marvellously ugly east window. The new church of S. Perpetue is beneath criticism.

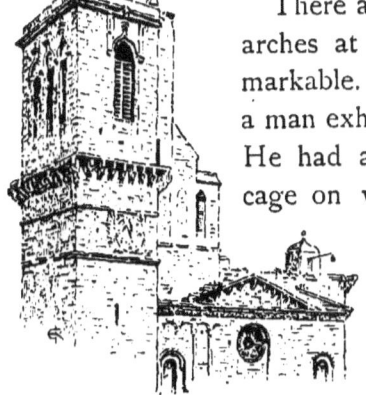

CATHEDRAL OF NIMES.—PART OF WEST FRONT.

There are two Roman triumphal arches at Nimes, but neither is remarkable. In front of one I found a man exhibiting a cage of canaries. He had a little table before the cage on which small cards, each numbered, were set out. Then he sold among the bystanders tickets with corresponding numbers. There were eighteen numbers, and each card sold for a sou, and the whole constituted a lottery for a chain and some seals that the fellow dangled before the eyes of the little circle of lookers-on. The lots were taken up after a little persuasion and chaffering. Then he opened the cage door; out hopped a canary that trotted up and down the little table, and finally picked up one of the cards. "Number nine," called the proprietor of the canaries. "Which monsieur is the happy possessor of card number nine?" A soldier stepped forward, presented his tally, and received the silver watch-chain. Then all those who had been unsuccessful restored their cards, and the same process was repeated, this time among women, for a silver thimble.

Nimes struck me as one of the very brightest, pleasantest towns I have ever visited, and the one in which, if forced to live out of England, I think I could live most happily in. I have said not one word about the museum at Nimes, which is within the Maison Carrée, and yet the museum contains some objects deserving of attention. There are two altars with wheels carved on them, both small, the largest only two feet three inches high, and that has on it not the wheel only, but the thunderbolt. These are altars to the Gaulish god of the sun. The second bears an inscription " et terræ matri." It was dedicated doubtless to the "sun and to the earth mother," but the first portion of the legend is lost. In the Avignon Museum is a statue of a Gaulish Jupiter in military costume, with his right hand on the wheel, and with the eagle on his left.*

Moreover, in the Nimes museum are some bronze circular ornaments, found in 1883 in the caves of S. Vallon in Ardèche, representing the wheel. On the triumphal arch of Orange are Gaulish warriors with horned helmets, and wheels as crests between the horns. The wheel, as symbol of the sun, was very general everywhere, in the east as well as the west, among the Germans as well as among the Gauls, but among the latter it assumed a very special importance, and it is due to this fact that in the French cathedrals

* Others at Trèves, Moulin, and Paris.

the west window is a wheel window. At Basle there is a round window in the minster with figures climbing and falling on the spokes, and Fortune sits in the midst. It is a wheel of Fortune. It is the same at Beauvais, at Amiens, and elsewhere. At Chartres is a representation in stained glass of the Transfiguration; and Christ is exhibited in glory in the midst of an eight-spoked wheel. A curious statue at Luxeuil, now lost, represented a rider protecting a lady whilst his horse tramples on a prostrate foe; his raised hand over the woman is thrust through a six-rayed wheel. On the Meuse a similar peculiarity has been noticed in a fragment of a sculptured figure, it is a hand holding a four-spoked wheel. In the Museum Kircherianum at Rome are bronze six-rayed wheels, the spokes zigzagged like lightnings, found at Forli, others at Modena. All these were symbols of the sun. Now when Constantine professed to have seen his vision, which was in all probability a mock-sun, he thought that the rays he saw formed the Greek initials of Christ, and he therefore ordered these initials, *forming a six-rayed wheel*, to be set up on the standards of his soldiers. The only difference between his "Labarum" and the symbol of the Gaulish sun-god was that his upper spoke was looped to form the letter P. No doubt whatever, that his Keltic soldiers hailed the new standard as that of their national god, and that when they marched against Maxentius and met him at Saxa Rubra, eight miles from Rome, they thought that they, as Gauls, were marching to a second capture of the capital of the world, under the protection of their national god.

Among men of note that have been associated with Nimes is Fléchier, born at Pernes in Vaucluse in 1632, who became Bishop of Nimes in 1687. He was the son of a tallow-chandler. From his eloquence he was much regarded as a preacher, but unfortunately his discourses contain very little except well-rounded sentences of well-chosen words. He was a favourite of Louis XIV., who respected his integrity and piety. One day a haughty aristocratic prelate about the Court had the bad taste to sneer at him for his origin. "Avec votre manière de penser," replied Fléchier calmly, "je crois que si vous étiez né ce que je suis, vous n'eussiez fait, toute votre vie—que de chandelles."

CHAPTER XVI.

AIGUES MORTES AND MAGUELONNE.

A dead town—The Rhônes-morts—Bars—S. Louis and the Crusades—How S. Louis acquired Aigues Mortes—His canal—The four littoral chains and lagoons—The fortifications—Unique for their date—Original use of battlements—Deserted state of the town—Maguelonne—How reached—History of Maguelonne—Cathedral—The Bishops forge Saracen coins—Second destruction of the place—Inscription on door—Bernard de Treviis—His Romance of Pierre de Provence—Provençal poetry not always immoral—Present state of Maguelonne.

AIGUES MORTES is a dead town, and differs from Maguelonne, to be presently described, in this, that it is a dead *town*, whereas Maguelonne is only the ghost of a dead town. It is a great curiosity, for it is a dead mediæval town surrounded by its walls, and dominated by its keep. But first about its name, which signifies Dead Waters. If the reader will remember what has been already said about the structure of the delta of the Rhone, he will recall the fact that the river is constantly engaged in changing its mouths. When it has formed for itself a new mouth, it deserts its former course, which it leaves as a stagnating canal. This occasions the delta to be striped with what are locally termed Rhônes-morts, whereas a flowing branch is called a Rhône-vif.

Moreover the stagnant masses of water left by floods are called Aigues Mortes—Dead Waters; and it is precisely on such that the little fortified town I am now writing about, stands. I know of no point on the littoral of the Rhone that offers so excellent an opportunity of observing the processes of that river than at Aigues Mortes. The river has, indeed, long ago deserted the branch that once discharged itself here, and it has left four lines behind it, making successive stages of advance, four bars, with their several backwaters, now converted into ponds or meres. The Canal of Beaucaire now passes by Aigues Mortes, and reaches the Mediterranean nearly three miles below the town.

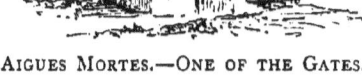

AIGUES MORTES.—ONE OF THE GATES.

It was from Aigues Mortes that S. Louis sailed on his Crusades in 1248 and 1270; and it has a little

puzzled many people to account for his having chosen such a wretched place as this for the assembly of his Crusaders and for embarkation. But he could not help himself.

As soon as Louis had, in 1244, made his vow to assume the cross, his first care was to obtain on the shores of the Mediterranean a territory and a port sufficient for the concentration of the troops that were to from his expedition. But he encountered great difficulty. The king was not *suzerain* over the southern provinces of France, and possessed as his own not a single town on the coast. The port of Narbonne was choked with sand, and belonged to the viscounts of that town. The port of Maguelonne was under the sovereignty of the bishop.

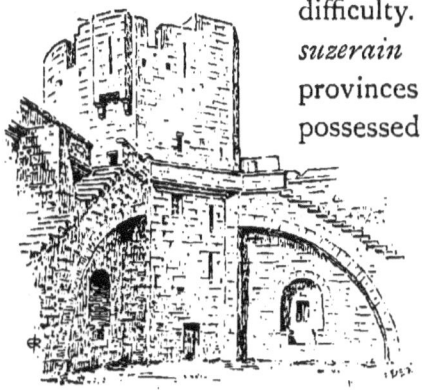

AIGUES MORTES.—TOWER OF THE BOURGIGNONS.

The lagoons and their openings into the sea of Montpellier were under the King of Aragon. The ports of Agde and S. Gilles were subject to the counts of Toulouse, and independent Provence was not to be attached to the crown till three centuries later. The marshy district of Aigues Mortes was alone available; it was under the abbey of Psalmodi, planted amidst the swamps on a little sandy elevation. Louis IX. entered into negotiations with the abbot, and in exchange for certain royal domains near Sommière, he was enabled to acquire the town of Aigues Mortes and all the zone of lagoons between it and the sea.

At that time there existed but a single fortification—the tower of Matafera—erected about five centuries before as a place of refuge from the Saracens. S. Louis restored this tower, or rather rebuilt it, in the form in which it remains to this day. Then he constructed a quay, and scooped out a canal through the lagoons to the sea. This is the old canal, now full of sand, and up this vessels were able to proceed through two lagoons to the tower of Matafera, which acquired later the name of Tour de Constance. But the old canal had an ephemeral existence; every inundation of the lagoons of the Rhone altered their depths, and disturbed the canal. A century or two later another canal was cut between the old one and that now in use, that also was destined in time to be choked up; but the old discharging and lading place of the vessels can still be distinguished by the heaps of ballast thrown out, consisting of stones from Genoa and Corsica. It is quite a mistake to suppose that Aigues Mortes was on the sea in the thirteenth century. The Crusaders embarked in the canal cut by S. Louis, and sailed through the lagoons before they reached the open Mediterranean.

The most ancient maps show us Aigues Mortes bathed by one of those branches of the Rhone, now deserted, which go by the name of Rhônes-morts. At a time before history—at all events the history of Gaul begins, the Rhone had its principal mouth in the great Etang de Maugio; but it choked up its mouth there, and advanced eastward in several stages, leaving in its rear, as the river thus shifted its quarters, a series of dwindling and then dead channels.

What is now the Petit Rhône, reaching the sea at Les Saintes Maries, was then the main stream, which has long ago turned away, and now discharges its greatest body of water into the Mediterranean at Saint Louis. It has left behind it, not only the dead or stagnant Rhones, its neglected beds, but also, as already noticed, its old bars, and these are very dis-

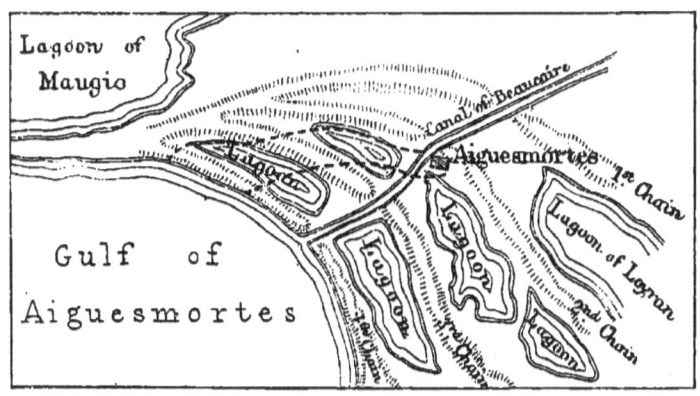

SKETCH MAP OF AIGUES MORTES AND ITS LITTORAL CHAINS.

tinctly marked at Aigues Mortes. The first chain gives us the primitive beach, which began at the lagoon of Maugio, traversed the entire Camargue, and can be traced to Fos. It is formed of an almost uninterrupted succession of sandhills crowned with a tolerably rich vegetation; on it grow the white poplar, the aleppo and the umbrella pines. To the south of this lay the prehistoric sea; the ground is horizontal, and although subjected to culture shows sufficient evidence that it was at one time sea-bed, covered with more recent alluvium. Here is the great lagoon of Loyran, which, before many years are passed, will be completely drained, and its bed turned up by the plough.

Still advancing seaward, we reach a second littoral chain, not so distinctly marked as the first, but nevertheless distinguishable by its low line of sandy dunes, on which a scanty growth of tamarisks and coarse grass is sustained. Then we come to a succession of lagoons, once united into one, and after them the third bar, presenting exactly the same features—a low range of sand and pebbles, and beyond it once more lagoons, cut off from the waves of the Mediterranean by a fourth and last chain, the most recent, that belongs to the historic epoch.

But that is not all : the wash of the sea, its current settling west, and carrying with it the mud of the Rhone is gradually, but surely building up a fifth bar or bank, which will in time close the gulf from the point of Espignette to the bathing-place of Palavas, when the Gulf of Aigues Mortes will be converted into a second Etang de Berre.

Aigues Mortes is surrounded by its mediæval fortifications just as they were left by Philip the Bold, son of S. Louis. The plan of the town is almost quadrilateral, it has six gates and fifteen towers. Only one angle of the parallelogram is cut off, where stands the stately circular tower of Constance. The streets are laid out in the most precise manner, cutting each other at right angles ; there are four churches, of which the principal is Notre Dame des

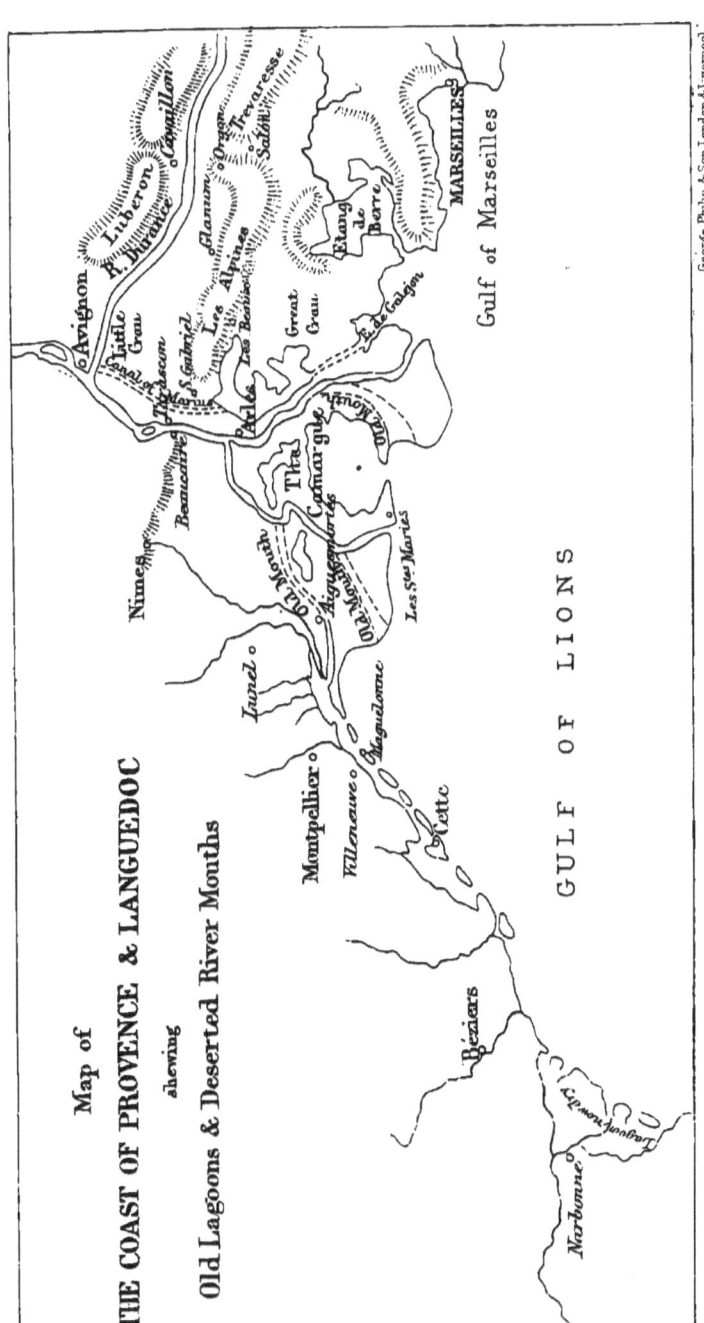

Sablons. The others were all formerly attached to monasteries or convents.

The plan of the fortification is precisely that adopted by the Crusaders wherever they built defences, in Syria, in Cyprus, in Palestine. The walls are crenellated, usually without machicolations, pierced with long slots, and with square holes through which beams were thrust, supporting wooden balconies which commanded the bases of the walls, and enabled the besieged to protect themselves against the efforts made by the assailants to sap the bases of the ramparts, or to escalade the walls. Towers, round and square at intervals, strengthened the walls, and formed points of vantage and of assembly for the besieged. Precisely similar fortifications were raised about the same period at Tortosa, Antioch, Ascalon, Cæsarea, &c.; but all these have been destroyed, only Aigues Mortes remains, an unique and perfect example of the systematic fortification adopted by the Crusaders everywhere.

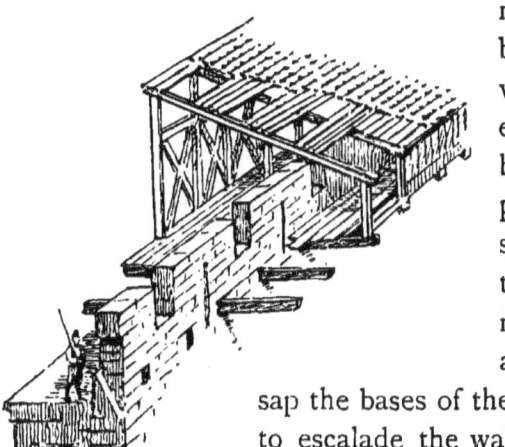

ORIGINAL USE OF BATTLEMENTS.—(*From Viollet-le-Duc.*)

The reader, probably, has not given a thought to the original purpose of a battlement, so common on towers and churches and castles. I therefore venture to show what it was originally. It was a wall broken through with doorways into the wooden gallery that overhung, and through which the assailants could be kept from approaching too near to the base of the walls. But, after a time, these wooden galleries were found to be inconvenient. Means were taken by the besiegers to set them on fire. Consequently they were abandoned, and their places were taken by projecting galleries of stone, supported, not on wooden

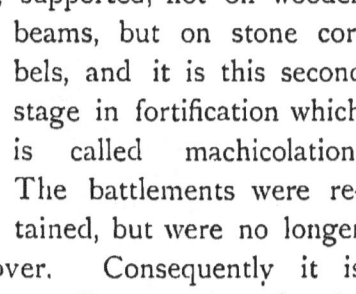

SECOND STAGE OF BATTLEMENTS.

beams, but on stone corbels, and it is this second stage in fortification which is called machicolation. The battlements were retained, but were no longer roofed over. Consequently it is possible to tell approximately the epoch of a Mediæval fortification, by a look at the battlements, whether they stand back flush with the walls, and have the beam-holes, or whether they stand forward, bracketed out from the walls.

Aigues Mortes is a dead town. About a third of the area within the walls is devoted to gardens, or is waste. The population, which in the thirteenth century numbered 15,000 souls, has shrunk to a little over 3,000, a number at which it remains stationary. It does a little sleepy trade in salt, and sees the barges for Beaucaire pass its walls, and perhaps supplies the boatmen with wine and bread. The neighbourhood is desolate. The soil is so full of salt that it is impatient of tillage, and produces only such herbs as love the sea border. But its lagoons are alive with wild fowl, rose-coloured flamingoes, white gulls, and green metallic-throated ducks.

And now for Maguelonne. I said that Aigues Mortes was a dead town, but Maguelonne was the ghost of one. The best way to reach this latter very singular spot is to take the train from Montpellier to Villeneuve de Maguelonne, and walk thence to the border of the Etang. There one is pretty sure to find fishermen—they catch little else than eels—who will row one across to the narrow strip of land that intervenes between the lagoon and the sea. The littoral chain here is not of sand and gravel only, for a mass of volcanic tufa rises to the surface, and originally formed an islet in the sea, then, when the process began of forming a littoral belt with a lagoon behind it, the sands clung to this islet and spread out from it to left and right.

On this volcanic islet stood first a Greek and then a Roman city, but of its history nothing is known till the sixth century, when it was attacked from the sea by Wamba, King of the Visigoths. It had been an episcopal city for a century before. After the Visigoths came the Saracens, who gave the place their name, and the harbour of Maguelonne was called Port Sarasin. In 737, Charles Martel, in order to clear the pirates completely out of their stronghold, destroyed the city to its last foundation, with the sole exception of the old church of S. Peter. The bishop took up his abode on the mainland at Villeneuve, and the seat of the bishopric was moved to Castelnau near Montpellier. For three centuries the islet was abandoned and left a heap of ruins. But it was restored in the eleventh century. The walls were again set up, and flanked with towers, and a causeway consisting of a chain of wooden bridges was carried across the lagoon to Villeneuve. The entrance to the port was closed lest it should invite Saracen pirates, and another opened under the walls of the town which could be rendered impassable by a chain at the first sign of danger. The newly-built town speedily showed vigour, became populous, and the harbour was filled with the merchandise of the Mediterranean. Two popes visited the city, Gelasius II. in 1118, and Alexander III. in 1162. In addition to the Cathedral of S. Peter, other churches were raised, dedicated to S. Augustine and S. Pancras. A castle with keep was erected.

For several centuries Maguelonne was a sort of ecclesiastical republic, in which the bishop exercised the office of president. It became very rich and luxurious. The bishop, not too scrupulous, forged imitation Saracen coins, and was called to order for doing this by Clement IV. in 1266. It seemed to the sovereign pontiff a scandal, not that the bishop should forge the coins, but that he should forge them with the name of Mahomet on them as "Prophet of God." In 1331 statutes for the monastery on Maguelonne were drawn up, which proved that the discipline kept therein left much to be desired; and a monastic treatise on cooking that came thence shows that the monks and canons were consummate epicures.

Maguelonne was ruined first by Charles Martel.

It was again, and finally ruined, by Louis XIII. The castle, the walls, the towers, the monastic buildings—everything was levelled to the dust, with the sole exception of the cathedral church. The stones of the dismantled buildings encumbered the ground till 1708, when they were all carried off for the construction of the new canal which runs along the coast through the chain of lagoons from Cette to Aigues Mortes.

"A church and its archives," says the historian of Maguelonne, "that is all that the revolution of fate has respected of one of the principal monastic centres in the south. A church in which service is no longer said, and archives that are incomplete. Even the very cemetery of Maguelonne has vanished, as though Death had feared to encounter himself in this desert, where naught remained save the skeleton of a cathedral. Yet what dust is here! Phœnician, Greek, Celtic, Roman, Christian, Mahomedan, French: A few tombs escaped the observation of the stone collectors of 1708, and even fewer inscriptions, excepting such as are found within the church, that is all! What a realization is this of the sentence on all things human, *Pulvis es.*"*

The islet of Maguelonne is but one knot in the long thread of *cordon littoral* that reaches from Cette to Aigues Mortes, and it can be reached on foot by land from Palavas, but the simplest and shortest route is by boat in half an hour over the shallow mere, nowhere over three feet six inches deep. The boats of the fishermen are all flat-bottomed, and the men have

* Germain: "Maguelonne et ses Évêques," 1859.

to row gingerly, lest their oars strike the bottom, or else they punt along. One can see as one crosses, the points of rest of the old causeway. The church, like that of Les Trois Maries, is feudal castle as much as cathedral, calculated, on occasion, to give refuge within to the inhabitants of the town, whilst the garrison stood on the flat roof and showered arrows, stones, molten sulphur and pitch upon the besiegers. The whole of this coast was liable to the descent of Moorish and Saracen pirates, consequently the same type of church prevails all along it. The western tower is ruinous, but the remainder of the church is in tolerable condition. It is cruciform, with an apse, has but very narrow windows, high up and few. The roof is slabbed with stone, so as to form a terrace on which the besieged could walk, and whence they could launch their weapons through the slots and between the battlements. At the southwest end of the church is a curious entrance door of the twelfth century, with a relieving arch of coloured marbles over it, and the apostles Peter and Paul rudely sculptured as supporters of the arch. They occupy a crouching position, and are sculptured on triangular

EAST END OF THE CHURCH OF MAGUELONNE.

blocks. In the tympanum is the Saviour seated in glory. But what in addition to its quaintness of design gives peculiar interest to this doorway is the inscription it bears :—

> AD PORTVM VITE SITIENTES QVIQVE VENITE.
> HAS INTRANDO FORES, VESTROS COMPONITE MORES.
> HINC INTRANS ORA, TVA SEMPER CRIMINA PLORA.
> QVICQVID PECCATVR LACRIMARVM FONTE LAVATVR.
> B. D. IIIVIS FECIT HOC ANNO INC. DO. CLXXVIII.

> Let those who will come thirsting to the gate of Life.
> On entering these doors compose your manners.
> Entering here pray, and ever bewail your crimes.
> All sin is washed away in the spring of tears.
> Bernard de Trevies made this, A.D. 1178.

Now Bernard of the Three-Ways is a man who did something else—he was a novelist and a poet. A Canon of Maguelonne, gentle and pure of heart, he wrote the story of 'Pierre de Provence et la belle Maguelone,' a charming monument of the old Languedoc tongue worthy to range alongside with 'Aucassin et Nicolette.' It has been translated into most European languages, Greek not excepted, and has become a favourite chapbook tale. It is still read in all cottages of France, sold at all fairs, but sadly mutilated at each re-edition, and in its chapbook form reduced to a few pages, which is but a wretched fragment of a very delightful whole. No idea of its beauty can be obtained without reference to the old editions, where it occupies a goodly volume.

The story of Pierre de Provence is not one of extraordinary originality, but its charm lies in its general tone, healthy, pure, gentle, full of the freshness of chivalry in its first institution, and of religion in its simplicity. We probably have not got the poetic romance quite in its original form as it left the hands of Bernard, for Petrarch, whilst a student at Montpellier, was struck with it, and added some polishing touches, and it is the version thus improved by his master-hand that is believed to have come down to us. I shrink from still further condensing a story spoiled already by condensation, and yet do not like altogether to pass it over without giving the reader some idea of it.

The story tells of a Peter, son of the Count of Melgueil, who, hearing that the King of Naples had a daughter of surpassing loveliness, determined to ride and see her. He had himself accoutred in armour, with silver keys on his helm, and on his shield; and when he reached Naples jousted in tournament before the fair princess, whose name was Maguelone, and loved her well, and she him. But, alas! the king had promised to give her to the Prince of Carpona in marriage, and as she felt she could not live without her Pierre, and Peter was quite sure he could not live without her, they eloped together. When the sun waxed burning hot she became very weary, and he led her beneath a tree, and she laid her head on his knee and fell asleep. Then he saw how she had in her bosom a little silken bag, and he lightly drew it forth and peered within to see what it contained. Then, lo! he found three rings that he had sent her by her nurse. Afraid of waking her, by replacing the bag, he laid it beside him on a stone, when down swooped a raven and carried it off. Peter at once folded his mantle, put it under the head of the sleeping girl, and ran after the bird, which flew to the sea and perched on a rock above it. Peter threw a stone at the raven and made it drop the bag into the water. Then he got a boat, moored hard by, jumped into the boat and went after the floating bag with the rings. But wind and waves rose and brushed him out to sea, and carried him across the Mediterranean to Alexandria, where the Sultan made him his page. In the meantime the fair Maguelone awoke in the green wood, and finding herself alone, ran about calling "Pierre! Pierre!" but received no answer. She spent the night in the forest, and then took the road to Rome, and encountering a female pilgrim, exchanged clothes with her. Maguelone pursued her journey, prayed in S. Peter's Church at Rome, unnoticed by her uncle, who, with great state, passed by her kneeling there, and threw her alms. Then she went on to Genoa, where she took boat to Aigues Mortes. Hearing at this place that there was a little island off the coast suitable for a hermitage, thither she went, and with her jewels she had brought from Naples built a little church and a hospital, in which she ministered to sick people. The Countess of Melgueil, hearing of the holy woman, came to visit her, and won by her sympathy, with many tears told her how she had lost her dear son Peter, who had gone to Naples, and had not been heard of since.

One day, a fisherman caught a tunny, and brought it as a present to the count. When the tunny was opened, in its stomach was found a little bag that contained three rings. Now, no sooner did the countess see these than she knew they were her own, which she had given to Pierre, and she hasted to tell the anchorite on the isle of the wondrous discovery, and to show her the rings. It need hardly be told that Maguelone also recognised them.

Now the Sultan of Alexandria had become so attached to Peter, that he treated him as his own son, and finally, at Peter's entreaty, allowed him to return to Provence, having first extracted from him a promise to come back to him. Peter carried with him a great treasure in fourteen barrels, but to hide their contents he filled up the tops with salt. Then he engaged with a captain of a trader to convey him across to Provence. Now one day the vessel stayed for water at a little isle, called Sagona, and Peter went on shore, and the sun being hot, lay down on the grass and fell asleep. A wind sprang up. The sails were spread. The captain called Peter. The men ran everywhere searching for him, could not find him, and at length were reluctantly obliged to sail without him. On reaching Provence the captain was unwilling to retain the goods of the lost man, and so gave them to the holy woman who ministered to the sick in the hospital she had built on a tiny islet off the coast. One day when Maguelone was short of salt she went to fetch some from the barrels given her by the ship's captain, and to her amazement found under the salt an incalculable treasure. With this she set to work to rebuild the church and her hospital.

In the meantime, Peter awoke, and found himself deserted. For some time he remained in the island, but from want of food and discouragement fell ill, and would have died had not some fishermen, chancing to come there, taken him into their boat. They consulted what to do with the sick man, and one said that they had best take him to Maguelone. On hearing the name Peter asked what they meant. They told him that this was the name given to a church and hospital richly built and tended to by a holy woman, on the coast of Provence. Peter then entreated them to carry him to the place that bore so fair a name. So he was conveyed, sick and feeble, into the hostel; but he was so changed with sickness that Maguelone did not recognise him, and as she wore a veil he could not see her face.

Now Maguelone, whenever she went by his bed heard him sigh, so she stood still one day, spoke gently to him, and asked what was his trouble. Then he told her all his story, and how sad his heart was for his dear Maguelone, whom he had lost, and might never see again. She now knew him, and with effort constrained her voice to bid him pray to God, with whom all things are possible. And when she heard him raise his voice in prayer with many sobs, she could not contain herself, but ran off to the church, and kneeling before the altar gave way also to tears, but tears of joy mingled with psalms of thanksgiving. Then she arose, and brought forth her royal robes, and cast aside those of an anchorite, and bade that Pierre should be given a bath and be clothed in princely garb. After which he was introduced into her presence. Of the joy of the recognition, of the restoration of the lost son to his parents, of the happy wedding, no need that I should tell. The church and hostel of Maguelone remained ever after as testimony to the virtues and piety of La Belle Maguelone, its foundress.

Such is the merest and baldest sketch of this graceful tale, told by the very man who cut the inscription I copied from the door of the church, in which he served as canon. When Vernon Lee says of Provençal poetry that adultery—rank adultery was what it lauded, we must not forget that there is another side to be considered—and that the Provençal poets turned their pens as well to drawing pure and artless love.

The land and the old church are now the property of a private gentleman, a M. Fabre, who has a great love for the place. I remember the church, when I was a child, full of hay and faggots. It is now restored to sacred uses, but Mass is only said therein once in the year. The proprietor has built a farm-house near it, and has moved his children's bodies to the old cathedral, and purposes to be laid there himself, when his hour strikes—surrounded by waters : the sea on one side, the great mere of Maguelonne on the other.

CHAPTER XVII.

BÉZIERS AND NARBONNE.

Position of Béziers—S. Nazaire—The Albigenses—Their tenets—Albigensian "consolation"—Crusade against them—The storming of Béziers—Massacre—Cathedral of Béziers—Girls' faces in the train—Similar faces at Narbonne, in Cathedral and Museum—Narbonne a Roman colony—All the Roman buildings destroyed — Caps of liberty — Christian sarcophagi—Children's toys of baked clay — Cathedral unfinished — Archiepiscopal Palace—Unsatisfactory work of M. Viollet-le-Duc—In trouble with the police—Taken for a German spy—My sketch-book gets me off.

THE position of Béziers is striking. It crowns a height above the Orb, its grand fortified church of S. Nazaire occupying the highest point, where it stands on a platform. This fine church is not the cathedral. In La Madeleine is the bishop's throne, a church that, with the exception of the tower and exterior of the apse, has been modernised out of all interest. But S. Nazaire is a stately and beautiful church of the twelfth to the fourteenth century, in the style of the country, very little ornamented externally, and very strongly fortified; even the windows being made impenetrable by their strong *grilles* of iron. There are two western towers, small, with an arch thrown between their battlements, over the rose window, and this battlemented archway is in fact a screen behind which the besieged sheltered whilst they poured down molten pitch on those who assailed the gateway of the cathedral. For this purpose there is an open space between the screen and the façade. The apse of eight sides, internally is fine; and there is a beautiful octagonal apsidal chapel on the north side, entered from the transept.

Beziers is the scene of a horrible slaughter in 1209, after the siege by the Crusaders under Simon de Montfort. It had been a headquarter of the Albigenses. As we are now entering the region reddened with the blood of these heretics, it will not be improper here to give a little account of them.

The Albigenses are often erroneously confused with the Waldenses, with whom really they had little in common. Actually, the Albigenses were not Christians at all, but Manicheans. The heresy was nothing other than the reawakening of the dormant and suppressed Paganism of the south of France. There are plenty of documents which enable us to understand their peculiar tenets and practices.

They held a dualism of good and evil principles in the world, equally matched; and they taught that the evil principle was the origin of all created matter. Accordingly they rejected the Old Testament, and declared that all the world and man's body were of diabolic origin, and that the spirit only was divine.

An Entrance to Carcassonne.

With regard to the person of Christ they were divided in opinion. Some said He had a phantom body, and that He seemed only to die on the cross. The real Christ was incapable of suffering. But another school among them declared that He had a true body born of Mary and Joseph, and that this was due to the evil principle, and that this body did hang on the cross. It was the Evil God of the Jews who slew Pharaoh in the Red Sea. They held that the Good God had two wives, Colla and Coliba, from whom he had many generations of spiritual beings. Of the Good Christ, the spiritual, they asserted, that He neither ate nor drank, that He was the source of all mercy and salvation, but that the Bad Christ was the carnal one following the Good Christ as the shadow follows the body; that this Bad Christ had Magdalen as his concubine. They were not agreed as to the future of man. Some denied the existence of souls, some said that the souls were fallen angels inhabiting men's bodies, others that the soul was pure and could only attain to blessedness by emancipation from the body, all the works of which were evil.

The faithful of the Albigenses were divided into two orders, the "perfect," who wore a black dress, abstained from flesh, eggs, cheese, and from marriage; and the "believers" whose salvation was to be attained by a certain ceremony called the "consolation." This sacrament of consolation was performed by one of the perfect laying his hands on the believer; and after consolation, the newly-consoled must starve himself to death. A great number of trials of Albigenses have been collected by Limborch in his history of the

Inquisition. One only can we now give. It is that of a woman who had herself consoled, and sending for a surgeon, ordered him to open her veins in a bath, that so, the blood running out more freely, she might sooner die. Also she bought poison, as the bleeding did not succeed, and procured a cobbler's awl wherewith to pierce her heart, but as the women with her were undecided whether the heart were on the right side or the left, she took the poison, and so died.*

We can understand what alarm this great heathen reaction in Provence and Aquitaine awoke in France, and in the minds of the popes.

Innocent III. at first employed against the Albigenses only spiritual and legitimate weapons; before proscribing he tried to convert them, but when they murdered his emissary, Peter de Castelnau, in 1208, he proclaimed a Holy War against them. It was a war undertaken on the plea of a personal crime, but in reality for the dispossession of the native princes who were believed to be in favour of the heresy. "The crusade against the Albigensians," says M. Guizot, "was the most striking application of two principles

---

* We have got the Acts of the Inquisition at Toulouse during sixteen years, between 1307–1323. The whole number of cases reported is 932. The usual sentence on one found guilty—unless guilty of causing death by "consolation"—was to wear a tongue of red cloth on the garments. Of such there are 174 sentences. If a case of relapse, there was sentence of brief imprisonment, 218 cases; 38 were reported as having run away; 40 were condemned to death for having caused the death of dupes by "consolation;" 113 were let off penances previously imposed; 139 were discharged from prison, and 90 sentences were pronounced against persons already dead. *See* Maitland's Tracts and Documents on the Albigenses, 1831.

equally false and fatal, which did as much evil to the Catholics as to the heretics; and these are the right of the spiritual power to coerce souls by the material force of the temporal power, and the right to strip princes of their title to the obedience of their subjects—in other words, denial of religious liberty to consciences, and of political independence to states."

In 1208 Innocent summoned the King of France to

BÉZIERS.—CHURCH OF S. NAZAIRE.

sweep from southern France these heretics, "worse than the Saracens," and he promised to the leaders of the crusade the domains they won of the princes who favoured the heresy. The war lasted fifteen years (from 1208 to 1223) and of the two leading spirits, one ordering and the other executing, Pope Innocent III. and Simon de Montfort, neither saw the end of it. During the fifteen years of this religious war, nearly all the towns and strong castles in the regions between the Rhone, the Pyrenees, the Garonne were taken, lost, retaken, given over to pillage, sack, and massacre, and burnt by the Crusaders with all the cruelty of fanatics and all the greed of conquerors. In the account of the war by a Provençal poet, we are told that God never made the clerk who could have written the muster-roll of the crusading army in two or even three months. One of the first victims was the young and gallant Viscount of Béziers, who, the same author assures us, was a good Catholic, but whose lands and towns the rapacious horde lusted to acquire. When they sat down before Béziers, then the Catholics within the walls made common cause with the heretics, and re- fused to surrender.

FOUNTAIN IN THE CLOISTER OF S. NAZAIRE, BÉZIERS.

Then the city was stormed, the walls scrambled up by a rabble rout of camp-followers, in shirts and breeches, but without shoes, who burst over the parapets whilst the envoys of the town were being amused by mock conferences with Montfort and the other leaders of the crusading host. A general massacre ensued; neither age nor sex were spared, even priests fell. It is said that news of what was being done was brought to

Arnauld, Abbot of Citeaux, one of the commanders of the crusade, and he was told that faithful and heretics were being slaughtered alike. "Slay them all," said he, "God will know His own."

The story is told by a contemporary, but only as an *on-dit*, and may therefore be quite untrue. But Simon de Montfort, the hero of the crusade, employed like language. One day two heretics, taken at Castres, were brought before him, one of whom was unshakable in his belief, the other expressed himself open to conviction. "Burn them both," said the count; "if this fellow mean what he says, the fire will expiate his sins; and, if he lie, he will suffer for his imposture."

An attempt has been made to exculpate the leaders of the crusade from the atrocities committed at the capture of Béziers, and to clear them of the charge of treachery. It is so far certain that the town was captured and the massacre begun by the camp-followers, but the Crusaders soon joined in and accomplished the work begun by the "ribauds;" and no attempt was made by the leaders to stay the carnage. In the cathedral church of S. Madeleine some seven thousand who had taken refuge there were butchered without regard to the sanctity of the spot. The city was then set on fire and the cathedral perished in the flames.

After all, it was well that the cathedral should be purged with fire, and rebuilt. One could not pray, one would not like to see the service of God rendered in a building that had been thus bespattered with blood. S. Nazaire is later. It was almost wholly rebuilt in the fourteenth century, and within it one can forget the horrors of that hateful siege and butchery.

As I travelled on to Narbonne, there entered the carriage in which I was two girls with remarkable profiles, and I wondered whether they bore the features of the Ligurian race that first peopled all this coast, now probably represented by the Basques—a race akin to the Lap. These girls had fine dark eyes and hair, sallow complexions, and their full faces were not unpleasant, but their profiles were certainly most remarkable. Now curiously enough, on entering the cathedral at Narbonne, I saw a tomb of the eighteenth century with mourners represented on it—some six to

TYPES OF FACES, NARBONNE.

MODERN.   SIXTEENTH-CENTURY TOMB IN CATHEDRAL.   CLASSIC BUST IN MUSEUM.

eight, and they had all the same type of face. Not only so, but in the museum of the town is a Classic bust, found among the remains of Roman Narbona, and the same type is there.

Narbonne was once a great capital. It stood on a lagoon, and did a large trade in the Mediterranean. It was a Roman colony, founded at the same time as Arles, and had its forum, capitol, baths, amphitheatre, theatre, and temples. But, alas! the necessity for fortifying the city in the Middle Ages induced the inhabitants to go to these Roman buildings and pull them to pieces in order with them to construct the walls and towers surrounding the town, and now not one of all these monuments remains. The walls have served, however, as a rich quarry of antiquities that have supplied the two great collections in the town, one in the Hotel de Ville, the other in a ruined church. These collections are only second to the Avignon museum, and abound with objects of interest.

Among the monumental stones for the dead are several with caps figured on them. The like are to be seen at Nimes, Avignon, and elsewhere. These are freedmen's caps. When a noble Roman died he left in his will that so many of his slaves were to be given their liberty, and then this was represented by caps sculptured on his tombstone.

FREEDMEN'S CAPS, NARBONNE.

Thus it happened that the cap came to be regarded as the symbol of liberty. The museum contains a Christian sarcophagus on the staircase, with an orante, a woman praying with uplifted hands in the midst, on the sides the striking of the rock and the multiplication of the loaves. On the lid is the portrait of the lady who was buried in it, with hair dressed in the fashion worn by the Julias of the Heliogabalus and Alexander Severus epoch, with whose busts one becomes so familiar at Rome, 218-223—a fashion that never came in again, that I am aware of. Another Christian sarcophagus has on it the multiplication of loaves, the denial of Peter, and a representation of Christ unbearded, which is the earliest form. Another, again, represents him unbearded holding a scroll, on the right St. Peter and two other apostles holding rolls, and three apostles on the left; on the lid is an orante.

In this museum may be seen one or two examples of bronze Gaulish sun-wheels with four and eight spokes; and, what is to me very touching, a number of children's toys made in clay, found in children's tombs—cocks and hens, pigs and horses, very rude. Similar toys are to be found in the Arles and the Avignon museums. I remember in the catacomb of S. Agnes at Rome is a whole collection of toys found in a Christian grave there, ivory dolls, a rattle, bells, and an earthenware money-box, just such as may be bought for a sou now in a foreign fair. De Rossi, the curator of the catacombs, has had them all put together under glass in proximity to the little grave where they were found. In a child's grave at S. Sebastian was found a little terra-cotta horse dappled with yellow spots. I suppose parents could not bear to see the toys of their darlings about the house, and so enclosed them with their dear ones in the last home. I remember a modern French grave, near La Rochelle; in the centre of the head-cross was a glass case, with a doll dinner-service enclosed, that had been a favourite toy with the poor little mite lying under the cross. So human hearts are the same as centuries roll by and religions alter.

CHILDREN'S TOYS IN THE MUSEUM, NARBONNE.

The cathedral of Narbonne is very delightful, after a course of castellated fortress-churches of early date. It is of the fourteenth century, light, lantern-like, with glorious flying buttresses.

The church is unfinished, it has no nave, only the lovely soaring choir, standing alone, like that of Beauvais; and as was that of Cologne till the last thirty years. Unfortunately this choir is so built round with houses that it is only in one place at the east end that it can be seen, and just there, out of delightful play of fancy, the architect has thrown a bow across from one flying buttress to another high up, and through this stone rainbow one sees the pinnacles and the sweeping arches of the buttresses crossing each other at every angle.

The archiepiscopal palace was a fortress, with two strong towers. M. Viollet-le-Duc was invited by the town to take them in hand and construct between them a façade in keeping with their architecture, which was to be thenceforth the façade of the Hôtel de Ville. There was not a man in France who had a more intimate knowledge of Gothic architecture than he; but, unfortunately, like Rickman in England and Heideloff in Germany, he was incapable of applying his knowledge. The consequence is that he has produced a façade which is disfiguring to the two grand towers between which it is planted. Viollet-le-Duc was delighted with the grand effect of the face of the papal palace at Avignon, where the buttresses run up unstaged and then are united by bold arches that sustain the parapet and battlements, so he attempted the same thing at Narbonne on a smaller scale. Now these buttresses or piers at Avignon are 5 ft. 1 in. by 2 ft. 9 in., whereas the measurements of M. le-Duc's little props are reduced to 1 ft. 2 in. by 1 ft. 6 in. Relative proportions are changed as well as sadly reduced. The result is that they are ludicrous. Moreover, instead of sinking his façade modestly—a little, eighteen inches would have been enough—he has carried the face of his niggling little buttresses flush with the massive walls of the great towers. I wished I could have had M. Viollet-le-Duc there by both his ears and knocked his head against the abomination he has created. He had a splendid opportunity, and through incapacity he lost it.

I got into trouble at Narbonne.

As I was walking on the platform of the station, a man in plain clothes with very blue eyes came to me, touched his hat, and asked if he might be honoured with a few words privately. I at once suspected he was going to beg or borrow money, and said I was willing to hear what he wanted to say on the spot. He smiled, and said that he thought perhaps it would be better that we had our conversation elsewhere, outside the station. After a little hesitation, I complied, and when we were by ourselves, "Monsieur," said he, "I must request you to show me your papers and allow me to identify you. I am in search of some one uncommonly like yourself. I am—the *chef* of the secret police down here. Will you come to my office, and bring your luggage?"

"Certainly, delighted to make your acquaintance. I will get my Gladstone bag, and my roll of rugs in a moment. There is a—a hurdy-gurdy——"

"I know there is," said the *chef* sternly. "It is that *vielle* that is suspicious."

So all my luggage was conveyed to the office of the police. I showed no concern, but laughed and joked.

"What countryman do you say you are?"

"English."

"Impossible. You have not the English accent when you speak. It is rather German than anything else."

"You think I am a German?"

"But certainly. Your bag has a German address on it, written in German characters." So it had. I had been in Germany before going to Rome, and had never removed the address, which, as he said, was in German characters. I explained, but the *chef* was unsatisfied. I became now convinced that he thought I was a spy.

"Here are German newspapers and a German book in your bag!" said the *chef*.

"Certainly. Why not? I have been in Germany."

"Yet you say you are English?"

"Here is my passport." I extended one to him. He looked at it, shook his head, and said: "It is a very old one of 1867." That was true, and I had not had it *viséd* since.

"Then," said the *chef*, "this passport is for you and your wife. Where is the wife?"

"Minding the babies. Thirteen of them—a handful," said I.

I had to produce card-case, letters, all of which the *chef* examined carefully, and yet he was not satisfied. Then, suddenly, a bright idea struck me.

"Monsieur!" said I, "I see what you take me to be. It is true I have been sketching in Narbonne, and along the whole coast. Would you like to see my drawings? Here is the result of my studies in Narbonne: the very remarkable profile of a Narbonnaise girl, the face of a lady carved in the cathedral, of another in the museum, some sketches of children's clay toys found in Roman tombs, and sundry Gaulish and Merovingian bronzes; also! yes, see, a bone toothcomb discovered among the remains of the fortifications."

The *chef* laughed, especially over the beauties of Narbonne, ran his eye through the book, took it over to his assistant to look at and laugh over the wonderful girls' faces, returned it to me, and let me off.

"And the *vielle*," said I, "what do you think of that——"

"Mais! with the *vielle* over your shoulder, and that book of sketches and thirteen babies—*assurément*—you could only be an Englishman."

CHAPTER XVIII.

CARCASSONNE.

Siege of Carcassonne by the Crusaders—Capture—Perfidy of legate—Death of the Viscount—Continuation of the war—Churches of New Carcassonne—*La Cité*—A perfect Mediæval fortified town—Disappointing—Visigoth fortifications—Later additions—The Cathedral—Tomb of Simon de Montfort.

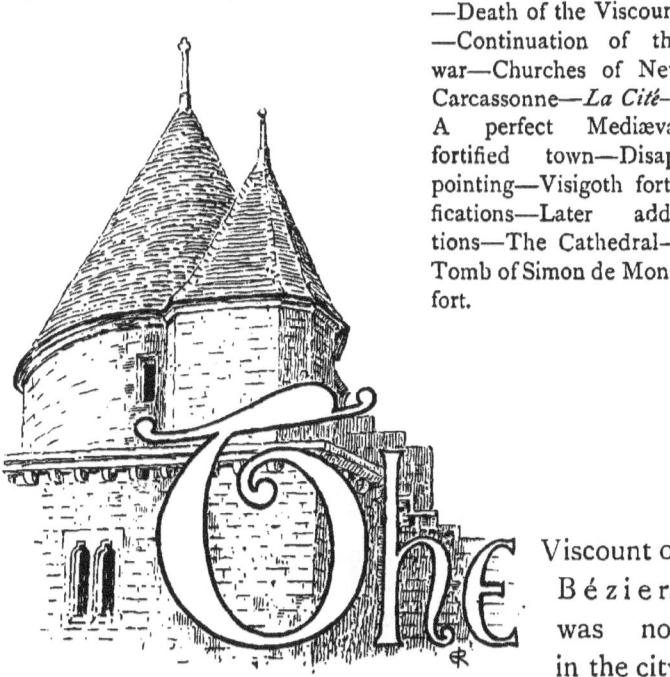

The Viscount of Béziers was not in the city from which he took his title when it fell. He had hurried on to Carcassonne to prepare that for defence. There he exerted himself with the utmost energy, with rage and despair, to be ready against the bloodthirsty, and yet blood-drunken ruffians who were pouring along the road from smoking Béziers, to do to Carcassonne as they had done there. Pedro, king of Aragon, interfered; he appeared as mediator in the camp of the Crusaders. Carcassonne was held as a fief under him as lord paramount. He pleaded the youth of the viscount, asserted his fidelity to the Church, his abhorrence of the Albigensian heresy; it was no fault of his, he argued, that his subjects had lapsed into error, and he declared that the Viscount had authorised him to place his sub-

TOWERS ON THE WALL, CARCASSONNE.

mission in the hands of the legate of Pope Innocent. But the Crusaders were snorting for plunder and murder. The only terms they would admit were that the young viscount might retire with twelve knights; the city must surrender at discretion. The proud and gallant youth declared that he had rather be flayed alive than desert the least of his subjects. The first assaults, though on one occasion led by the prelates chanting the 'Veni Creator' ended in failure.

Carcassonne might have resisted successfully had it

been properly provisioned, or had the viscount limited the number admitted within its walls. But multitudes of refugees had come there from all the country round. The wells failed. Disease broke out. The viscount was obliged to come to terms, to accept a free conduct from the officer of the legate, and he endeavoured to make terms for his subjects.

Most of the troops made their escape by subterranean passages, and the defenceless city came into the power of the Crusaders. The citizens were stripped almost naked, and their houses given up to pillage, but their lives were spared, with the exception of some fifty who were hanged and four hundred who were burned alive. The viscount had given himself up on promise of safe conduct; but no promises, no oaths were held sacred in these wars of religion, and the perfidious legate seized him, cast him into a dungeon, and there he died a few months later of a broken spirit and the pestilential prison air.

The law of conquest was now to be put in force. The lands of the heretic the Pope was ready to bestow on such as had dutifully done his behest. The legate assembled the principal crusading nobles, that they might choose among them one to act as lord over their conquests. The offer was made, successively, to the Duke of Burgundy, the Count of Nevers, and the Count of S. Pol; but they all three declined, saying scornfully that they had lands enough of their own without taking those of another. They were, perhaps, fearful of the perilous example of setting up the fiefs of France to the hazard of the sword. Simon de Montfort was less scrupulous, or more ambitious, and he took immediate possession of the lands that had been acquired. The Pope wrote to him and confirmed him in the hereditary possession of his new dominions, at the same time expressing to him a hope that, in concert with the legates, he would continue very zealous in the extirpation of the heretics.

From this time forth the war in southern France changed character, or, rather, it assumed a double character; with the war of religion was openly joined a war of conquest; it was no longer merely against the Albigenses and their heresies, it was against the native princes of the south of France, for the sake of their dominions, that the crusade was prosecuted.

If it came within my scope to speak about Toulouse, I should be constrained to tell more of this sanguinary story. I am thankful that I need not prosecute the hateful tale; but so much it was not possible for me to withhold from the reader, as it is with these memories that Carcassonne and Beziers must be visited and looked at.

Carcassonne is a double city, a city on a hill and another on the plain, each ancient, but that below with the modern element leavening it, that above wholly steeped in mediævalism.

In the lower town are two fine churches, very peculiar in design, forming vast halls without pillars, and with small chancels and apses. There can be no question that they look uncomfortable without pillars, that the choir does not grow out of the church naturally, and is devoid of dignity. These two churches are S. Vincent and S. Michael. The latter is of the thirteenth century, and seems to have formed

BÉZIERS FROM THE RIVER.

the pattern upon which the other was built in the fourteenth and sixteenth centuries. There is no west portal, but it has a fine rose window. The church is entered by a small door on the north. The other and later church, S. Vincent, has a very fine tower, which has, unfortunately, not been completed. It also has no west door, and is entered by a small portal at the side. These churches have their lateral chapels arranged like those in the cathedral at Munich between the buttresses, and the church is lighted by windows above them. Such buildings make admirable preaching-halls, but as churches are not pleasing internally.

To the east of New Carcassonne flows the river Aude crossed by a bridge, with a quaint little chapel recently restored beside it. From this bridge a view of Old Carcassonne, *La Cité*, as it is called, bursts on the sight. It stands on a height about 125 ft. above the river, and this height has two peaks, one is occupied by the citadel, the other by the old cathedral of S. Nazaire.

The whole of this *Cité* is surrounded by its walls and towers, quite as perfect as when originally built, for they have been very carefully restored by M. Viollet-le-Duc. Consequently we have before us a French fortified town of the Middle Ages come down to us unaltered. That it is picturesque is unquestionable, that it is *eminently* picturesque cannot be allowed. The builders had no concern for making a beautiful picture, they thought only of making an impregnable place. It is precisely this that differentiates it from a score of German fortified towns. The burghers of these latter were resolved to make their towns miracles of beauty as well as strong places. Consequently they varied the shapes of their towers, they capped them quaintly, hardly making two alike. Here, at Carcassonne, every tower, or nearly every tower, resembles its fellow, and all have sugar-loaf caps that irritate the eye with iteration of the same form. The citadel has no character of massiveness, no grand donjon to distinguish it from the rest of the fortifications, and the cathedral has only two mean little donkey's ears of towers that are most ineffective, peeping over the walls of the south-western angle of the town. In looking out for a study for a picture one has to get where some of the sugar-loaf towers are eclipsed, and there is only one point in the whole circumference where a really satisfactory grouping is obtainable, and that is at the angle outside immediately below the cathedral platform to the west, where the one respectable turret of the castle stands up boldly from

A BIT OF CARCASSONNE.

the rock, and the flanking turrets overlap and hide each other.

Interesting, most interesting is Old Carcassonne, and picturesque in its fashion; the regret one feels is that, with its opportunities, it is not more so. I do not think that M. Viollet-le-Duc's restoration is in fault, but that the original architects had no idea of anything better, were men of mediocre abilities, or cared only to make the defences strong at all costs, and to sacrifice everything else to this one consideration.

But the same fault is inherent in all French castle-building and city-fortification of the Middle Ages. It is picturesque when in ruins. On the other hand, the German castles and fortified towns look their very best when in perfect repair. Let the reader take up Albert Dürer's delightful little engraving of the Hermit, and compare the background of a German walled town and castle on a height with *La Cité*, Carcassonne, and he will see how vast is the difference in quality of picturesqueness between the two.

The *Cité* is actually enclosed within double ramparts, and a portion of these dates from the time of the Visigoths. Their walls were composed of cubic blocks of stone, with alternate layers of brick, were double-faced, and filled in with rubble bedded in lime, forming a sort of concrete core. The towers were round outside with flat face to the town, and large round-headed windows which were closed with boards. These in later times were built up. The interior walls and towers are the earliest, and were those besieged by the Crusaders. It was in one of the towers of the

s

INSIDE THE WALL, CARCASSONNE.

castle that the unhappy young viscount died. The outer fortifications were erected by Louis IX. and his son, Philip the Bold. The Visigoth walls were defended by thirty-two towers, of which only one was square. Louis IX. constructed a great barbican below the castle, commanding the bridge over the Aude, but that was destroyed some years ago.

The *Cité* underwent a second siege in 1240, whilst Louis IX. was on his crusade, and Queen Blanche was regent. Very curious letters exist from Guillaume des Ormes, the seneschal to the regent, describing the siege of Carcassonne by the troops of the viscount; but for these, and for a detailed account of the fortifications, I must refer the reader to M. Viollet-le-Duc's account, in his treatise on the Military Architecture of the Middle Ages.

The old town of Carcassonne, crowded within the walls, has very narrow streets and tiny squares; the only open space being before the citadel and the cathedral. This latter has a fine Romanesque nave that was consecrated by Pope Urban II. in 1096, with its west end designed for defence, after the customary manner in the south. It is supported by massive piers, alternately round and square. To this plain nave is added a light and lovely choir with transepts, of the beginning of the fourteenth century. Here the glorious windows are filled with rich old stained glass — barbarously restored. And here, on one side of the high altar may be seen a slab of red marble—rightly blood-red—marking the tomb of the infamous Simon de Montfort, Earl of Leicester, the cruel and remorseless right hand of the Pope, with which this fair region was deluged with blood. He was killed on June 20th, 1218, by a stone flung from the walls of Toulouse, which he had been unsuccessfully besieging for nine months. From the south side of the old *Cité*

ENTRANCE TO THE CASTLE, CARCASSONNE.

a delightful view is obtained of the Pyrenees, snow-clad when I was there in April; but the mountain forms of the chain as it approaches the Mediterranean lose boldness and picturesqueness of outline, as they also dwindle in altitude.

CHAPTER XIX.

AVIGNON.

How Avignon passed to the Popes—The court of Clement VI.—John XXII.—Benedict XII.—Their tombs—Petrarch and Laura—The Palace of the Popes—The Salle Brûlée—Cathedral — Porch — S. Agricole — Church of S. Pierre—The museum — View from the Rocher des doms — The Rhone—The bridge—Story of S. Benezet—Dancing on bridges—Villeneuve —Tomb of Innocent VI.—The Castle at Villeneuve—Defences—Tête-du-pont of the bridge.

We leave Languedoc and are again in Provence, or what was Provence, till the Popes by a fraud obtained it. Avignon belonged to Provence, which was claimed by Charles of Anjou in right of his wife, and it had descended to his son, Charles II. of Naples. On the death of the latter it fell to Robert of Naples, and from him to his grand-daughter, Joanna, the heiress of the Duke of Calabria.

The Papal residence was now at Avignon, and

there it remained for a century and a quarter. Joanna fell into trouble, her kingdom of Naples was invaded by Louis, King of Hungary, who asserted his right to her throne. She fled to Provence—to Avignon—where at once Pope Clement VI. seized the occasion to purchase this portion of her Provençal inheritance of her at the price of eighty thousand gold crowns. He kept the principality, but never paid the money.

The Popes have left their indelible mark on the place in the glorious palace, a vast castle, of the boldest structure, wonderful in its size and massiveness.

The Papal court at Avignon, under Clement VI., "became," says Dr. Milman, "the most splendid, perhaps the gayest, in Christendom. The Provençals might almost think their brilliant and chivalrous counts restored to power and enjoyment. The Papal palace spread out in extent and magnificence; the Pope was more than royal in the number and attire of his retainers; the papal stud of horses commanded general admiration. The life of Clement was a constant succession of ecclesiastical pomps and gorgeous receptions and luxurious banquets. Ladies were freely admitted to the Court, and the Pope mingled with ease in the gallant intercourse. The Countess of Turenne, if not, as general report averred, actually so, had at least many of the advantages of the Pope's mistresses—the distribution of preferments and benefices to any extent, which this woman, as rapacious as she was handsome and imperious, sold with shameless publicity."

Under the Papal rule, with such an example before it, Avignon became the moral sink of Christendom. To see what its condition was, and how flagrant was the vice in all quarters, the letters of Petrarch must be read. He speaks of the corruption of Avignon with loathing abhorrence; Rome itself, in comparison, was the seat of matronly virtue.

But I must step back for a moment to John XXII. because of the lovely monument to him in the cathedral, and because thereon we have his authentic portrait.

This Pope was a cobbler's son of Cahors; he was a small, deformed, but clever man: the second cobbler's son who sat on the seat of S. Peter. He had gone, when a youth, to Naples, where his uncle was settled in a little shop. There he studied, his talents and luck pushed him into notice, and he became bishop of Frejus. But he preferred to live on the sunny shores of Naples, and to keep within the circle of the king, where lay chances of higher preferment, and he troubled his diocese little with his presence. He became a cardinal, and in 1316 was elected Pope at the conclave of Lyons. He at once dropped down the Rhone, and fixed the seat of his pontificate at Avignon. Able, learned though he was, he was not above the superstitions of his age. He had been given a serpentine ring by the Countess of Foix, and had lost it. He believed that it had been stolen from him wherewith to work some magic spell against his health. The Pope pledged all his goods, movable and immovable, for the safe restoration of his ring: he pronounced anathema against all such as were involved in the retention of it. It was rumoured that one of those involved in the plot by witchcraft to cause his death through this serpentine ring was Gerold, bishop of his own native city, Cahors. The alarmed and angry sovereign Pontiff had the unhappy bishop degraded, *flayed alive*, and torn to pieces by wild horses.

John XXII. issued an edict of terrible condemnation against all such as dealt in magical arts, who bottled up spirits, made waxen images and stuck pins into them, and the like. He died at the age of ninety, having amassed enormous wealth by drawing into his own power all the collegiate benefices throughout Christendom, and by means of reservations, an ingenious mode of getting large pickings out of every bishopric before the institution of a new bishop. The brother of Villani the historian, a banker, took the inventory of his goods when he was dead. It amounted to eighteen millions of gold florins in specie, and seven millions in plate and jewels. His face, on his monument, is indicative of his harsh, grasping, and cold character.

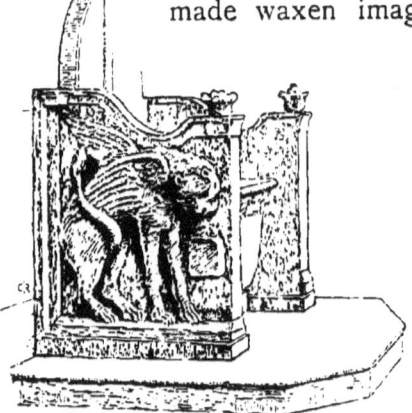

PAPAL THRONE IN THE CATHEDRAL OF AVIGNON.

Now look at this other face, it is that of the

successor of John, of James Fournier, who took the name of Benedict XII. He lies in the north aisle of the cathedral.

On the death of John XII. twenty-four cardinals met, mostly Frenchmen, and their votes inclined to a brother of the count of Comminges, but they endeavoured to wring from him an oath to continue to make Avignon the seat of the Papacy. He refused ; and then, to his own surprise, the suffrages fell on the Cistercian abbot, James Fournier.

JOHN XXII.

"You have chosen an ass!" he said, in humility or in irony.

But he did himself an injustice : he was a man of shrewdness and sagacity, he lacked only courage and strength to have made a great Pope. His whole reign was a tacit reproach against the turbulence, implacability and avarice of his predecessor. The court of Avignon was crowded with fawning courtier bishops seeking promotion : he

BENEDICT XII.

sent them flying back to their sees. He discouraged the Papal reserves, the iniquitous system whereby Pope John had amassed his wealth ; he threw open the treasury of his predecessor, and distributed some of the coin among the cardinals, the rest he spent in the erection of the huge castle-palace that is now the wonder of all who visit Avignon, and the construction of which made the money circulate among the poor and industrious artificers.

When Benedict died, after a brief reign of eight years, his reputation was disputed over with singular pertinacity by friends and foes.

"He was a man wiser in speech than in action, betraying by his keen words that he saw what was just and right, but dared not follow it. Yet political courage alone was wanting. He was resolutely superior to the Papal vice of nepotism. On one only of his family, and that a deserving man, he bestowed a rich benefice. To the rest he said, 'As James Fournier I knew you well, as Pope I know you not. I will not put myself in the power of the King of France by encumbering myself with a host of needy relatives.' He had the moral fortitude to incur unpopularity with the clergy by persisting in his slow, cautious, and regular distribution of benefices; with the monks by his rigid reforms. He hated the monks, and even the Mendicant Orders. He showed his hatred, as they said, by the few promotions which he bestowed upon them."*

AN ANGLE OF THE PAPAL PALACE, AVIGNON.

The bitter hatred begotten in return was displayed

* Milman : 'Latin Christianity.'

in the epitaph set up over him, describing him as a Nero, as death to the laity, a viper to the clergy, a liar and a drunkard.* But malignity of disappointed ambition and repressed vice did not go so far as to caricature his face. The graver had to copy the epitaph given him, but the sculptor reproduced the face of the man himself, and that face, sweet, gentle, and pure, tells its own tale. It is quite another face from that of John XXII. John has a magnificent shrine of incomparable Gothic pinnacle-work; but Benedict is laid in a very humble tomb, yet over it is the best of monuments, his own good face. Of this "Nero" there is not recorded one single act of cruelty; and he was guiltless of human blood shed in war.

Here, at Avignon, and writing of the very epoch in which he lived, it is not possible to withhold the pen from some lines relative to Petrarch, and I feel the more disposed to write about him, for I think that the words used relative to him and Laura in Murray's Handbook are not quite just. Speaking of Vaucluse, the author says: "It is more agreeable to contemplate Petrarch in these haunts, as the laborious student retired from the world, than as the mawkish lover sighing for a married mistress."

Petrarch was an exile, living at Avignon in exile, when he saw his Laura in a church there, and lost his heart. He was then aged twenty-one, and she was twelve or thirteen; she belonged to the illustrious family of Sade. Now it so happens that the chief

* "Ille fuit Nero, laicis mors, vipera clero,
 Devius a vero, cuppa repleta mero.''

authority for the history of Petrarch is the Abbé de Sade, who set to work with a determination to show that his family were lineal descendants of Petrarch's Laura, and he ingenuously left out such particulars as militated against his doctrine. The great family of Sade, who had their castle between Avignon and Vaucluse, had not the smallest intention of suffering a daughter of the house to become allied to an exile of no great birth and prospects; accordingly every impediment was put in the way of a meeting. Petrarch's love for her was well known, indeed his imprudence was great, he allowed his poems in her honour to pass from hand to hand. It was impossible for her relatives to suffer this to continue. She was placed with her aunt Stephanette de Romanie; and died unmarried. Her father was Hugo de Sade, and her mother Laura de Neves; and the Abbé de Sade, and all who follow him, suppose that Petrarch was in love with the mother, whereas there is abundant evidence that the object of his passion was the daughter.*

Whether Petrarch's love for Laura was as pure as he represents it in some of his sonnets—whether the unhappy Laura did not suffer from his pursuit in honour as she certainly lost in repute, is uncertain. Petrarch in some of his poems exalts his passion for her into the most pure platonic affection, but other verses addressed to her have a very different complexion.

The vast fortress-palace of the Popes at Avignon has stood a siege. It was at the time of the Great Schism,

---

* The whole matter has been thoroughly discussed, and I think the story of his love for the wife of Hugo de Sade refuted by Bruce-Whyte ('Hist. des Langues Romanes,' t. iii. c. 38).

The Cathedral and the Palace of the Popes, Avignon.

when three grey-headed claimants to be representatives of S. Peter and Vicegerents of Christ were thundering anathemas against each other and the supporters of their rivals. Benedict XIII. was then Pope in Avignon, but there was a general desire in Christendom that the scandal should be terminated. All his cardinals except two deserted Benedict, and the King of France required his renunciation of the tiara. "Pope I have written myself; Pope I have been acknowledged to be; Pope I will remain to the end of my days," was his answer. Then he was besieged in his palace and forced to capitulate, and thrown into prison, where he lingered under the jealous ward of the cardinals for five years.

LANTERN AT THE CATHEDRAL, AVIGNON.

The palace has been restored, and is now a barrack. In it is shown a hall, the principal dining hall, called now la Salle Brûlée, as in 1441 the Papal Legate brought together into it the burghers and nobles of Avignon, and in the height of revelry withdrew himself, and had fire applied to barrels of gunpowder under it, and blew the guests into the air. This was done in revenge for the murder of his nephew, a young libertine who had dishonoured a maiden of good family in the town.

Adjoining the palace, on higher ground, the Rocher des doms, is the cathedral of Nôtre Dame, small and early. With barbarous taste, the fine Romanesque west tower has been finished off with an octagonal structure supporting as apex a gigantic figure of the Virgin, leaning against a lightning conductor that is screwed into her head and back, and looks much like

ANGEL AT W. DOOR, CHURCH OF S. AGRICOLE.

the apparatus of a photographer to steady her for a successful *carte*. To the cathedral ascent is made by flights of stone steps, and it is entered by a porch that is made up of Corinthian pillars taken from a Classic temple. Some have thought the whole porch to be of Roman architecture, but it is not so. For some time Provençal architecture was much influenced by the remains that covered the soil, and from which the builders of churches not merely drew their ideas but also appropriated materials.

The dome of the cathedral is noticeable within from the bold and effective manner in which it is sustained on four successive receding arches. There is a fine north aisle, the vaulting of which starts as though it were about to spread into the fan-tracery of English Perpendicular. It is curious as showing French architects on the eve of reaching the same marvellous development attained in England.

There is a fine church at Avignon, S. Agricole, of

noble proportions, the vaulting and arcades springing from the pillars without capitals. In the south aisle is a curious fourteenth-century shrine. The west front of the church is of very poor design.

S. Pierre is a flamboyant church, the details passing into Renaissance. In the north aisle is a superb Renaissance altar-piece, representing Christ between S. Peter and S. Paul. Underneath is the Last Supper. It was too fine and good to be appreciated, and a modern vulgar altar and altar-piece have been erected at the side for use. The choir-stalls are really wonderful. They are also of Renaissance woodwork, with painted panels in the back representing architectural scenes alternating with vases of flowers. They are separated by Corinthian columns gilt, and very sumptuous, yet the whole effect is subdued and pleasing, not gaudy. In this church also the arches spring from the pillars without capitals. Altogether this church deserves careful study.

A BIT OF THE OLD WALL, AVIGNON.

The museum of Avignon is the richest in antiquities in the south of France. Unfortunately the substance of the collection was gathered by a M. Calvert who made no note as to *where* he got the various articles he collected, and this naturally deprives much that is there of its value. However, there is a great deal there to be seen; notably a bronze cavalry standard, Roman, in admirable preservation; a stamp in bronze with the letters $^{\alpha}_{V}{}^{\iota}_{N}$ and the seven-branched-candlestick between, clearly a Jewish stamp. A magnificent gold necklace and gold bracelets with a large medallion of a Roman Empress in gold in the midst. The head is said to be that of Orbiana, third wife of Severus Alexander, unknown to history, and known only by her coins.

Among the statues preserved there is the Venus Victrix found at Pourrières, and a very rude but interesting Gaulish warrior, discovered at Montdragon in 1834, cut in sandstone. He is leaning on a huge shield. There are several busts of Roman emperors, a good one, but with nose broken, of the Elder Drusus, Lucius Verus, Tiberius, Trajan, a Plautilla—and some that are doubtful.

Of the paintings in the *Musé* I cannot say much, as I looked at two only—two perfectly delicious Brueghels, a Flemish Fair, and, I think, a wedding. I won the heart of the *concierge* by studying them. He found me careering about the gallery, like an owl in sunlight, looking for Brueghel, and when he found what I was after, led me back to them, one on each side of the entrance door. "Why do you want to see Brueghel?" he asked. "Why? because I love his oddities." "Are you a Belge?" "No." "But you seem to know the Flemish artists. I am by ancestry a Belge. My grandfather came from Brussels." So we talked over

AVIGNON.

dear, delightful Belgium for half-an-hour, and I had the most eager, amiable guide to all that was of interest in the museum, after that. And it is a collection! The mediæval and Renaissance sculptures alone deserve a visit.

One can hardly bear to think of the amount of good work that has perished in Avignon. The city possessed before the Revolution sixty churches, and of these only eighteen remain; of between two and three hundred towers and spires, not one-tenth are left standing. There is, however, a very fine tower and east end in S. Didier, a church of the fourteenth century, another in the Hôtel de Ville built round with a tasteless Classic structure that obscures it from view. The Musée Requien is in an old convent, the chapel of which is given up to the Protestants; it has a rich flamboyant window to the north, unfortunately blocked.

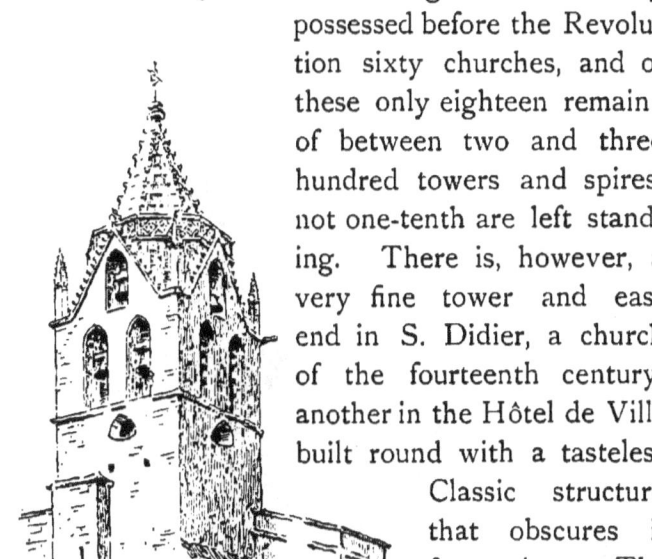

PART OF CHURCH OF S. DIDIER, AVIGNON.

A quaint and picturesque tower stands by itself in the Rue Carréterie; it is machicolated and has a delicate little spire. It is all that remains of the

T

church of the Augustinians. Nearly opposite is a rich flamboyant portal.

Avignon is completely surrounded by its old walls and towers. Much of the space inside is now occupied by gardens and vineyards; apparently in the time when Avignon was the seat of the Papacy, it was far more populous than at present. I should like the clergy of Rome to see Avignon with its fifty-two

BRIDGE AND CHAPEL OF S. BENEZET.

desecrated churches and its thirty-five abandoned convents, and compare it with Rome where nearly everything is left them; then perhaps they would be inclined to salute their king and queen.

What a lovely view that is from the gardens on the Rocher des Domes! To the east rises Mont Ventoux, a spur of the Alps thrown out into the plain, and in April veiled in snow. To the west the chain of the

Cevennes, and the plain gleaming with water from the many windings of the Rhone, and from its branches, as it splits and circumvents islands clothed with willow and poplar.

Above Avignon is a very large island, and below it the Durance enters the Rhone through a lacework of rubble-beds with scanty growths upon them, the water flickering in a thousand silver threads between. Then, immediately under the Rocher des Domes is the mighty river sweeping on with strong purpose, and half-bridged by a quaint old structure, built between 1177 and 1185, under the direction of S. Benezet. On the second pile is a little chapel, erected in honour of the founder, in which Mass is still said on his day, April 14th. S. Benezet was a shepherd, he was baptised by the name of Benedict, but, being a very little man, he received the diminutive that has adhered to him. He heard of the accidents that happened to those who crossed the rapid Rhone in boats, and he considered in his mind that it were well if the prelates and burghers of Avignon would devote their wealth to making a good bridge, instead of squandering it in show and riotous living. So he came into the city, and adjured the Pope and the bishop of the see to construct a bridge. The haughty ecclesiastics scoffed at him, and, as he would not desist from his urgency, sent him to the city governor to be chastised. Unshaken by this treatment, the shepherd persisted. He went among the citizens, he sought out the clergy, he collected knots of men to listen to him in the market-place, preaching the advantage of a bridge. It was his one idea. He was ignorant, perhaps foolish, in other matters, but he was possessed with the belief that God had sent him to induce the Avignonese to build a bridge. After a while, nothing was talked of in the

AT VILLENEUVE.

place but the great question of this same bridge. Its advantage was apparent to all. Finally it was decided by acclamation that they must have a bridge, and when it was built, and the shepherd died, "Really," said the good people of Avignon, "he must have been a saint to have roused us out of our apathy."

The poor shepherd's body was not respected by the revolutionists, though he was a sans-culotte, but he was a sans-culotte who was a constructor and not a destroyer, therefore—to the dogs with him.

There was a saying—

> " Avenio ventosa
> Cum vento fastidiosa,
> Sine vento venenosa."

That may be rendered in French—

> " Avignon venteuse
> Avec vent ennuyeuse,
> Sans vent pernicieuse."

Windy it was when I was there, and when I went out on the broken-down bridge of S. Benezet I was nearly blown off it. This bridge in French nursery rhyme takes much the same place as does London Bridge in English children's jingles. We have :—

> " London Bridge is broken down,
> Dance over my Lady Lee."

And the French have :—

> " Sur le Pont d'Avignon tout le monde danse, danse ;
> Sur le Pont d'Avignon tout le monde danse en rond."

Why dancing should be associated with bridges I cannot tell for certain, but there is probably some mythologic origin. It was customary in Pagan times to sacrifice a human being when the foundations of a bridge were laid, by burying the victim alive under it, and every year an offering of a life was made to the river to propitiate it, and ensure the stability of the bridge. Our nursery games of children dancing in a round, and one being taken by the casting of a kerchief, is a relic of an old heathen *sors*, by which a victim for immolation was selected ; and it is very probable that the dancing on bridges had something to do with this. One out of the chain that danced over the bridge, or the ring that wheeled on it was chosen, and cast over the parapet as an offering to the river.

CASTLE OF S. ANDRÉ, AT VILLENEUVE.

This superstition lingered on through the Middle Ages, in spite of Christianity. We say in Devon :—

"The River Dart
Every year demands a heart."

Anciently the Dart was *given* his victim; now, however, he *takes* it.

The bridge of S. Benezet is broken down and

abandoned, but a suspension bridge unites Avignon with the farther bank of the Rhone, and this must be crossed to reach Villeneuve, which stood to Avignon as Beaucaire to Tarascon. Villeneuve was French, and Avignon Papal down to the Revolution, when in 1791 it was annexed to France. At Villeneuve the army was assembled that besieged Pope Benedict XIII. in his palace.

Villeneuve is full of picturesque points. It was originally well fortified, and was a frontier fortress of Languedoc. The old Hôpital contains the tomb of Pope Innocent VI., which may be compared with that of John XXII. in the cathedral. Innocent was a native of Limoges. There was a strange struggle at his election.

On the death of Clement VI. a conclave of cardinals assembled to consider about choosing John Borelli, Carthusian superior, but, when Cardinal Talleyrand warned them that a man of such stern simplicity would in a very few days order their stately caparisoned horses to be turned to toil at the plough, they were alarmed, and looked elsewhere. But first of all they passed a law by unanimous vote that the College of Cardinals should become a dominant, self-elective assembly, superior to the Pope, and that one-half of the revenues of the Papacy should be diverted into the pockets of the cardinals. Then they proceeded to elect, and chose Stephen Aubert, a distinguished canon lawyer, who assumed the title of Innocent VI., and his first act was to emancipate himself from the oath he had taken, to rescind and declare null this statute of the Conclave. He was a severe disciplinarian.

He drove away a great portion of the swarm of bishops and beneficed clergy, who passed their time in Avignon in luxury and indolence, on the look-out for rich emoluments. One story is told of his conduct with regard to preferments. A favourite chaplain presented his nephew, a boy, and asked for him a rich benefice.

"You are already the holder of seven," said the Pope, "give him one of those." The chaplain looked discouraged. The Pope compelled him to choose three of the best. "These must suffice thee and the boy," said Innocent, "I will give the others to poor and deserving clerks."

It was under Cardinal Albornoz, the martial legate of this Pope, that Rienzi was subdued, and Rome recovered to the Papal chair.

AT VILLENEUVE.

The castle of Villeneuve was built by Philip the Bold in the thirteenth century, and is interesting in many ways. It contains a little chapel of an earlier date with a small apse and little round-headed windows. The whole of the body is under a very low-pitched roof supported on an almost Classic cornice. The fortifications of the castle are an example of a stage of defence carried beyond what was attained at Aigues Mortes. There, as we saw, the upper portion of the walls was covered with a balcony of wood on to which the besieged stepped through the doorways left in the battlements.

When, in sieges, the catapults were made to fling barrels of flaming tar over these balconies, and set them on fire, recourse was had to structures of stone, and the wooden *hourdes*, or balconies, disappeared. Then came the machicolated galleries. But even these were deemed insufficient, and *échauguettes* were erected, sentry-boxes between the towers standing forward beyond the curtains, and with double slits in the floor, through which two streams of flaming combustible or of stones could be sent down on the besiegers. The palace of the Popes at Avignon exhibits these on piers standing forth from the wall. They are also to be seen at Villeneuve.

A WELL AT VILLENEUVE.

The fine Gothic church of the Chartreuse is ruinous;

in that stood the tomb of Innocent VI. A grand tower, erected by Philip the Fair, formed the Tête du Pont of the bridge of S. Benezet. It was erected after the bridge had been constructed, as a protection against the troops of the Papacy. Thereupon the popes raised a tower of defence at their end of the bridge. There were originally seventeen arches in the bridge, resting on eighteen piers.

CHAPTER XX.

VALENCE.

A dull town—Cathedral—Jacques Cujas—His daughter—Pius VI.
—His death—Maison des Têtes—Le Pendentif—The castle of
Crussol—The dukes of Uzes—A dramatic company of the
thirteenth century.

What a sleepy place Valence is! There was supposed to be a fair there when I was at Valence, but even that could not wake it up. But the fair was in a condition of the utmost somnolence itself. Why—I did not suspect till I reached Vienne, when I found that this latter place had drawn to it all that was enterprising, startling, attractive, and left only the very dregs of fairings to poor Valence.

It has a great boulevard, very wide, very inviting, but the spotted boys, and fat girls, and bearded women, would have nothing to say to it—they herded to Vienne. It has a vast terrace, planted with trees, where any amount of stalls might stand, but there were erected there only some very inconsiderable ranges of boot and shoe tables, and of old cutlery, and slop clothes.

The cathedral is interesting and fine. The apse at the east end is early and curious; in place of buttresses receding in stages are Corinthian pillars tied into the walls they are to support at their heads by caps laid on them. There is no clerestory to the church, only an arcade of rude character. The walls of the cathedral are of sandstone, and have been so gnawed by the wind and rain, that the whole pile looks like a piece of very decayed cheese. The interior, however, is quite sound, reposeful, and lovely. That weatherbeaten exterior, with its calm sweet interior, struck me as a picture of many a good Christian, buffeted and worn by storm and trial without, whose inner self is ever still and untouched.

CATHEDRAL OF VALENCE.

The church was consecrated in 1095 by Pope Urban II. in person. A new western tower has been erected and a very fine west entrance in the Romanesque style, all very good, except the topmost stage of the tower, which has probably been confided to an inferior architect, who has managed to mar a work of great promise.

Jacques Cujas, born at Toulouse in 1520, one of the most famous lawyers of his time, taught at Valence. He was a candidate for the chair of laws in the university of his native city, but was refused it ; a certain Forcadel was elected instead, whose chief merit seems to have been that he was a wag. Cujas, on leaving Toulouse, turned, and shaking the dust off his feet against it said, " Ungrateful fatherland, in you my bones shall not rest." He kept his word, he died and was buried at Bourges. After he was gone from the place and his fame was sounded abroad, the university of Toulouse wanted to recall him, and sent a letter to him nominating him to the chair of laws. His answer was, " Frustra absentem requiris, quem præsentem neglexistis." "In vain do you desire him absent whom present you flouted."

At Valence he had eight hundred scholars, who attended his lectures. So great was the reverence shown for his opinion, that it is said that in the schools of Germany, when the professors quoted him they were wont to raise their hands to their caps. And he deserved it. His burning ambition was to break down the system of injustice to the accused which prevailed in French courts, where one charged with a crime, if the crime were unproved did not obtain complete acquittal. He wrote in the cause of humanity against the abuses of tyranny and ignorance. " Where there is not complete proof of guilt," said he, " there let there be no condemnation," a maxim observed in England, but not in France. " What is not full truth," is a saying of his, "is full falsehood." It was his hope, his prayer, that he might live to see the injustice of the French laws swept away. That he was not destined to see. He was a kind professor to all his scholars. When he found that some were needy, he assisted them with money and books. "I was once a poorer lad than you," said he to one whom he assisted, "and very grateful if any one would have pity on me."

He had a daughter, unworthy of her virtuous father. When his scholars were caught flirting with the damsel, they were wont to excuse themselves by saying that they were only "commenting on the works of Cujas."

DOORWAY IN THE HOUSE DUPRÉ LATOUR, VALENCE.

On this the following epigram was composed :—

"Videras immensos Cujaci labores
Æternum patri commeruisse decus :
Ingenio haud poterat tam magnum æquare parentem
Filia; quod potuit corpore fecit opus."

In his will Cujas desired that none of his books should be sold to a Jesuit; and that his library should be sold in parcels, lest any one should use his ill-digested notes for publication. His behest was obeyed. The booksellers of Lyons purchased his MSS. and used them as binding for books. It was not till sixteen years after his death that Alexander Scott of Carpentras, one of his pupils, collected his works.

At Valence died and was buried the unfortunate Pope Pius VI. who had been treated with great harshness, and had been loaded with insults by the French. His was, indeed, a strange story. He began his pontificate in splendour in 1775, and set to work at once to aggrandise his family, the Braschi. He was a man of rapacious avarice; of this one glaring instance is given. He persuaded, or compelled, a certain Amanzio Lepri to constitute him his heir, and hand over to him the title-deeds of an estate worth many millions of lire. The natural heirs of Lepri were greatly annoyed at this, and instituted proceedings before the tribunals, which gave judgment sometimes for them and sometimes for the Pope, and the matter might have dragged on indefinitely, had not public opinion begun to manifest itself with such force that Pius thought it best to agree to a compromise.

In everything relating to himself and his family the Pope showed unbounded extravagance and ostentation. He had pedigrees manufactured to prove the descent of his family from ancient Scandinavian heroes, and that of his nephews, on whom he heaped honours, from the Dukes of Benevento. He collected all the proudest devices of heraldry to incorporate them as quarterings into his arms, and this gave rise to an epigram from the pen of an ex-Jesuit, to this effect: "The eagle belongs to the Empire, the lilies of the field to France, to heaven belongs the stars—to Braschi what? Puff."

His extravagance had become so great that the States of the Church were practically bankrupt long before the French overran and pillaged them. In his money difficulties he laid his hands on the funds appropriated to pious works, and so barefaced were his robberies at last, that ten years before the French invasion he had appropriated 36,000 pounds weight of silver from the Holy House of Loretto. Then came the crash. This luxurious and splendid Pope, in his old age, was reduced to be a prisoner, and to be hustled about from place to place by the French. He had been sent first to the Certosa, near Florence, with only two companions; then, by order of the Directory, was conveyed to Parma. There he was allowed to remain only thirteen days, and, in spite of his age and growing infirmities, was conveyed to the citadel of Turin. One day was there allowed him for repose, and then he was carried over the Alpine pass of Mont Genèvre in April to Briançon. There he was left in peace, but sick and feeble, till the end of

June, when he was hurried away by Gap towards Dijon, but at Valence he became so ill that he could be no further moved, and there he died on the 29th August 1799, three days after his arrival.

The story is told that the official at Briançon on

DOORWAY AND NICHE IN THE MAISON DES TÊTES, VALENCE.

receiving him, sent to headquarters a formal receipt couched in these terms: "Reçu—un pape, en fort mauvais état."

There is not much of interest in domestic architecture at Valence, with the sole exception of the Maison des Têtes, which stands near the market-place, and which is sculptured over with great richness, with heads representing the seasons, and Roman emperors. The enrichment of this house is in the style of Flamboyant passing into Renaissance; the façade being in sandstone has been sadly gnawed by the tooth of Time, has indeed lost all edge to the sculpture, but within the entrance porch, where protected, the sandstone retains its sharpness. Curiously enough, no one knows for whom this gorgeous mansion was raised. It has a pretty interior court, but there is not much sculpture therein. One cannot quite forgive the original owner and edifier of the mansion for a bit of ostentation and vulgarity of which he has been guilty. The house has one portion looking on to the square, but at the side bends away at an obtuse angle down the street. As the whole façade was not visible at a single glance, only that portion which was most seen was sculptured, and that with overpowering richness, whereas the other portion in the street was left bare to baldness. Wind and rain and frost are engaged in rubbing down all the decoration, and flattening the surface of the decorated portion to the simplicity of the other part.

The same destroying agencies are at work upon a very quaint mausoleum, on the north side of the cathedral, called *Le Pendentif*, which was erected in 1548 in Classic style as a monument to the Mistral family. It is quadrangular, and consists of four great piers at the angles, and is adorned with pillars and with arches in the sides sustaining a vault. In the rusticated space that fills the sides, quaint sculptures of monsters and birds of foreign plumage may, or rather might have been traced, the honeycombing by weather has made them almost undiscoverable. Probably the structure is more picturesque now in its decay than it ever was before.

Immediately opposite Valence, on the farther side of the Rhone, rises a bold scarp of sandstone cliff, crowned with the ruined castle of Crussol above the village of S. Peray at its feet, where is made a very capital sparkling wine, not at all inferior to champagne. There is also there an odd château, designed, it is believed, by Marshal Vauban, on the plan of a mimic fortress, with bastions, curtains, glacis, portcullis, and loopholes. It is now the residence of the owner of the great vineyards where the S. Peray effervescing wine is made.

The view of the cliff of Crussol and the village of S. Peray from the terrace of Valence is spoiled by the river being at some distance from the base of the terrace, and the flat land that intervenes being covered by poplars, manufactories and cottages, so that the Rhone is shut out from sight.

Originally, certainly, the cliff on which stands the cathedral, as well as that now converted into a promenade, were swept by the Rhone, but it has thrown its gravels on to the left bank and cut its way farther to the west.

The castle of Crussol belonged to the Dukes d'Uzès, and occupies a headland formed by the torrent at its side, that has sawn a chasm through the soft sandstone in its course to join the Rhone. Within the walls may be seen the remains of a small town that clustered there, much like Les Baux, but now completely deserted. The family of Crussol was not of much note till Louis de Crussol gained the favour of Louis XI., and was created his chamberlain, and governor of Dauphiné. The son married the heiress of Uzès, and with her the title of viscount passed to their son Charles, whose son Anthony obtained the title of Duke d'Uzès. There is nothing very remarkable in the story of the Crussols, but the origin of the Uzès is of romantic interest.

There were three brothers, Ebles, Guy, and Pierre, who had a little estate and castle at Uzès near Nimes. There they lived together, unmarried, and in very pinched circumstances. So, one day Ebles said to his brothers that it was a shabby life for three gentlemen thus to live scraping a few coppers together whilst all was beautiful beyond Uzès. Let them all three leave the crumbling walls and leaky roof of Uzès to the bats and owls, and seek their fortunes in the courts of princes.

His advice was relished, and they invited their cousin, named Elias, a comic poet, to travel with them. Now Guy, the youngest of the brothers, and Ebles the eldest, had a pretty gift at poetry, and the second brother, Pierre, had a pleasant pipe, so they agreed that Ebles should write *sirventes*, and Guy *chansons*, and that Pierre should sing them. Moreover, Elias should compose little comedies that could be performed by their small party, and the profits were to be equally shared between them. They also put their hands together and vowed to be true and friendly, and not to separate till they came back to ramshackle Uzès.

So the company started, and went first to the court of Reynald, Viscount of Albuzoni and of Marguerite his wife, who received them with pleasure, both of them being fond of Provençal poetry. The brothers and cousin had great success with their songs and comedies, sent round the hat, and got a handsome sum. Then, when they had sucked their orange, they went farther, mounted like paladins, and passed into the territories of the Countess of Montferrat, who received them quite as cordially as had the Viscount of Albuzoni. There they sang and twanged the guitar, but having unhappily composed some satirical verses under the title of "The Life of the Tyrants" in which the morals and greed of the popes and some of the princes of Europe were chastised, the Papal Legate complained and threatened them with public punishment; he finally imposed silence on them, under threat of excommunication. Then the little company returned home laden with treasures, but sad at heart; and Guy died about 1230. The company must have done pretty well, if Guy founded with his share of the profits the family which later became one of viscounts. I fear dramatic and musical companies nowadays have not the same success.

CHAPTER XXI.

VIENNE.

Historic associations—Salvation Army bonnets—The fair—A quack—A vampire—The amphitrite—A *carousel*—Temple of Augustus and Livia—The Aiguille—Cathedral—Angels and musical instruments—S. André-le-Bas—Situation of Vienne—Foundation of the Church there—Letter of the Church on the martyrdoms at Lyons.

WENT on to Vienne with mind full of thoughts of the Burgundian kingdom of which it was the capital in the fifth century, of S. Avitus, of King Clovis, of Calixtus II., of the condemnation of the Templars at the Council of Vienne in 1307—one of the most cruel and iniquitous deeds done by the Crown of France in compact with the Papacy—and I found myself plunged, unexpectedly, suddenly, into the vortex of a great popular fair. I had passed from a fair in a condition of languor into one in full flush of life.

Which was to be done first, the temple of Augustus and Livia, the remains of the Roman theatre—microscopic I found afterwards—the cathedral of S. Maurice, or the shows?

But surely, the proper study of mankind is man, so I resolved on seeing the fair first, and after that of studying the antiquities, and indulging in antiquarian and historic dreams.

The weather was sorry: wind and threatenings of rain. Moreover it was cold and overcast. Yet nothing damped the ardour of the sellers, and the acquisitiveness of the buyers. But—had I come upon a nursery of hallelujah lasses? Were the nights to be made hideous with Salvation Army howls? On all sides of me were great girls and little girls, matrons and maids, in Salvation Army straws. I turned sick and faint with dismay. In the city of S. Mamertius, of S. Avitus and of Ado—"General" Booth's great Religious Speculation! It was not so, however, I was rejoiced to find, only all the women had been buying straws in the fair of the Salvation Army shape that were selling cheap, and having bought them ran home, trimmed them, and then out they popped again and marched about to show them.

An avenue of booths and stalls. Boots, straw hats and Salvation bonnets, ribbons, kerchiefs, books and engravings. There was even a reduced household selling off all their worldly goods, lamps, chairs, prayer-books, kettles, crocks, linen—and a spinning-wheel. I looked lovingly, longingly at that spinning-wheel, and might have bought it for a franc and a half, and would have done so, had I not been encumbered with the hurdy-gurdy. *That* had brought me into such difficulties that I felt convinced a hurdy-gurdy + a spinning-wheel would lodge me in a lunatic asylum. So reluctantly I left it.

A gust of wind, and away went the straw hats from the stall, up into the air, over the heads of the crowd, spinning along in the gutters ; one, a very kiss-me-quick, was blown slap in the face of an old priest trudging along reading his breviary. Then such outcries, entreaties, objurgations, as the straw hats and bonnets were run after and recovered, or sought to be recovered.

Here—a quack with an assortment of bones that were so brown they looked as if they had been devilled, but they had acquired their tone from his hands. He held up a distorted piece of spine and pelvis, and declared he had a plaster so curative—fifty centimes, ten sous—that it would restraighten the most curved back. As for corns! He raised a horrible foot, applied to it some tow steeped in green fat, rapidly narrated the treatment he recommended—*et voilà !*—he drew away the tow, and the supposed corn was lodged in the midst of it. An inflammation of the lungs ? a darling child sick ? He opened a coffin and exposed a baby skeleton. "Look! your *cher enfant* will be like this, but for fifty centimes I will save it, I guarantee. Pelt me with rotten apples, with addled eggs, if I fail. This plaster placed here (he applied it to the breast of the skeleton), and your child breathes thus (drew a long inhalation)—is well. Warts (a labourer held up a horny hand, the middle joint of the little finger disfigured with such excrescences)? Nothing easier! You take this bottle—warts are my speciality— you rub the wart with this. Thank you, fifty centimes. Come here next Sunday. If the wart be not gone—I do not say it will not leave a scar, but the scar will disappear in a month—here is a knife, stick it into my heart. I give you leave. I will not resist. I will not budge."

Here—a man selling silvering-liquor, to be applied to vulgar yellow spoons, only a franc a bottle, and a whole set turned into

HOUSE IN VIENNE.

purest silver-plating, plating that will not wear out through all your lives.

Then, among the shows :—Cora, the Beautiful Serpent Charmer. Cora was outside beating a drum, and was quite the reverse of beautiful; she may have had the faculty of charming serpents, but not men. A cluster of young soldiers stood without, shook their heads, and would not be allured within.

"Galerie des actualités artistiques"—a peep-show at photographs from the Paris Exhibition.

"The real Vampire, alive, living on BLOOD. Called by the Chinese, from its powers of traversing twenty kilometres in an hour, 'The Flying Horse.'"

The showman was outside, haranguing. His system was to thrill the audience with horror, till they precipitated themselves in a spasm of terror into his show. Just as when one is on a height, a nervous, uncontrollable impulse fills some men to throw themselves down out of very fear of falling, so did this great artist in horrors work up the feelings of his audience to such tension that it became insupportable, they must go headlong in, and see the vampire, if they died for it.

"The vampire is to be seen—smacking his lips—thirsting, ravening, for BLOOD. A live rabbit will be offered him; he will roll his eyes, look at the human beings present, try the bars of his cage—he cannot reach them. En fin, a rabbit is better than nothing! Mesdames, je vous implore! Do not bring your babes within. A stern necessity—a care for the consequences would prevent me from admitting them. The sight of a human babe rouses

At Vienne.

in the vampire the sanguinary passion to a paroxysm of frenzy. In its natural state the vampire sucks the blood of men. This vampire has sucked that of KINGS, and to have to descend to—RABBIT!"

I did not expend my sous to see the wretched bat, but I did lavish thirty centimes on the amphitrite next door. The programme was so characteristically French that I give it:—

"Amphitrite vivante. Tous les soirs au couche du soleil elle laisse son palais royal de coraux et d'algues, et sort des vagues sombres pour jouir de son amour idéal. Légère et vaporeuse comme un ange, elle caresse les ondes, et observe d'un doux regard son idéal, et réplonge au fond de l'océan. Dépeindre avec quelle perfection on présente cette expérience au public est impossible!!!"

Thirty centimes, reserved seats; twenty, unreserved. As it turned out, there were no seats at all, but a slushy soil on which one stood, where the water had run in under the sides of the booth, and which sightseers had, with their boots, churned into mud.

I supposed I was to see a nautilus; it was légère et vaporeux, it could not then be a seal. No, a nautilus. Thirty centimes—here goes for a sight of the nautilus. But it was touching to observe the confidence of the showman. He refused the entrance fee.

"No, gentlemen. You shall yourselves decide whether the amphitrite is worth six sous. If you say not—go forth; I am content, but I pity you."

A piece of drugget served as a curtain, which cut off what may be termed the stage. At a signal the drugget was withdrawn, and the spectators looked into a cave, the sides made of painted calico. Beyond this was the rippling ocean, with the evening sun sparkling on it, much like the scene in "Oberon," only on a very small scale, and with no stage. At a word from the showman, Amphitrite arose. By Ginger! not a nautilus, not a seal, but a living girl of sixteen summers, in fleshings, who floated in the air, made revolutions, waved her hands, stood on her head, touching nothing, precisely as if she really were devoid of all specific gravity. Only when hand or foot touched the calico-rocks did these same rocks begin to wave about.

I supposed at the time, I suppose still, that the trick is done by means of mirrors. But *how*—I cannot conceive. Presently the hat went round for Amphitrite's special benefit: her *amour idéal* had something of the sordid mammon in it. As every-one put a copper into the hat, "Merci, monsieur;

merci, madame!" was what she said. So that there is a difficulty in supposing that the phenomenon was achieved by reflectors. She watched and acknowledged every offering made, as she calmly folded her arms and floated in mid-air, with head on one side, observant.

I can't explain it—I am puzzled still. I paid my thirty centimes with alacrity, so did every one else. The show was worth the money.

There was a merry-go-round—a *carousel ;* the only feature in it with which I was unfamiliar was a ship, sails spread, on a pivot athwart the ring, so that it swayed as on a rolling sea when the *carousel* was in revolution. I would not have entered that ship for twenty francs. Before the orchestrion that accompanied the merry-go-round had accomplished the first strain of Strauss's waltz I should have been feebly calling for the steward. I observed that those silly youngsters with nautical proclivities who did scramble into the swaying ship, got out with livid lips, and did not ask to go in again.

Some years ago I was at Innsprück with a friend. We were sauntering together in the afternoon, not exactly knowing what to do with ourselves, when we found one of these *carousels.* We went farther ; then I said, " We will return and go and see the Xaverianum "—a collection of paintings, mostly daubs, at Innsprück. " No," said my companion, "I don't feel inclined for the Xaverianum, I'll go down by the river." So we parted. Now, I had not gone far along my way in the direction of the Xaverianum, before I said to myself, " I don't want to see the Xaverianum either ; but, as my friend is away—

upon my word—I am unknown here! I'll—yes, I will—by Jove, I will—I'll go and have a round on the whirligig."

So I retraced my steps, and, on reaching the merry-go-round, what should I behold but my friend seated on a piebald horse, with a short sword in his hand, aiming at the targets he passed in his revolution. He was a bald-headed man, with a long grey beard. His face and head became like a beetroot when he saw me; but I comforted him. At Würzburg, in the Episcopal palace, is a *carousel*, in which the bishop—a prince elector—was wont on rainy days to go round and round, seated in a purple velvet chair with the Episcopal arms embroidered on the curtains, and the mitre over it.

Enough of the fair. Now to graver matters; and first the temple of Augustus and Livia. I do not know whether it was that the weather was gloomy, or that the fair had set me out of tune for antiquities; but somehow this temple did not impress me as did the dear little Maison Carrée at Nimes. For one thing the stone is dingy, whereas that of Nimes is bright and white; and the proportions did not please me. I believe the knowing ones say that the Nimes temple is not proportioned according to the laws of Vitruvius, and this at Vienne is. If that be the case, then I am sorry for Vitruvius. The temple is structurally perfect—as perfect as that of Nimes.

Another object of interest is the Aiguille, a Roman obelisk seventy-six feet high. There is a square base, pierced by arches in each face, and the obelisk, or pyramid rather, stands on this. It is not very beautiful, but it is worth examining. It is thought that the monument to Marius at Pourrières was somewhat similar.

The cathedral of Vienne is of sandstone, and has decayed accordingly. The west end, which was very rich, and is rich still, has suffered from corrosion in the upper part; but a firmer, less friable sandstone was fortunately employed for the lower stage, in which is the richest sculpture, and that is fairly perfect. Murray pooh-poohs this west front: "It is rich in flamboyant ornaments, but they are clumsy and without delicacy." The sculpture was adapted to the material, and any other would not have looked well. After the severe and bald west fronts in Provence, I was disposed, I suppose, to be pleased with the rich façade at Vienne. I confess that "clumsy and without delicacy" though it might be, I thoroughly enjoyed it.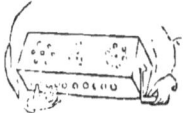

HURDY-GURDY PLAYED BY AN ANGEL.

But that façade caught me quite by my weak point. There is a central doorway, and one into each aisle, and round the archways into these lateral doors are sculptured angels playing upon musical instruments. As I have told the reader, ancient forms of musical instruments are my hobby, or rather one of my hobbies. I at once pulled out my sketchbook and drew them; there are angels with fiddles, angels with viols—no, not hurdy-gurdys!—but twanged with the fingers, angels with pipes and horns, one with a harp, two with portable organs of ten pipes in each, two angels with bagpipes with single drones. Conceive of a salutation on bagpipes from the celestial choir!

An angel plays the cymbals, and another with a plectrum strikes a metal disc.

The interior of the cathedral is remarkable for the peculiarly fine sculpture of the capitals of the pillars. The foliage is of exquisite loveliness and variety ; but over the transept door is a very Brueghel creation of horrors—in fact, the zodiacal signs worked up together into a nightmare.

CHURCH OF S. ANDRÉ-LE-BAS.
THE TOWER.

A church of remarkable interest in Vienne is S. André-le-Bas ; it has in it two Roman marble Corinthian columns supporting the arch of the apse, and a Corinthian capital used as a font.

The situation of Vienne is remarkable, it resembles one of the towns on the Rhine, where the river is contracted among hills. The mountains rise immediately behind the city, and are crowned with old castles. The space between the river and the bases of the heights is small, and the city is somewhat cramped accordingly. But the Gère issues from the hills on the north, and gives some scope for the suburbs of the old town to creep up its banks.

Vienne is one of the most ancient towns of Gaul, it was the capital of the Allobroges; it claims as the founder of the Church there Crescens, disciple of S. Paul. Crescens, it will be remembered, was sent by Paul into Galatia. That was quite sufficient for these Gallic enthusiasts, who desired to give to the French bishoprics Apostolic founders. They supposed that Galatia was a slip of the pen for Gallia, and argued, if to Gallia, then to Vienne, the most ancient and important city therein, *q.e.d.* But no bishop of Vienne appears fixed with any certainty before Verus, who attended the Council of Arles in A.D. 314. It is, however, quite certain that the Church was founded there before A.D. 150; for one of the most precious and authentic records of the early Church we have is the letter written by the Vienne Christians to those of the East, recording the martyrdom of the bishop Pothinus of Lyons.

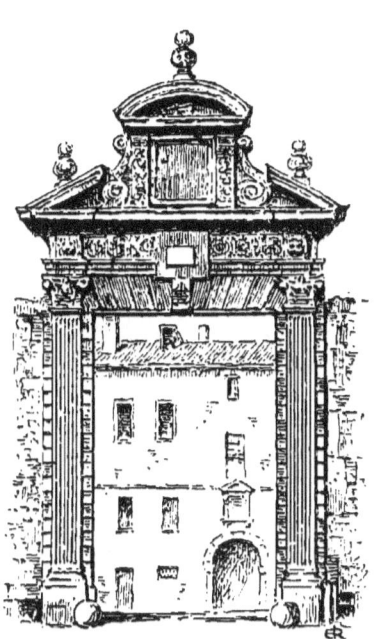

PORTE DE L'AMBULANCE, VIENNE.

X

It used to be said of the old Gallo-Roman city that its wealth was so great that the streets were paved with mosaic. Now one would be thankful for a bit that was smooth. The pavement is almost as bad as that of Arles.

CHAPTER XXII.

BOURGES.

The siege of Avaricum by Cæsar—The complete subjugation of Gaul—The statue of the Dying Gaul at Rome—Beauty of Bourges—The cathedral—Not completed according to design—Defect in height—Strict geometrical proportion in design not always satisfactory—Necessity of proportion for acoustics—Domestic architecture in Bourges—The house of Jacques Cœur—Story of his life—A rainy day—Why Bourges included in this book—A silver thimble—*Que de singeries faites-vous là Madeleine ?*—Adieu.

BOURGES stands in the very forefront of Gaulish history marked by a great disaster. There, on a little height at the junction of the Yèvre and the Auron, the gallant Bituriges had their capital, Avaricum. In six campaigns Cæsar had, as he believed, broken the neck of all resistance, and Gaul was under the iron heel of Rome. "My aunt Julia," said Cæsar, "is, maternally, the daughter of kings ; paternally——" he passed his fingers through his curled and scented locks—" paternally, she is

X 2

descended from the immortal gods." After that, even barbarians must feel that it was in vain to strive against a man thus preordained to mastery. Yet they did not see it.

When Julius Cæsar was in Rome, after six years of stubborn conflict, after incredible suffering and bloodshed, the heart of the people though bowed down was not broken.

There lived among the Arvernians, in the high mountainland, among the volcanic peaks of Auvergne, as it is now called, a young chief, whose real name is not known, but whom history calls Vercingetorix, that is, Head over a Hundred Tribes. The time was come for an united, determined, and desperate resistance. He sent messengers throughout Gaul. The downtrodden inhabitants rose to a man and invested Vercingetorix with the chief command.

In the year of Rome 702, B.C. 32, Cæsar was suddenly informed in Italy that his work of six years was threatened with ruin. Most of the Gallic nations, united under a chieftain hitherto unknown, were rising with one common impulse, and recommencing war.

Cæsar at once returned to Gaul. He had one quality, rare even amongst the greatest men, he remained cool amidst the hottest alarms. He was always quick, never hasty. He placed himself at the head of his troops, and, in the early part of March, moved to what is now Sens, the very centre of revolt, and looked round to decide where first to strike.

Vercingetorix from the outset knew that the ill-armed and worse disciplined Gauls could not cope in the open field with Cæsar and the Roman legions ; he therefore formed a plan of campaign that required great sacrifices on the side of the Gauls, for the sake of the common safety. No walls, he assured the confederates, could withstand the skill of the Romans in engineering, no array maintain itself in the field against their phalanx. But he reminded them that through the winter and early spring the soil on which the enemy trod could not furnish him with provision. He must disperse his troops among the fortresses. Let then, said he, no further attempts be made to defy the Roman in the open field ; let him rather be followed in detail, and cut off when separated into cantonments, and above all, let the towns that served him for magazines be destroyed by the hands of the inhabitants themselves. He recommended in fact the very course pursued more than eighteen hundred years later by the Russians against the French Cæsar, a course which proved fatal to him.

The assembled council of Gaulish states assented gallantly to this proposal. In one day twenty cities of the Bituriges were flaming, and similar havoc was made throughout the territories of the allies. But when the fate of Avaricum (Bourges) came to be discussed, the hearts of the Bituriges failed them. Their deputies knelt to the assembled chiefs and interceded for the preservation of their beautiful, and as they deemed it, impregnable city. The council yielded. In vain did Vercingetorix urge them to carry out their determination without exception. They would surrender every other city to the flames, but not their loved capital, not Avaricum.

The situation was admirably calculated for defence. It stood on rising ground, and the only approach to it then was a causeway between the river and a morass. The garrison laboured night and day to strengthen their defences with earthworks and with palisades of sharpened stakes. The Romans at once moved from Sens and surrounded the place. The story of its fall I will take from the graphic pen of Dean Merivale:—"Whilst the Bituriges within their city were hard pressed by the machinery which the Roman engineers directed against their walls, the forces of the proconsul on their side were harassed by the fatigues of the siege and the scarcity of provisions. Cæsar is lavish of praise in speaking of the fortitude with which his soldiers bore their privations; they refused to allow him to raise the siege,

A STREET CORNER, BOURGES.

and when he at last led them against the enemy's army, and finding it too strongly posted for an attack, withdrew them again within their lines, they submitted to the disappointment, and betook themselves once more without a murmur to the tedious operations of the blockade. The skill of the assailants at length triumphed over the bravery of the defenders. The walls were approached by towers at various points, and mounds constructed against which the combustible missiles of the besieged were unavailing. Finally, a desperate sally was repulsed, and then, at last the constancy of the Bituriges began to fail. Taking advantage of a moment when the watch on the walls had relaxed its vigilance, Cæsar marshalled his legions behind his works, and poured them suddenly against the opposing ramparts. They gained the summit of the walls, which the defenders abandoned without a blow, rallying, however, in the middle of the town, in such hasty array as the emergency would allow. A bloody struggle ensued; both parties were numerous, and the assailants gave no quarter. The Gauls were routed and exterminated, their women and children mercilessly slaughtered, and the great central city of Gaul fell into the hands of the conquerors without affording a single captive for their triumph." After that the fate of the insurrection was sealed. The war was carried on with fluctuations of fortune even into an eighth campaign, and then the yoke of Rome, iron, and doubly weighted with the wrath of the conqueror, was riveted on to the neck of prostrate Gallia, never again to be shaken off.

Now, day after day at Rome during the winter had

I stood before the Dying Gaul in the Capitoline Museum, that statue of incomparable pathos :—

> "He leans upon his hand—his manly brow
> Consents to death, but conquers agony,
> And his drooped head sinks gradually low—
> From the red gash fall heavy, one by one,
> Like the first of a thunder-shower; and now
> The arena swims around him—he is gone,
> Ere ceased the inhuman shout which hailed the wretch who won."
>
> *Childe Harold.*

The statue is not of a Dying Gladiator, but of a Gaulish chief, who has dealt himself the death-wound rather than fall into servitude to the Roman, and then has broken his sword.

And, after having looked and dreamed over that figure, could one come to Bourges and not think of that heroic and fatal struggle?

Bourges was a beautiful city in those times, loved by the Bituriges so that they could not resolve to destroy it; but oh! how beautiful it is now, with its quaint Mediæval and Renaissance houses, and above all that most glorious cathedral, one of the very finest creations of art in the world. And yet, it is not perfect. The original design was not carried out. The nave has not the height proposed. Funds failed, and it was finished off as best might be. It wants about forty-six feet of the height it should have had, to be in correct proportion. The flying buttresses outside were designed and executed to carry a vaulting some forty-six feet higher than the present one, and they are now of no use; they sustain nothing, all the outward thrust of the central vault is thrown on the second stage of buttresses. Fine as is the interior, it ought to be finer. The clerestory windows are dwarfed, and the height of the side aisles is felt to be out of all proportion to that of the nave. Moreover, there is nothing of the wonderful skill of design in the apsidal chapels, that is seen at Amiens, Vezelai, Beauvais, &c. Instead of forming an integral portion of the plan, they are mere excrescences in the sides of the apse.

However, in spite of defects, partly in design, but mainly through lack of means to carry it out, the cathedral of Bourges is of singular beauty. In one point the architect was a greater man than the designers of Amiens and Cologne. These two cathedrals are in strict proportion in all their parts. The designer of each, like the architect of York Minster, was a great man with the compasses. But an architect should be artist as well as geometrician. I have ever felt in York Minster, in Amiens and Cologne, that there is a lack of genius, of the human soul in the creation. There is strict formality, exact rule, that is all. No allowance has been made for effect of perspective, for the foreshortening to the eye at distances; there is no poetry in these three cathedrals. The designers drew them out on paper without having the faculty of seeing them in their minds' eye rise before them out of the soil. These churches made better sketches than they do structures. They are in admirable proportion on paper, but they are out of proportion when seen in stone. Now such architects as the men who designed Beauvais and Bourges were geniuses. They were not tied hard and fast by rule of compass. They worked from a definite geometric plan, but deviated from it where their taste and feeling for beauty taught them that such deviation was advisable. Now at Beauvais and at Bourges the exact proportions have been abandoned. For instance, at Bourges, to be exact, each of the two side aisles should have been half the width of the nave. But the architect was perhaps afraid of the great span, perhaps he dreaded too great formality, and he made the aisle next to the nave about 2 ft. 3 in. less than the width it ought to have had, if in exact proportion. The outer aisle was given almost, but not quite, the exact proportional width.

The great defect of our modern architects is that they do not work from a foundation of geometrical proportion, but design out of their own heads by eye; we are sometimes distressed at finding that our churches recently built are bad acoustically. This is very generally due to the fact that they have been built regardless of geometric proportion.

If Bourges had been carried out as intended, the crown of the vault would have been exactly seven times half the width of the nave. S. Servin, Toulouse, has the keystone of the vault exactly five times the half width. If we desire to have good acoustic qualities in our churches and halls we must observe some such rule. So with the plan. The length of Autun is seven times the width of the nave; Beauvais the same, or would have been, had the nave been completed. Amiens has exactly the same proportion, measured to the end of the apse. So Noyon. In fact, the Mediæval architects were careful to build so as never to give even proportions. Twice, four times, six times, would have had bad acoustic effects. There would have been an echo.

Of the sculpture on the west façade, the richly, deeply-recessed portals, I will not speak. That has been sufficiently observed and admired by other writers. I am not writing a guide-book, and I do not as a rule notice at any length what may be found in easily-accessible works. Here, as at Rouen, is a butter tower, so called because built with money paid for indulgence to be allowed to eat butter in Lent. Does the reader know how strictly the observance of Lent was enforced down to the Civil Wars in England? I have gone through some episcopal registers of our English bishops since the Reformation, and find that in James I.'s time a bishop's licence was sought to obtain permission to eat meat in Lent. Not only so, but all schoolmasters, surgeons, and midwives were required to obtain an episcopal licence before being permitted to practise in the diocese.

In Bourges one feels that one is removed altogether from the influences that moulded architecture in Provence. There the abundance of Classic remains affected the minds and formed the taste of the Mediæval builders. In Central France there were few traces of the Roman conquerors, and Gothic architecture developed freely according to its own genius. The domestic architecture is different. We come now to the gables standing over the street. There are many and charming specimens in Bourges. Among the houses is that of Cujas, concerning whom some anecdotes have already been told. Bourges was famous for its University and School of Laws, and Cujas was invited to a professorship in it. The house is of brick, of the sixteenth century, and richly adorned. Another interesting house is that of Charles VII., with a graceful staircase, and an old hall with open fireplace. But the most striking mansion of all is that of Jacques Cœur, the Bourges jeweller, father of an Archbishop of this his native city. Throughout the house is introduced his canting device, a human heart and the scallop-shell of S. James. His motto is also graven, "A vaillants cœurs rien impossible."

PART OF JACQUES CŒUR'S HOUSE.

I hate doing a thing again and in an inferior manner that has already been done inimitably; and Madame Parkes-Belloc, with her fresh pen dipped in sunlight has written about Bourges and Jacques Cœur's house in her charming book, 'La Belle France,'* and I dare not tread after her. So I simply quote her words—I fear her pleasant book is not much sought after and read now:—" His dwelling must have fitted Jacques Cœur as its skin fits an animal. All its quaint architectural corners seem, as it were, wrinkles and creases, whereby it adapted itself to the nature and genius of the man. We, in our day, know nothing of such a style of building. If we want a large house we send for an architect, who submits his plans to our enlightened judgment; allotting ample stairs, a sufficiency of best bedrooms, kitchen, butler's pantry, &c. If rather less, then rather cheaper; and as to making the slightest difference in style on account of our late pursuits, as whether, for instance, we were a retired candlestick-maker, or a Lord Chancellor, or a physician, the very idea would savour of lunacy. Not so Jacques Cœur. This man wished, in dying, to leave a beautiful shell behind him, so that the passers-by might say: 'Here lived a great merchant; he had a wife, sons, and a daughter, and numerous domestics. He liked his money, but loved art more. He kept a negro; he was pious, also loyal. He didn't mind fighting, if needs must be; but preferred commerce and politics. He loved Bourges, and Bourges loved him; for he paid his workmen well.' All this, and more, Jacques Cœur continued to write in legible characters on the walls of his house,

* Published in 1868.

some of it on the outside, some of it on the inside."

He had humour, a quaint conceit, this man of gold and jewelry. He had the very knocker to his door made to strike upon a *heart*. Under the eaves of his observatory he had his negro sculptured hugging his money-box, and a little beyond an angel exhibiting his newly-acquired coat-of-arms. The one led to the other—the money-box brought on gentility. Hard by is the shield of an allied commercial family, their coat one of *fleurs-de-lis* interspersed with woolsacks. The Fuggers of Augsburg, when desiring a coat, asked Maximilian for lilies—for, said these wealthy spinners—as for the lilies, " *They* toil not, neither do they spin." With droll invention Jacques had one of his fireplaces made like a fortress, with little windows above, out of which folk are peeping. He had a gift for pungent mottoes. Here are some he had wrought into the decorations of his house :—

> " A close bouche
> Il n'entre mouche."

Another is :—

> " Entendre, taire,
> Dire, et faire,
> Est ma joie."

I remember a merchant's house, very sumptuous, at Schaffhausen, on which he had written this bitter device—"God preserve me from my friends; I will protect myself from my enemies." Another man altogether from Jacques Cœur.

The ending of this bright, merry, pomp-loving

merchant was sad. He fell into disgrace with his king—he had probably lent him too much money; he was accused falsely of several crimes—forging money and selling arms to infidels, and was thrown into prison. The king then seized his wealth, tore up the bills in his name, and left one of Jacques' sons only a remnant of his treasure and the house. Jacques Cœur managed to escape from prison, got to Rome, and was taken into favour by Nicolas V. and Calixtus III., and was appointed captain of an expedition against the Turks. He is thought to have been wounded in a skirmish with them, for he is known to have died in Chios. And so he passed his old age, and laid his bones far from the house he had built for himself in which to end his days, and was not buried in the chapel of the cathedral which he had constructed as his mausoleum.

TURRET IN THE HOTEL LALLEMAND.

Another very delightful old house in Bourges is

STAIRCASE IN THE HÔTEL LALLEMAND.

the Hôtel Lallemand, constructed after the great fire of 1487; there is another in the Rue des Toiles, and another again in the Rue S. Suplice.

The reader may ask —If you are writing a book on Provence and Languedoc, why give us Bourges? Bourges, which is in Berry, which is in the very centre of France? For the same reason that I began with Florence. One does not drop out of a balloon into Provence, nor ascend out of it by one. One must stay somewhere in going there, and stay somewhere and see something on leaving there. And as my stay at Florence led on as a sort of preface to my flight up and down in Provence, so will this chapter on Bourges serve as an epilogue. For, in verity, as my encounter with the Jew dealer served me as an introduction so shall a little incident I met with in Bourges serve me as an easy mode of making my exit with a bow.

It was raining. It had rained all day. The interior of the cathedral, dark at all times with its deep-dyed (and dirty) glass, was in darkness, too deep to see and study much. The gurgoyles were spouting, the eaves dripping, the gutters running as mountain torrents. However, towards sunset, the windows of heaven were closed, the rain ceased, and folk who had been indoors all day came out with umbrellas and pattered and splashed about.

Now, by some fatality a thimble had been brought down from the roof of one of the houses by a descending water-spout; perhaps a dragon-gurgoyle had spat it disdainfully down. How had the thimble got on the roof? That was the question, not how it got down into the gutter. Had a cunning jackdaw, as in the 'Gazza di Ladra' carried it off, or had a child tumbled it out of an attic window on to the leads?

I was not the only person interested in this thimble. There was a young man, a student, a French exquisite, who also observed it; and I saw him poking at it in the water with the ferrule of his umbrella. Indeed it was his behaviour towards the thimble that attracted my attention to it. Presently he managed to extricate the thimble from the flood, to lodge it on a paving-stone, but it was slippery and round, and rolled off between two cobbles. Then he put up his eye-glass and studied it. Was it worth soiling his fingers over or not? Was it of silver or of brass? He walked

Y

round the thimble, with his eye-glass up, stood astride over the little torrent that had brought it down, stiffened his back, clapped the umbrella under his arm, and pursed up his lips to consider. Then he formed his resolution, stooped, and with the extreme point of his forefinger turned the thimble about. Then he stood erect again, pulled out a pocket handkerchief—saw it was of spotless cleanliness, considered that it would cost him two sous to have it washed if he dirtied it by drying thereon his forefinger, replaced it, and put his finger up his back under his coat tails and wiped it on the calico of his waistcoat.

He had made up his mind to have nothing more to do with the thimble, when along the *trottoir* came tripping a pretty damsel, with the purest of white caps, a sallow face, with fine dark eyes and abundant black hair. She bore over her shoulder, expanded, a plum-coloured umbrella. It had ceased raining, but the plum-colour threw out her pleasant face into relief: she knew that, and tripped on without folding it.

Instantly down bent the student, and, regardless of the dirty water, picked up the thimble. It slipped from his fingers into the gutter. Boldly he plunged his hand in, soiling thereby his *manchette;* but he recovered the trifle. The girl was abreast of him, and had passed before he was prepared.

He now pulled out a dogskin glove and polished the article. It *was* silver. He affixed it to the end of his little finger and waited his opportunity.

Three ladies approached. The youth plucked up courage—holding out his little finger shod with the thimble. It was like Paris and the Three Goddesses.

The ladies looked at him, at his thimble, then at each other, tossed their heads, and walked on.

Then came a very ugly woman—the exquisite put the thimble resolutely behind his back.

Next—back, under her plum-coloured umbrella, returned the grisette. At once the dandy stood forward.

"Mademoiselle, as you passed just now, assuredly you dropped this."

SCULPTURE OVER THE KITCHEN ENTRANCE AT JACQUES CŒUR'S HOUSE.

"Mais, Monsieur! ce n'est pas possible. Ce n'est pas à moi."

"Pardon, mademoiselle, you dropped it; I saw you. I heard it fall."

"Cependant,—it is not mine."

"Then it is nobody's. I will throw it away."

"Mais, monsieur, it is of silver."

"Take it, mademoiselle, I pray."

She held the little silver thimble between thumb

and forefinger, turned it about, studied it, hesitated, was inclined to take it, but did not wish to place herself under an obligation to a fop, and a stranger—knitted her brows—when up came a young workman, with a lead pencil in his hand—in his blouse.

"Mais! que de singeries faites-vous là, Madeleine?" said he, and flip!—with his pencil he sent the thimble out from her hand, flying—neither he, nor the girl, nor I saw whither it went, or where it fell.

And—just thus stands the author of this little work, offering his trifle to the gentle and well-disposed reader, who is inclined, may be, to be pleased with it, and to adopt it. But up comes the envious reviewer, and with his pen—flip—he sends the poor little article away—away—away, into the limbo of forgotten books, "que de singeries faites-vous là—avec cette bagatelle là?

JACQUES CŒUR'S KNOCKER.

APPENDIX.

A.—Monuments from the Alyscamps.

1. THE inscription to Cornelia, daughter of Marius, is something of a puzzle. Against its genuineness may be urged that he is represented as conqueror of the Cimbri, whereas the Cimbri were not defeated till the following year, near Vercelli. Now it is strange that he should have left his daughter at Arles instead of moving her into Italy; and it is also odd that, if she were left there, he should be designated as conqueror of the Cimbri, whereas in the engagement with the Cimbri he shared the glory with Catulus; and he alone was victor over the Teutons and Ambrons near Aix. Moreover, one would have supposed that at Arles he would have been entitled the conqueror of these latter, the terror of whom had fallen on the province, and not of the Cimbri who did not menace it.

On the other hand, the inscription is in shockingly bad Latin; Calpurnia is made conqueror of the Cimbri, not her father, by a grammatical blunder; and one would suspect a forger would have avoided such a grotesque error, which is quite in agreement with other blunders made by the sculptors of monuments in the Alyscamps, who were clearly Gallo-Greeks, and hardly understood Latin.

Also—and this is remarkable—the name of the girl is Calpurnia; and Caius Marius was a native of Arpinum, and when this town was taken by the Romans from the Samnites, in B.C. 188, the franchise was given to the inhabitants, who were enrolled in the Calpurnian *gens*. Now this is a little fact that it is most improbable a forger would know—but it quite explains the girl receiving the name of Calpurnia, if genuine.

2. The Tomb of Julia Tyranna. The inscription runs :—

    IVLIÆ . LVC . FILIÆ . TYRANNIÆ .
    VIXIT ANN . XX . M . VIII .
    QVÆ MORIBVS . PARITER . ET .
    DISCIPLINA . CETERIS . FEMINIS .
    EXEMPLO . FVIT . ANTARCIVS .
    NVRVI . LAVRENTIVS . VCXORI .

It was raised to her memory by her father-in-law Antarcius, and by her husband, Laurentius. The organ is represented with seven pipes.

3.
    O DOLOR . QVANTÆ
    LACHRIMÆ . FECERE
    SEPVLCRVM . IVL . LV
    CINÆ . QVÆ . VIXIT . KA
D .   RISSIMA . MATRI . FLOS . Æ   M .
    TATIS . HIQ . IACET . INTVS .
    CONDITA . SAXOO . VTINAM .
    POSSIT . REPARARI . SPIRITVS . ILLE .
    VT . SCIRET . QVANTVS . DOLOR . EST .
    QVÆ . VIXIT . ANN . XXVII . M . X . DIE XIII .
    IVL . PARTHENOPE . POSVIT . INFELIX MATER .

"O Grief! what tears have watered this tomb of

Julia Lucina who in life was very dear to her mother. Carried off in the flower of her age, here she lies, buried in this marble tomb. Would that her spirit might be restored, that she might learn how great is my grief. She lived twenty-seven years, ten months, and thirteen days. Julia Parthenope, her unhappy mother, raised this."

4.   HYDRIÆ TERTVLLÆ
           C . F . CONIVGI . AMANTISSI
           MÆ ET AXIÆ OELIANÆ .
           FILIÆ DVLCISSIMÆ .
           TERENTIVS MVSEVS
           HOC SEPVLCRVM
           POSVIT .

" Terentius Musæus placed this to his most loving wife, Hydria Tertulla, and to his most sweet daughter, Axia Œliana." On this is a child with a cock in hand, an oblation to the infernal deities.

5.   F . MARIO . MF .
           MARINO .
           EXS . TESTA MENTO .

Observe in this, as in No. 3, the queer spelling, in both phonetic :—HIQ, SAXOO, EXS.

6. Here is a Christian inscription :—

INTEGER . ATQVE . PIVS . VITA . ET . CORPORE . PVRVS .
ÆTERNO . HIC . POSITVS . VIVIT . CONCORDIVS . ÆVO .
QVI . TENERIS . PRIMVM . MINISTER . FVLSIT .
IN . ANNIS .
POST . ETIAM . LECTVS . COELESTI . LEGE . SACERDOS

TRIGINTA . ET GEMINOS . DECEM . VIX . REDDIDIT .
ANNOS .
HVNC . CITO . SIDEREAM . RAPTVM . OMNIPOTENTIS .
IN AVLAM
MATER . BLANDA . ET . FRATER . SINE FVNERE
QVÆRVNT .

"Intact and pious, pure in life and body, here lies buried, but eternally lives Concordius, who in his tender years shone first as a deacon, afterwards chosen by the celestial law a priest; he lived hardly fifty years. Transported too soon to the starry hall of the Almighty, his gentle mother and his brother seek him without bewailing him."

This is on a sarcophagus of white marble with a colonnade carved on the face, the pillars channeled and spiral. In the centre is Jesus Christ, seated on a throne, instructing His apostles and a crowd, which is seen through the arcade, at the right a man, on the left a woman, on the cover are the twelve apostles with rolled volumes before them. This sarcophagus belongs to the fourth century.

7.   PAX ÆTERNA
DVLCISSIMÆ . ET . INNOCEN
TISSIM . FILLIÆ . CHRYSOGONE . IV
NIOR . SIRICIO . QVÆ . VIX . ANN . III .
M . II . DIEB . XXVII . VALERIVS . ET . CHRY
SOGONE . PARENTES . FILLIÆ . KARIS
SIMÆ . ET . OMNI . TEMPORE . VI
TÆ . SVE . DESIDERANTISS .
M . A . E .

"Peace eternal to the most sweet and innocent girl, Chrysogone (the younger) Siricio, who lived three years, three months, and twenty-seven days. Valerius and Chrysogone, her parents, raised this monument to their most dear daughter, whom they will regret all their lives."

The bones were found in a leaden coffin enclosed in one of stone. The body of the little Chrysogone had been enveloped in a rich brocade of gold thread and silk.

8. A curious column dedicated by the good people of Arles to Flavius Valerius Constantinus (Constantine the Great), son of Constantius, long served the boatmen on the Rhone to fasten their vessels to, and it is sadly furrowed by the chains and cords so employed. It bears the inscription :—

IMP . CÆS . FL . VAL . CONSTANTINO
P . F . AVG . DIVI CONSTANTI .
AVG . RII . FILIO .

Constantius Chorus also bore the names of Flavius Valerius.

B.—THE CAMPAIGN OF MARIUS.

For determining this the following points must be settled :—

I. *Where was his camp?*

To fix the position of his camp we must see where he could best watch the barbarians cross the Rhone, in such a place as he would have his rear covered, and where he could keep open his communications with Rome, and receive both reinforcements and victuals.

Now there is absolutely no point that answers these requirements like S. Gabriel. It was certain that the barbarians would not cross at Arles, for they could not advance thence south of the chain of Les Alpines, owing to the lagoons and morasses, and the desert of the Great Crau. They must cross below Avignon and at or above Tarascon. Now, as they would almost certainly march along the high table-land that extends from Montpellier by Nimes to Beaucaire, and not wade through the marshes below these hills, they would arrive with dry feet at Beaucaire, and there, naturally would cross and follow up the valley of the Durance. S. Gabriel was a natural watch-tower, whence Marius could observe them. It is an ancient Roman settlement. Numerous Roman remains have been found there. Marius had but to mount the heights behind the little town, and he commanded all the country to the north-west and south for a vast distance. Then, again, by means of his canal, connecting the lagoons, he was able to bring ships with supplies under his walls. His canal opened out of the Etang de Galéjon, with a station at Fos, not at the exact entrance of the canal, which was low and marshy, but at the entrance of the channel of Martigues that opens into the Etang de Berre. Through Galéjon it ran north, cutting through a chain of lagoons, passed under Mont Majeur to S. Gabriel, and there probably received the waters, the overspill of the Durance, above Château Renard. Plutarch says that it was connected with the Rhone, but this was probably an error. Its course to S

Gabriel remained in use and falling into decay in the Middle Ages as the Canal des Lonnes. Between S. Gabriel and the Etang de Galéjon it could also be traced, and bore the name of Le Vigueirat. This canal of Marius was perfectly protected from the barbarians by the morasses that intervened between it and the Rhone.

II. *To determine his march.*

The old pre-Roman road from Nimes to Aix certainly followed the high and dry ground to Tarascon, thence traced up the valley of the Durance. It could no longer follow the high ground, as that is broken into limestone peaks, but it followed up the river below them, carried above the rubble of the Durance. The first station after Tarascon was Glanum, now S. Remi. Then it went to Orgon, where it touched the Durance for the first time, and whence branched the roads to Italy—one by Mont Genèvre, the other by Aix and the coast. I suppose that Marius, following the barbarians, he on the heights, they in the valley, observed the direction they took to right or to left, from the precipitous crags of Orgon. It must be remembered that Marius had an army made up of demoralised soldiers, who had escaped from defeat by the barbarians, and of raw levies, and all were in deadly fear of their savage foes, so that he dare not bring them to a pitched battle till they had become accustomed to the sight of the Teutons and Ambrons, and were themselves impatient to come to blows with them.

The host of invaders turned south towards Aix. Marius pursued: there can, I think, be little question that he pursued the same tactics, exchanging a sandstone range for one of limestone, and following them steadily step by step, keeping the heights.

Now, if the camp of Marius was at S. Gabriel, and if the Teutons marched up the Durance valley to Orgon, and then turned to Aix, then, it seemed to me, on the spot, that no one save an idiot in command of the Roman soldiers could have done anything else than strike for the sandstone ridge and march along that, still observing the enemy.

Another theory relative to the Roman road is that it ran south of the chain of Les Alpines. This would not matter for the course of Marius, but would explain the fact of the monument of Marius being found at Les Baux; and Les Baux would then be the cliff whence he watched the march of the barbarians.

III. *To determine the position of the battles.*

Plutarch does not distinguish between sites. He says that there were two battles separated from one another by two days, and that in the first Marius defeated the Ambrons. In the second he defeated the Teutons. He leaves us to infer that both battles were fought on the same field. But there are difficulties in supposing this.

1. The field of Pourrières does not answer the description of the first battle site; it does that of the second.

2. The Ambrons alone were engaged in the first battle, and no Teutons came to their help. We may therefore fairly suppose that the two great bodies of barbarian invaders had separated.

3. There was a very tempting bait, Marseilles lying to the south, inviting attack and pillage.

Following M. Gilles in his monograph on the campaign of Marius, I believe that the first battle was fought at Les Milles, the first station out of Aix on the Marseilles road, and that the Ambrons had parted company with the Teutons so as to try their luck with Marseilles, or perhaps only so as to ravage the coast, if they could make no impression on a walled city.

Now, the sandstone ridge along which Marius and his army were marching, as I suppose, ends abruptly above Les Milles. Below flows the river Are, making a loop in which is a rich green meadow, and under the hill ooze out countless rills of water. Indeed, the bottom of the hill is dense with irises loving the slushy percolated soil. There is no water on the sandstone heights. Here, if I am right, Marius came out and saw the Ambrons below, and wanted to form his camp, but was deterred by an engagement being begun by the water-carriers of the camp going down to the river and springs with their pails, and being attacked by the Ambrons. Aix lies away to the north in a broad basin, and at some little distance, two kilos., from the river. The battle could not have happened there. There is no other place save Les Milles where we have hill, river, green plain and springs together, as in Plutarch's narrative. Let us then suppose that Marius fought the first battle at Les Milles and there defeated the Ambrons. Those not slain would fly along the Aurelian road that leads from Aix through the plain of Pourrières, crosses a low *col*, and enters the valley of the Argens, and leads to Fréjus, where

I suppose Teutons and Ambrons designed to meet again, and pursue their course westward together. In the meantime the Teutons had been advancing up the Are valley along the Aurelian way. A mile and a half out of Aix they reached the Are, five miles above Les Milles, and thence followed up the river for three miles, when they left it. Their road now lay due east before them, across the almost level plain of Pourrières, below the limestone precipice to the north of Mont Victoire. But there is a curious formation here. South of Mont Victoire is a semicircular sandstone chain, inferior in height, precipitous towards the plain, called Le Cengle, "the Belt," dying into the limestone mountain at the point where the latter attains its greatest altitude, above the village of Puyloubier. This sandstone girdle slopes easily inward to the precipice of Mont Victoire, and its rills flow together into a little stream that reaches the Are at the point where the Aurelian road left it, *i.e.* seven and a half miles from Aix.

M. Gilles supposes that Marius followed on the heels of the flying Ambrons along the Aurelian way, and that he detached Marcellus at this point to go up this little stream behind the Cengle and come out farther east so as to gain Pain de Munition.

I do not think this is tenable, for there is a long tract of bare hill-slope between the extremity of the Cingle and the conical fortified hill of Pain de Munition, and even if Marcellus were concealed whilst ascending this little lateral valley, he would emerge in full view of the barbarians for the last five or six miles of his march. My belief is that Marcellus was despatched up the valley of the Infernet, behind Mont Victoire, by which means his march would be concealed throughout, nor would it be much longer.

Also, I do not think that Marius pursued the Teutons the whole way along the road. According to Plutarch's account, the second time he came on them so as to cause them surprise. Again, if he had pursued a certain plan up to the first engagement, and it had succeeded, it is likely that he would follow the same plan up to the second and final engagement. Now hitherto he had kept to high ground always to the south of the advancing horde. From Les Milles he very probably, as I think, only followed the traces of the flying Ambrons along the road till he struck the Are in the open plain of Pourrières, and then at once crossed to the south bank of the river, and marched along on ground that slopes up to the south, so that he had the river between him and the enemy. If, as is probable, this hill-slope, along which the rail now runs, was then, more than now, dense with broom and pine, his march would not be seen by the enemy. And so I conclude Marius by a forced march reached Trets. Then, as I have said in my text, he had the enemy in a trap. Behind them was the fortified camp of Pain de Munition into which he had thrown Marcellus, and behind him he had the chain of Mont Aurélien and Mont Olympe, with another fortified camp. Between him and the enemy was a slope, and this was cut by streams that had torn their way through a friable marly soil. Moreover, he had a natural screen of rock between him and the enemy, with the low face towards him, and an easy slope towards the barbarians.

The actual site of the camp of the Teutons is fixed without very much doubt. They would certainly camp in the first available situation near water. Now they had been marching for five miles without water, and on reaching the Are at the station Tegulata, they found an admirable site, three tofts of dry level sandstone apparently made for their purpose. Moreover, opposite them is the ruin of the monument of Marius. About the ruin there might have been doubts whether it was Roman, and whether it referred to the victory, but for the discovery there of the statue of Venus Victrix, which sets that question at rest for ever.

M. Gilles supposes that the battle was fought along the road, when the Teutons saw Marius overtake them in pursuit, and that it began at a point about a mile due west, at Le Logis Neuf. If it had been so, then surely the monument would have been on the west side of Tegulata, and north of the Are. The tradition that it raged from north to south between the bridge and Trets is only of value from its being based on the masses of weapons, bronze and flint, found on the south side of the river, and not on the north.

There is something too to be said for what common sense would point out. Standing on the red sandstone hill above Les Milles, and looking at Aix, and away east, one tries to imagine the barbarian hordes marching along the Aurelian way; and then one asks, " Now had I to fight them, what would I do?" The answer I gave to myself was, " Common sense bids me make with forced marches away to Trets, keeping my flank protected by the river, and surprise them again." I am not a general—but it appeared to me that it would be hard for any one on the spot in the position of Marius, if he had his wits about him, not to see that the barbarians had given him a splendid chance, and that he must catch it, and take them unawares when they had stepped into his net.

C.—THE UTRICULARES.

There are twenty-three inscriptions relative to the Colleges of Utriculares in Provence. M. Lenthéric gives five in the appendix to his volume, 'Les Villes Mortes du Golfe de Lyon,' and nineteen in that to his volume " Le Grèce et l'Orient en Provence,' but of these one is from Temesvar in Hungary.

Then M. Gilles, in his 'Campagne de Marius,' engraves a medal of the Guild of Utriculares of Cabelio (Cavaillon), which is now in the Cabinet of Medals at Paris. It was found on the hill-slopes of the Luberon. On the obverse it bears a representation of an inflated skin of a beast (a calf?); on the other side the inscription—

Colle(gium)utri(culariorum) Cab(ellionensis) L(ucius) Valer(ius) succes(sor).

I will give a few of the inscriptions on stones.

1. *D. M. G. Paqui, Optati lib(erti) Pardalæ, sextum (viri) Aug(ustalis) col(oniæ) Ju(liæ) Pat(ernæ) Ar(elatensis) patron(i) ejusdem corpor(is), item patron(i) fabror(um) naval(ium), utricular(iorum) et centena(riorum) C. Paquius Epigonus cum liberis suis patrono optime merito.*

" To the manes of G. Paquius Pardalas, freedman of Optatus, sevir Augustal of the Colony of Julia Paterna of Arles, patron of the same body, and also patron of the shipbuilders, of the utriculares, and of the centenares. C. Paquius Epigonius and his children to a well-deserving patron."

This was found under the porch of S. Cæsarius at Arles. The Centenarii were the men who made the patchwork beds that covered towers and walls in war as a protection against the ram and against fire.

2. *D. M. L(ucio) Secundia eleutheria navicular(io) Arel(atensi) item sevir(o) Aug(ustali) corpor(ato) c(oloniæ) J(uliæ) P(aternæ) A(relatensis) secundia Tatiana fil(ia) patri pientissim(o).*

"To the manes of Lucius Secundius Eleutherius, boatman of Arles, and Augustal sevir, incorporated in the colony of Julia Paterna of Arles. Secundia Tatiana, his daughter, to the most tender of fathers."

Found on the banks of the Rhone, at Arles.

3. *D. M. M(arco) Junio Messanio, utricul(ario) corp(orato) Arelat(ensi), ejusd(em) corp(oris) mag(istro) quater, fi(lio), qui vixit ann(os) octo et viginti menses quinque, dies decem, Junia Valeria.*

"To the manes. To Marcus Junius Messianus of the corporation of the utriculares of Arles, four times president of the same; Junia Valeria to her son, who died at the age of twenty-eight years, five months, and ten days."

This is on a stone sarcophagus in the museum at Arles.

4. *M(arco) Frontoni Eupori, sevir(o) Aug(ustali) col(oniæ) Julia(e) Aug(ustæ) Aquis Sextis, navicu-*

lar(io) Mar(ino) Are(late) Curat(ori) ejusd(em) corp(oris) patrono nautar(um) Druen(ticorum) et utricularior(um) corp(oratorum) Ernaginensium. Julia Nice uxor conjugi carissimo.

"To Marcus Fronto Eupor, Augustal sevir of the Colony of Julia Augusta at Aix, mariner of Arles, curator of the said corporation, patron of the corporations of the mariners of the Durance and of the utriculares of Ernaginum. Julia Nice to her dearest husband."

Found in the church of S. Gabriel (Ernaginum).

www.ingramcontent.com/pod-product-compliance
Lightning Source LLC
Chambersburg PA
CBHW032042220426
43664CB00008B/824